COOL MADNESS

The Trial of Dr. Mollie Fry and Dale Schafer

✍

Vanessa Nelson

Published by Medical Marijuana of America
www.MedicalMarijuanaOfAmerica.com

For Cody, Caroline, Geoffrey, Heather and Jeremy
who watched with great courage and strength
during their parents' time of tribulation.

Contents

Introduction

Nestled in the foothills of the Sierra Nevada Mountains is the tiny town of Cool, California.

Visitors need not bother with jokes about the name. The locals have heard them all, many times over. When it comes to unusual place names, it turns out that El Dorado County has plenty of other jewels in its chest.

Its glittering streams sparked the California Gold Rush in 1848, and the miners who flooded the area christened places like Hangtown, Murderer's Bar and Fleatown. The prospectors were a straightforward lot, using a strong streak of literalism in the names they bestowed…and Cool is no exception. It is airy and laidback, seemingly secure in the midst of ongoing change.

The evaporation of the 19th Century mining industry drained out the county's population, and a sense of rural calm returned at that point. The mass of rowdy settlements transformed into a handful of mannerly communities by the end of the 20th Century. It was this small town charm that attracted Dr. Mollie Fry and Dale Schafer to the foothills in

The town of Cool sits quietly atop the Sierra foothills of northern California. Photo by Vanessa Nelson.

the late 1990s, and they found a nice place to raise their five children.

1

Although mom was trained in medicine and dad practiced law, the family didn't have the yuppie lifestyle of many other professionals. Instead, Fry and Schafer led a simple life, garnering respect for their community involvement and their devoted parenting. Their world was centered around home-schooling their children, going to little league games, and volunteering at their church.

Dr. Fry and Dale Schafer, along with three of their children, pose for photographers. Photo by Vanessa Nelson

It would have been a snapshot of idyllic Americana, were it not for what was lurking in the shadows.

For years, Fry and Schafer were under investigation by the federal government.

The indictment against them, filed in June 2005, accused them of being "major west coast drug dealers" who based their operations at Fry's medical offices. They were both hit with felony counts for manufacturing and conspiring to manufacture a Schedule I controlled substance.

One might imagine that the clean-living residents of Cool would be scandalized by the accusation that their neighbors had been using their trusted professions as a front for drug dealing. Not so with Fry and Schafer. In their case, the drug in question was medical marijuana, and the couple's efforts were widely perceived as admirable rather than illicit.

It was no secret that this country doctor was writing approvals for her patients to use medical marijuana. After all, it was a treatment she knew to be effective – marijuana had helped her through chemotherapy and a double mastectomy during her near-fatal battle with breast cancer. And it was a treatment she also knew to be legal – in 1996, California voters had passed an initiative allowing patients to grow and possess marijuana with the approval of a licensed physician. Two years later, with her husband at her side for legal consultation, Fry set up an office for evaluating patients who benefited from the use of medical marijuana. Given their professions and their profound personal experiences, the couple was perfectly poised to extend a hand of compassion to their community.

Well, *almost* perfectly poised.

Their trouble was that the federal government explicitly refused to recognize the state laws regarding medical marijuana. This situation created a dangerous conflict in legality, and no shortage of confusion. The problem was further complicated by instances in which local law enforcement officers participated in federal investigations, with the cross-over between jurisdictions allowing them to play both sides.

It was precisely this type of situation that led Fry and Schafer to claim they were victims of entrapment. They had conferred with the El Dorado County Sheriff's Department about their medical marijuana cultivation, and the deputies had assured them that their activities were legal…but then turned around and supplied the information to federal investigators.

It was another source of information, however, that was the lifeblood of the investigation: the couple's former employees. In exchange for leniency in their own criminal cases, these employees were abundantly forthcoming with government prosecutors about the marijuana-related activities of their former bosses.

"If Mollie and Dale are guilty of anything, it's trusting the wrong people," confessed Bobby Eisenberg, a representative of the Fry/Schafer Defense Committee.

There's no question that the defendants were innovative with their compassion, or that state law left room open for such pioneering. While California has allowed patients to possess medical marijuana, there has been ambiguity and wide variation in the ways patients can legally obtain it. On a practical level, access has all too often been thwarted by high costs and by scarcity. These were the conditions and the concerns, Fry insisted, that motivated her and her husband to explore ways of helping patients obtain their medicine.

Case discovery describes the couple selling various forms of marijuana to patients, including starter marijuana plants packaged in 'grow kits,' as well as processed bud distributed through the medical office and the United Parcel Service. Fry and Schafer publicly distanced themselves from these accusations, but outside of court they made general admissions about facilitating access to medical marijuana.

"We wanted our patients to be able to get their medicine at the lowest possible price," Fry told supporters a month after the indictment. By her explanation, recommendations aren't beneficial if patients can't afford marijuana or fail to find a source for it. "That's what we were trying to do – we wanted to teach the patients to grow their own medicine," the doctor insisted.

If these sentiments are sincere, then it's certainly true that no good deed goes unpunished. The road leading up to trial was especially rough for both Fry and Schafer, who describe instances of brutality and mistreatment by law enforcement. And their struggle was a long one as well, spanning nearly six full years.

The initial wake-up call occurred in September 2001, when DEA agents raided the couple's house, offices and storage facility. Fry reported being thrown face-down on the ground by armed officers who held her and her 14 year-old son Geoffrey at gunpoint during the search.

Assistant U.S Attorney Anne Pings has repeatedly bristled at Fry's descriptions. "The defendant has been quoted many times about being held at gunpoint, made to lie on the ground – things that just didn't happen," Pings complained during a pre-trial hearing. And the prosecutor was in a good position to make such assertions, given that she was personally present at the scene during the raid. "There's a lot of false information here that may be damaging," Pings warned ominously.

Dr. Fry stands alongside her son Geoffrey.
Photo by Vanessa Nelson

Fry's treatment during the bust was not the only dispute that developed a 'he said/she said' aspect while the case worked its way to trial. During the motions hearings that preceded the trial, it seemed that the defense and the prosecution couldn't even agree to disagree. Still, with regard to the raid, there were a few facts that went unchallenged. By the end of the ordeal, the defendants' home and office had been trashed, and their family was shaken. Federal agents seized 34 marijuana plants from the residence, as well as a lesser quantity of processed buds. However, Fry's greatest dismay came when she realized that the feds had confiscated over five thousand of her patients' medical files.

Immediately following the raid, Fry launched a legal struggle to force the return of the records. In the meantime, the government initiated a series of negotiations over a pre-indictment plea agreement. When all this wrangling proved unsuccessful, an eerie calm came over the case. Federal prosecutors watched and waited for years, closely monitoring the legal environment to determine the right time to strike. When the Supreme Court ruled in favor of the federal government in

Raich v. Gonzales, the U.S. Attorney decided the iron was hot and immediately issued an indictment against Fry and Schafer.

They were arrested in June 2005, and the arraignment brought some startling surprises. Even though their bust had only netted 34 marijuana plants, the indictment clearly charged Fry and Schafer with cultivating, and conspiring to cultivate, over a hundred plants. It was incongruous.

The 66 plants that made up the difference weren't in the government's possession. They would never be seized by law enforcement, nor would the prosecutor, the judge or the jury ever lay eyes on them. Nonetheless, Fry and Schafer were accused of cultivating these invisible plants. The charges, which were felonies, immediately put the defendants in jeopardy of 40 years in prison and $2 million dollars in fines.

To bolster their claims, government prosecutors used some fantastical mathematics. The trumped-up plant count relied on witnesses who were willing to testify that Fry and Schafer had grown marijuana during the two years before their raid. Since the statute of limitations was five years, prosecutors appeared to have some wiggle-room to add these prior harvests to the plant total. However, it would take a compelling argument to persuade jurors to convict on multiple marijuana crops that were never seized. The extra 66 plants in the charges were essentially from hearsay harvests.

Facing what seemed like flimsy charges, Fry and Schafer were confident they could prevail. They pled not guilty, and pushed forward to trial. Getting there wouldn't be easy, though. It was a dangerous path, and Schafer, a hemophiliac, faced heightened risks. While in jail in June 2005, he reported that he was kept tightly shackled for so long that he sustained severe internal bleeding. His injuries would require treatment through blood transfusions.

The misfortune continued to escalate after the pair was granted bail. First off, Fry discovered that her jailers had lost her most precious jewelry: her wedding ring and her treasured crucifix necklace. From then on, things went from bad to worse.

A magistrate judge set bail conditions that prohibited the couple from using marijuana while on release, a decision that would be enforced by mandatory random drug testing. The magistrate also denied subsequent motions for permission to use Marinol, a pharmaceutical drug that is a synthetic version of an active component in marijuana. Fry and Schafer then were forced into a last resort – treating their ailments with cocktails of prescription drugs that saddled them with a host of harmful side effects.

In precarious health, the couple relied heavily on the advocacy of their lawyers, a pair of prominent San Francisco attorneys from a group known as Pier 5 Law Offices. Fry secured representation by Laurence Lichter and Schafer hired J. Tony Serra, who had been the inspiration for the film "True Believer" and gained fame for his work with such celebrity defendants as Ellie Nesler, the Black Panthers, and the Symbionese Liberation Army.

Defense attorneys Tony Serra and Laurence Lichter withstood the government's attempt to have them removed from the case. Photo by Vanessa Nelson.

Lichter and Serra got right to work, filing an aggressive series of motions that sought dismissal of the case on a variety of grounds. But just when Fry and Schafer needed their lawyers most, the government made an attempt to have them removed.

Pier 5 had already had its hand in the case, Pings argued, and this created a conflict of interest. The prosecutor revealed that a Pier 5 attorney had represented Schafer's former assistant in a separate criminal case, but had dropped him as a client when he decided to reduce his sentence by giving the government information about Fry and Schafer. Serra and Lichter argued that there was no conflict of interest because Pier 5 was a "community of sole practicioners" and not a law firm.

Nonetheless, Pings was granted an evidentiary hearing to present her grounds for disqualifying the attorneys, and fellow prosecutor Matthew Segal was at her side for the battle. According to Segal, he had

7

watched Pier 5 spring up while he was working at the federal courthouse in San Francisco, and he had been waiting years for the chance to challenge the attorneys on conflict of interest. In spite of this zeal, however, the government's showing was paltry. It hinged on an assumption that a shared office is the same as a law firm, and the magistrate judge was unconvinced. Fry and Schafer were ultimately allowed to keep their high-profile attorneys. It was, they felt, their only chance for winning their case.

But even with the power lawyers, it seemed that the deck was stacked against Fry and Schafer. The majority of their pre-trial motions were flatly denied, including their attempt to present a medical defense. Serra tried to turn the tide, arguing all the way up until the trial confirmation hearing, but he was met with resistance from Judge Frank C. Damrell, Jr.

Standing outside the federal courthouse, Dr. Fry and Dale Schafer unfurled a U.S. flag made out of hemp. Photo by Vanessa Nelson

Introduction

Many U.S. District judges have ruled that state law is irrelevant during a federal trial, and Judge Damrell turned out to be no exception. The only time that California's medical marijuana law would be mentioned at trial, he decided, was in selecting the jury. This left Fry and Schafer in a difficult position – medical marijuana laws could not be mentioned as a defense, but the prosecutors could raise the topic in order to keep potentially sympathetic individuals off the jury.

In spite of impassioned argument from the defense attorneys, Judge Damrell stuck firmly to his resolution.

Fry and Schafer were forced to start the trial with a handicap, but they wouldn't take it lying down. Six years had passed since their bust, and they were determined to finally prove themselves in front of a panel of their peers.

Jury selection commenced on August 1st, 2007, and a ferocious tug-of-war began almost immediately. What followed was like something out of the movies – a dramatic trial with surprises that kept watchers on the edge of their seats and pushed the boundaries of permissible evidence.

This is the story of those proceedings.

Jury Selection

The morning of jury selection got off to a showy start. Before they even set foot in court, Fry and Schafer had become a spectacle. At their urging, dozens of medical marijuana activists gathered in front of the Sacramento federal courthouse to protest the proceedings. The demonstrators carried signs that read "Medical Marijuana Legal in Calif. Since 1996," "Uphold the Will of California Voters," and "Educate, Not Incarcerate."

Supporters for Dr. Fry and Dale Schafer protested outside the federal courthouse before the start of the trial. Photo by Vanessa Nelson.

In front of various news cameras, Fry made a case for the uniqueness of her trial. "I am the only doctor who has come to federal court," she emphasized into the microphones. "And there are at least 40 to 50 doctors I know who recommend marijuana."

In the courtroom, Judge Damrell assembled the prospective jurors and began the selection process by acknowledging the crowd that was clamoring outside. "There were folks outside with signs…you may or may not have noticed that," he said cautiously.

He received only blank stares in return. Clearing his throat, the judge edged closer to his point. "Were you approached by anyone as you came to the courthouse, about the use of marijuana or about your service as a juror?" he asked the group.

A timid "no" emanated from the back of the jury box, but the judge instructed responses to be given in the affirmative by raising a numbered sign. It was closely akin to the process of a silent auction…only no one was bidding on this particular lot. The prospective jurors made no indication that they had been approached.

Seeking to offer a small measure of clarification for his question, Judge Damrell started to explain. "Let me tell you a little about this case," he began. "Defendant Dale Schafer is an attorney." Schafer smiled at the jury from across the room, where he sat next to his lawyer, J. Tony Serra.

"His wife Mollie Fry is a physician in Cool, California," the judge continued. Fry beamed serenely as well, attorney Laurence Lichter at her side and rosary beads clasped in her hands.

As an attorney, Dale Schafer once specialized in workers' compensation law. Photo by Vanessa Nelson.

It all seemed pleasant and straightforward enough, but Judge Damrell's next statement was an egregious bumble. "They claim they were selling marijuana for medical purposes," he summarized mistakenly.

It took Serra a split-second to speak out against this characterization, and the objection led to the first of what would be a great many sidebar conferences at the judge's bench. The courtroom was washed out in white noise as the judge and attorneys conferred, and finally Judge

Damrell turned again to address the would-be jurors. "It is my understanding that the defendants claim they did *not* sell marijuana," he amended. "I said that they sold it for medical purposes. Do you understand that – is it clear?"

He then asked the group to raise their numbered cards if, based on the description of the case, they felt they could not be fair when considering these issues. One number went up. The woman who raised her card turned out to have a son who had recently received a DUI for driving under the influence of marijuana. "He's had a problem for a long time now, and I'm not real thrilled about that," she related with a grimace. "So, I don't know whether I could be impartial."

The admission stirred up more confessions from the group. Another mother spoke passionately about her son's drug addiction, describing him as being in and out of jail as well as rehab. When asked about which drug her son was addicted to, however, the woman drew a blank. "I'm not sure," she told the judge. "I think it's that one they *make* – crank or whatever."

"Do you mean meth?" Judge Damrell guessed.

"Yeah, that's it," she affirmed.

The two concerned moms were later dismissed from the case, but first the judge tightened up the specificity of his questions. "Does anyone in your family have a prescription for medical marijuana?" he asked the jurors. No one moved a muscle.

Perhaps the use of the term 'prescription' threw the panel off. Under state law, medical marijuana is *recommended* in written or oral form by licensed physicians, but *prescriptions* are not issued. Whether it was a problem with terminology or with bashfulness, there was one woman who held back on sharing her personal experience with medical marijuana until later in the questioning.

This woman, a resident of the same county as the defendants, did not open up until she was asked if she had heard or seen any media coverage of the case. She described the story of Fry and Schafer as being "all over the Mountain Democrat," the local newspaper for El Dorado County. When the judge inquired if she had formed any

13

opinions from the coverage, she replied with a hint. "No, not as a result of the *articles*," she said suggestively.

When prompted to explain what factors had influenced her opinions on the issues, she became suddenly grave. "I'm sorry – I'm going to get emotional here," she apologized as she began her revelation. "I had a niece die of breast cancer, and I watched her die. She did take marijuana so that she could eat, and it was just *pitiful* to watch her go."

Tearfully, the woman declared herself to be incapable of impartiality in a case related to medical marijuana, and the judge softly praised her honesty before moving on with his questioning.

A series of other inquiries followed, aimed at identifying various types of bias. There were a couple cards thrust up when asked about substance abuse amongst family members, and a slightly larger number of cards lifted to affirm that a close friend or relative had been convicted of a crime. There was a flurry of raisings, however, when the group was asked whether any friends or family had been employed by law enforcement. During individual questioning, it turned out that most of these 10 card-raisers had several close family members employed in corrections.

The challenge for Judge Damrell was to figure out if the prospective jurors would be influenced by their intimacy with officers, and thereby give greater weight to law enforcement testimony than to the testimony of other witnesses presented during the trial. In response to this question, only one woman responded affirmatively. She turned out to have a retired CHP officer for a husband, two stepsons in corrections, a daughter who works as a police dispatcher, and a son-in-law employed as a patrolman.

"Would you favor the testimony of law enforcement during trial?" the judge inquired.

The woman took a moment of thought. "Maybe if two witnesses were saying the exact opposite thing about the same circumstances…yeah, I'd probably believe the officer." She answered confidently at first, and then quickly hedged at the end. "I don't know."

14

The judge talked through some of the finer details of her situation, and then chose to put the deciding question in the hypothetical. "If you were the defendant, would you like 12 jurors of your frame of mind serving on your case?" he asked.

"No, I wouldn't," the juror answered frankly. She was thanked for her candor and soon thereafter released from service.

This response had inspired a lengthy round of applause from the audience, where every available seat had been packed with onlookers. Most of the attendees were supporters of the defendants, but the crowd also had a light sprinkling of current and future prosecutors. As the clapping erupted, the U.S. Marshals grew frantic, threatening the enthusiasts with expulsion. Joined with an admonishment from the judge, the threats served to quickly, and permanently, quiet the audience.

Once the issue of law enforcement influence was put to rest, the defense expressed its concern about identifying another kind of jury bias – a prejudice against lawyers. After taking a minute to thank the potential jurors for their time, Serra presented his argument. "I know, because I am a lawyer, that there is a lot of bias out there against lawyers," he began. "Some people just don't like lawyers...and for *good reason.*"

There was some tittering in reaction to the self-effacing humor, and Serra used the pause to ask the group if any of them had negative experiences with attorneys that could bias them against his client, or against *any* of the attorneys arguing the case. One woman spoke up, detailing a situation in which she felt she had been scammed. "I had an attorney put down on my credit card quite a lot of money," she explained. "Then I just found out in July that she's no longer an attorney and no one knows where she is."

Serra was appropriately sympathetic. "You had a bad experience," he said affably. "You got ripped off. You're angry, and you should be." Then, becoming more fanciful in his language, he announced, "When there's a revolution, they're going the kill all the attorneys first."

It seemed that most of the prospective jurors weren't quite sure what to make of Serra. Charismatic, engaging, and chronically whimsical, he was a different breed from the other attorneys present. Soon, however, he had the entire audience engrossed.

"Look at my guy over there – Dale Schafer," Serra commanded, gesturing towards his client. Schafer promptly stood and submitted to visual appraisals from the jury pool.

"Do you think that, because of this experience, you would be less than objective, less than utterly impartial about him?" Serra asked.

The jilted juror seemed to respond to the drama of Serra's approach, and soon admitted to reacting with disdain when watching lawyers on TV. She then added with zeal, "And when I see them walking around here, I think, 'I wonder who they're going to rip off next?'"

"Don't look at me!" Serra shot back, smiling. "I didn't rip anybody off!"

Giggles abounded, and the attorney appeared confident that he had made a demonstration of juror prejudice on this subject. "If you look at them like you want to bite them, that's bias," he concluded.

Serra then moved on to address the key issue of the case. After admitting that federal law prevented him from mounting a medical defense, he stated that the presentation of case evidence would inevitably bring up the medicinal nature of the marijuana. "The context of the case – and you can't strip it down naked to nothing – is that the defendants were involved in medical marijuana, both of them."

The words precipitated an objection from Assistant U.S. Attorney Anne Pings, and another sidebar was called. Upon returning, Serra abandoned the soliloquy and went straight into his question for the future jurors. "How many of you know that you can get permission on the state level to use marijuana?" he asked. The inquiry resulted in Pings accusing Serra of testifying rather than examining, but after yet another sidebar, the question was allowed to go through. It seemed not to matter, however, because no one was answering.

The group sat silent. "Anyone?" Serra prompted, only to be met with quiet stares and fidgeting from the potential jurors. "No one knows about Proposition 215?" he hinted in vain. Finally, he threw in a provocative query, "How many of you vote?"

That seemed to break the dam of reservations, and slowly a few opinionated individuals came out of the woodwork. One woman in particular gave a brief overview of the general facts of Proposition 215, correctly identifying the year of its passage and recapping its success in the polls. Serra acted surprised when this sudden outburst of knowledge broke the silence. No one else in the group, he noted, seemed to remember anything about California's medical marijuana law.

"Or they were afraid to mention it," the woman said pointedly, hitting the nail squarely on the head.

Further questioning revealed that this prospective juror had voted for Proposition 215. "I voted the way I thought was right," she said plainly. When asked whether this would affect her ability to be objective in the case, however, she threw the defense for a loop. "No," she answered thoughtfully, "because I believe there's a lot more involved here than just the medical marijuana. I don't know – I haven't read or seen anything – but I believe there's more to this case."

Her cynicism was based on mysterious grounds that were never fully discovered by her questioners, but she held fast and tight to her beliefs. The vagueness of her answers was at odds with the suspicion in her voice, and listeners were perplexed. Nonetheless, the tone had been set. From there, potential jurors offered medical marijuana stories that were increasingly ambiguous.

Next, an elderly woman, who identified herself as a widow with nine children, proudly declared that none of her children has abused substances. "I always say I did something right," she said with satisfaction about her offspring. "I have no drug dealers, no dope addicts, no alcoholics…and they all work for a living."

She did, however, have a grandson who used medical marijuana. "He got cancer when he was five years old," she related. "They gave him – they put the patch on him that has THC, which is, I understand, what they get from marijuana." If listeners were expecting to hear a conclusion in support of medical marijuana, however, they were soon disappointed. "If it's available other ways, then I just don't see why it has to be smoked," insisted the aged lady.

17

Following this outpouring of personal stories, Serra inquired whether any of the potential jurors were affronted by marijuana, or, for that matter, medical marijuana.

One woman spoke up, saying that she voted 'no' on Proposition 215, and that she felt that "an illegal drug is an illegal drug." The prosecutor's eyes widened with delight at the possibility of seating such a juror, but Serra had another idea entirely. He was intent on keeping this woman off the jury, and he pursued his plan with repeated questioning about the possibility of bias. As it appeared, this tactic worked perfectly. "I thought I could be positive about whether I could be impartial, but then you keep going on and on, and I just don't know," the woman finally admitted in distress.

"Well, how's your Pavlovian response?" Serra asked her, starting to get warmed up to full theatrics. "When you smell marijuana, do you get angry and want to destroy it and say, 'Where is it? I'll step on it!'"

By the end of his musing, Serra was shouting and gesturing wildly. The woman he was addressing, however, couldn't have been more placid in her response. "To be honest with you, I don't know that I've smelled marijuana," she said simply.

"Come to San Francisco, any day," Serra suggested in a lighthearted quip, before continuing to probe her about bias.

Finally, she gave in, agreeing to the defense attorney's characterization. "I just don't think there's a good medical use," she added, speaking about marijuana.

The defense wrapped up the examination, and the would-be jurors were sent out of the courtroom so that final decisions could be made. Serra had an air of victory about him, even beyond his usual glow of triumphant confidence, and quickly requested to strike the woman he had just questioned.

Pings, however, was outraged by his treatment of this potential juror. "Mr. Serra, in all his skill, has convinced her that if she voted 'no' on the proposition, then that's equated with fairness," the prosecutor told the judge. "Just because she believes that medical marijuana should not be allowed, doesn't make her unfair. In fact, that's exactly the law the jury will be asked to follow in this case."

18

Serra was quick to counter. "She agonized over the question, and ultimately pronounced herself to be unfair," he claimed. "I didn't lead her. It was because of her position on marijuana that she answered as she did."

After referring to Proposition 215 as the "so-called California medical marijuana law," Judge Damrell granted Serra's request and dismissed the woman who had voted 'no' on the initiative. A long period of quiet negotiating then commenced, with notes passed back and forth, and pensive frowns on both sides. The afternoon dragged by, and onlookers watched the clock apprehensively, wondering if the jury would be finalized in time for recess.

Nearing the end of the day, however, the process concluded and the jury was successfully seated. In the end, most of those who expressed opinions had been cut, and a rather homogenous group remained. The finalized jurors are overwhelmingly white and mostly middle-aged, with a sex ratio of seven females to five males. After all of the pointed rhetoric about bias regarding attorneys, it was surprising to find a lawyer sitting on the jury. Also seated was a woman who has worked for years at a plant nursery, a notable detail in a cultivation case.

Standing apart from the rest, however, is the juror who retained spot #1 throughout the selection process and into the confirmation. A 51 year-old black woman employed by the public defender, this juror might have expected the prosecution to dismiss her immediately due to her job, but she was spared every time there was a cut. She stayed firmly in her place in spite of her description of her daughter's felony drug conviction and, more amazingly, regardless of her revelation that her uncle had been the warden at Attica Correctional Facility during the violent inmate riots there.

Although not starkly revealing, the biographical information on some of the jurors presented a few gems of curiosity. There was not much time for the audience to assess them, however – as soon as the jury was seated, court was recessed until the next morning. At that time, the judge promised, opening arguments would begin and the trial would go into full swing.

After the jury left the courtroom for the day, defense attorney Laurence Lichter addressed the judge about a proffer relying on Conant vs. Walters. That case resulted in an injunction against prosecuting physicians for making medical recommendations, and Lichter announced that this will be a large part of the defense he presents on behalf of Fry. "She is protected by an injunction from being prosecuted for criminal conduct," Lichter argued about his client. "This ruling shielded doctors' activities, so that they could make a recommendation – either written or verbally – even if they know the patient will use that recommendation to break federal law."

Pings did not think highly of this defense strategy. In her view, it didn't even apply. "The ruling says that the DEA cannot revoke a license to prescribe medicine solely because the doctor had a 1st Amendment protected conversation about use," Pings was long-winded but adamant. "It's about DEA registration. It does not say that you can sell little baggies of marijuana hand-to-hand. It doesn't say you can cultivate marijuana plants or possess large amounts of marijuana…We're not talking about people getting a recommendation and then going elsewhere to get drugs. [Fry] sold them drugs hand-to-hand! She sold them plants hand-to-hand! She conspired with her employees to sell drugs hand-to-hand!"

Lichter's response was simple: since the judge would permit his proffer, he would make his proffer…and that was that. Otherwise, he had just one final comment to make about his client. "The defense will be that she acted as a doctor, not as a dope dealer," he said succinctly.

Fry herself echoed those words outside the courtroom.

"I am not a drug dealer – I didn't go to medical school for four years to be a drug dealer," she declared to the news reporters. "I consider drug dealers to be on a lower rung. I'm up *here*," she said proudly, gesturing slightly above forehead level. The first phase of the trial under

Speaking to the press, Dr. Fry distinguished between physicians and drug dealers. Photo by Vanessa Nelson.

her belt, Fry ended the day on a full tank of self-esteem.

Opening Statements

Before the attorneys could deliver their opening statements, the court took up a matter outside the presence of the jury…and it proved to be a hotly controversial one. At issue was the applicability of Conant v. Walters, a case that ultimately enjoined the government from prosecuting doctors for giving advice and recommendations to their patients. Raising this precedent sparked unanticipated debate in the courtroom, and each side had a slightly different take on its relevance.

In Judge Damrell's view, the Conant case was only about free speech. "She can talk to her patients about the use of marijuana," he said about Fry. "If that's all she did, then fine. But that's not the conduct she's charged with here. Understand what I'm saying?"

Lichter, the attorney who had made the proffer, ventured a guess. "That she may have crossed the line with her conduct?"

"You might argue that this is a mistake of law," the judge mused. "For instance, did she think Conant did other things? But Conant is very specific."

Indeed, the Conant decision does not allow doctors to assist patients in obtaining marijuana, nor does it give legal protections for cultivating or possessing marijuana for patient use. These were details that Pings was quick to point out.

"We're not talking about the ten thousand recommendations for asthma, sore elbows, PMS – that's not the case here," the prosecutor said, the ridicule apparent. "This is only about whether they tried to sell marijuana to the people who came in for recommendations. Period."

21

In spite of the verbal punctuation mark, Pings was not quite finished on this subject. "The government has prepared its case based on the charges," she clarified. "We have not prepared a case to attack the recommendation business. Our witnesses will only testify if they got the recommendation and if they bought marijuana from the defendants."

At first, Serra acted like he would stay out of the debate. Since he was representing a lawyer rather than a doctor, he felt the discussion on Conant didn't really apply to his client. "I don't have a dog in this fight," he told the judge at the outset.

But the intrepid defense attorney soon changed his mind. He couldn't stay out of the argument once the prosecutor stated that she did not intend to malign Fry's practice. "That's not the charge, but that's what they want to do – they want to dirty us up!" Not one for

Assistant United States Attorney Anne Pings acted as lead prosecutor in the trial of Dr. Fry and Dale Schafer. Sketch by Dr. Care.

morning grogginess, Serra was already infusing his spirited arguments with cartoonish voices well before 9am.

Serra, in fact, had much to say about the prosecutor's intent. "She will bring up bad acts, and say, 'These people are running a mill, they're profiteering, they're frauds!' That will be the sub rosa content of her case at some level. We have to counter that in some way and say, 'This is altruistic, they were helping people--'"

"I was not intending to ask them about diseases, illnesses, etc." Pings jumped in to clarify the point. She reiterated that the defendants were not charged with wrongdoing regarding the recommendation business, but quickly indicated her willingness to accommodate such charges. "If [the defense attorneys] want to do that, we can present a very large case about the insincerity of the recommendation practice."

For Judge Damrell, however, the matter was simple. "She made good faith recommendations," he summarized regarding Fry. "I won't get into why she made those recommendations. A physician is entitled to make recommendations under Conant. And we are not going to engage in the sort of discussion that Mr. Serra thought we might."

The judge then ordered the jury into the room, but was cut off by another request from Pings. Her snippy attitude had vanished, and this time she approached the lectern and spoke into the microphone with great gravity. "Your honor, I am going to ask for a special instruction," she began. "It would be that, everyday when the jurors come into the courtroom, you look them in the eye and ask them if they were exposed to any media about this case."

Responding to the judge's quizzical expression, Pings continued. "The reason I ask is because the defense has scheduled to be on a radio show. Yesterday, one of the things that Dr. Fry said on the air was, when a dismissed juror called in, 'Everyone here lies to you. They make you think you have to tell the truth, but you don't.' This violates the law."

There was visible dismay in Judge Damrell's eyes, but Pings wasn't finished with her report. "And at the end of the show, the host said, 'Come on, people, just play dumb and vote not guilty no matter what they tell you.' These are affirmative messages to taint the jury pool," Pings concluded.

Tough to beat to the punch, Serra got his statement in before the judge could muster a response. "I vigorously object to this instruction," he declared before launching into his list of the ways Pings had violated his client's civil rights. "She swallowed our defenses, she swallowed our 4th Amendment right, and now she wants to swallow what is our 1st Amendment right--"

"It's not your right if you're going to be on the radio telling [the jurors] not to follow my instructions!" the judge snapped. "You're not going to tamper with this jury under any circumstances."

"She took great liberty in exaggerating what was said," Serra noted about the prosecutor's characterization. About the jurors, he requested the judge have greater faith in their honor. "You told them not to listen, so that should be that. But to interrogate them everyday when they come into the courtroom is a form of intimidation."

"You're intimidating this jury, if that's what you're saying on the radio!" Judge Damrell bellowed back at Serra, livid at the revelation. "Bring in the jury," he ordered. "I'm going to ask them."

Once seated, the jurors were subjected to a full re-run of the previous day's lecture on media exposure. That concluded, Judge Damrell asked slowly and carefully if any of the jurors had been exposed to any media about the case. He turned in his chair to scrutinize them, looking straight into their eyes as the prosecutor had requested. "I take it by your silence that you have not," the judge eventually conceded.

The Prosecution Opens

Satisfied with the purity of the jurors, Judge Damrell allowed opening statements to commence. But the courtroom got a quick surprise – though she has been the lead prosecutor on the case for several years, Pings would not be making the opening statement for the government. Instead, the duty would fall to Assistant U.S. Attorney Sean Flynn, who gave the distinct impression of having some wetness behind his ears.

But Flynn was no stranger to Judge Damrell's courtroom. Just two months earlier, the young attorney helped convict two men for burning a cross in front of a Catholic church run by a Rwandan immigrant. Flynn had railed against racism in that case and he resurrected the passionate rhetoric for the Fry/Schafer trial, transferring his indignation to target "dope dealers."

In this effort, Flynn employed ample flair. He began with an anecdote about a mortgage appraiser who looked at the Fry/Schafer property in early 2001 and afterwards reported to police that he had discovered marijuana growing in a concrete bunker. "When he looked inside, he saw so many marijuana plants, he was frightened," Flynn said of the appraiser. "He realized he had come upon the property of drug dealers. This case is about those two drug dealers."

24

There was fervor in his tone, which dulled only slightly as he defined a few terms and outlined the elements that would need to be proven for each part of the charges against the defendants. Shortly, afterward, however, Flynn got his momentum going again. "The witnesses will tell you about how [the defendants] sold marijuana and even had a delivery service. They had a captive customer base for selling the marijuana. Dr. Fry and Dale Schafer had a medical and legal office where people would come to her as patients."

The prosecutor then explained how Paul Maggy, a former employee of Schafer, would testify that the defendants sold marijuana in a fire station parking lot across the street from their offices. According to Flynn, the jurors would also hear evidence from an undercover officer who posed as a patient at Fry's clinic. "You will hear Dr. Fry describe the volume of her business and her sales pitch," the prosecutor said, describing the evidence from the officer. "You will hear her encourage him to buy marijuana from her, and you will hear her badmouth her competition by saying another marijuana growing store was staked out by law enforcement."

Flynn then outlined the testimony of another ex-employee turned key witness, Mike Harvey. According to the prosecutor, Harvey outfitted various areas of the property for the defendants to grow marijuana, then drove the products of these grows to the defendants' customers in a manner similar to pizza delivery. Harvey was also expected to testify about building kits for growing marijuana and selling them at a price of $400 apiece, a plan he attributed to Schafer's requests.

The prosecutor informed the jurors that the distribution conspiracy included the defendants' daughter Heather Schafer, who allegedly put on marketing events known as cloning workshops. Not only did this seminar teach about growing marijuana from rooted plant cuttings, but Flynn also reported that it taught participants how to make Rice Krispie treats from hash oil.

Most notable to the prosecutor, however, was a detail from the law enforcement infiltration of the workshop. According to Flynn, when an undercover officer called Fry's office to ask if marijuana clones would be sold at the seminar, the agent was told the plants would be available for $5 each. That sale was never to happen, but the prosecutor quickly turned the lack of evidence around to serve his side.

"After the workshop, Heather Schafer said they didn't have any plants right now, since her family was cleaning out the house because her father was running for District Attorney of El Dorado County," Flynn summarized. "Well, when the house was later searched by law enforcement, they found out Heather Schafer was telling the truth – the house had been cleaned out."

Although only a couple dozen plants were found during the raid, the prosecutor assured the jury that officers found other evidence of large-scale cultivation. "They found the grow equipment the witnesses described. They found shopping bags full of processed marijuana in the living room and the bedroom. They found the plants on the hill, and they found Marion Fry's big ole greenhouse." The last phrase came across with a whimsical ring, and Flynn decided to end on this note.

But first he brought back the figure of the real estate appraiser, who would also testify that there had been massive marijuana cultivation at the Fry/Schafer residence. "He will tell you that some of the plants were nine feet tall," Flynn said of the appraiser, "and the plant number was so many that he was forced to call law enforcement." Although it was unclear what power had compelled the appraiser to make the police report, the prosecutor seemed pleased with his characterization. With this reference, Flynn's opening statement had come full circle back to its beginning, and he concluded contentedly.

The Defense Opens

Serra, ever dominant, made the first opening statement on the defense's side. He started out by asking the jurors to grant just one little favor to him and Lichter. "We're sitting way over there," Serra said, gesturing in an arc to the other end of the courtroom. "If it was foggy like it is in San Francisco, I wouldn't even be able to see you."

The grins from the jury box, however, were bright enough to be visible from across the room. The jurors appeared much beguiled by the fancies of Serra's illustrative language. Now that he had them smiling, the attorney finished his plea. "Even though the prosecution gets to sit closer and we're way over there, and even though it will take days before we can start our case, I beseech you to defer judgment."

It seemed a simple enough favor, but, as usual, Serra laid it on thick, continuing for another few lines by comparing ideal jurors to scientists who function objectively and remain neutral until the work is completed. At the judge's urging, the attorney finally moved on to the substantive part of his address, but it wasn't long before the judge was intervening again.

During his opening statements, Tony Serra stressed the disadvantages faced by the defense during trial. Sketch by Dr. Care.

"Dale Schafer is not contending that he did not grow marijuana," Serra put forth. "But he never conspired to grow more than a hundred plants, and he never grew more than a hundred plants… You'll hear that he agreed not to grow more than a hundred plants because he believed that was a line –"

After an objection by Pings and an animated sidebar, Serra returned to say, "I can't say what the reason for his belief was, but he had this belief and he would grow no more than a hundred plants."

Serra then backed up a bit, taking the time to give some background on his client's life and summarize what the character witnesses would say about Schafer. "They will testify that he is honest, credible, believable, trustworthy – in essence, a good person. They will testify that he is a law-abiding person, that he follows the law as he knows it, that he would not knowingly break the law."

In fact, Serra suggested, Schafer has been law-abiding all his life – not only did he take up the practice of law, but he used his expertise to ensure that his family's activities were legal. And, as the defense attorney described it, things were harmonious in their household for a while. "They were successful – not enormously so, but their family was intact, and their life was good, and their life was wholesome."

According to Serra, however, the good times came to an abrupt end with a crisis over Fry's health. "What happened next was so catastrophic it was overwhelming...Dr. Fry was diagnosed with breast cancer. She had both breasts removed but she was still imperiled. It was around this time that Proposition 215 was—"

The prosecution made an objection mid-sentence, but Serra interrupted the interruption. "We have to have context, your honor," he asserted to Judge Damrell.

"I object!" Pings insisted, visibly offended. "There is an objection!"

"I'm asking to proceed," Serra explained, calmly dismissive of the prosecution's concerns.

The spat resulted in yet another sidebar at the judge's bench. Upon returning to his podium, Serra apologized to the jurors in his classic affable style. "From time to time, there will be interruptions and sidebars," he explained. "Forgive me for precipitating them. But I would ask that you—"

"Just proceed," the judge broke in, his frustration only minimally concealed.

Serra obliged, going on to describe the physical ailments Schafer has suffered from: hemophilia, hepatitis C., polysite arthritis, and chronic pain from these conditions. "They used marijuana to help them in their conditions – hers being severe cancer, and his being the ailments I just described," Serra said of Fry and Schafer. "When marijuana became legal under state law, my client grew for them...He initially didn't grow to sell. It was to medicate their own serious illnesses."

The prosecution voiced its objection, leaving the defense attorney to take another route. He continued by focusing on Schafer's shortcomings as a grower. "He's not a farmer – he's a lawyer," Serra chuckled about his client. The idea here was to establish that Schafer's mortality rate was so high that he would need to start off with a large number of clones in order to have some probability of bringing a few plants to fruition. "You'll hear from marijuana experts about the problems Mr. Schafer had growing. You don't just throw seeds in the ground and they grow up to the sky. The preferred medicine is from the female and —"

Predictably, Pings made an objection, and Serra responded by shrugging at the judge, "I can't say 'medicine'?" A sidebar established that indeed he could not, and from then on Serra was made to say "preferred part" rather than "preferred medicine." However, his compliance with this rule immediately faltered.

"As time proceeded," Serra began, "Dr. Fry was issuing recommendations to patients that allowed them under California law to — "

"Counsel!" the judge warned sharply. "I already ruled on that."

"My client gave up his civil practice. He wanted to help his wife. He joined her office, and what he did was advise her patients to explain, to edify, to make clearer what patients could do with marijuana under state law." The reference to state law appeared to slide, so Serra went on to further expound. "This was a new thing. The California law was a new phenomenon. People flocked from all over to avail themselves with the medical and legal services—"

Judge Damrell turned to the jurors and told them to disregard the references to the words 'medical' and 'medication.'

But the references were there again, in Serra's next breath. "There came a time that, out of compassion, my client started to provide patients with what he called medicine – marijuana – because he believed people buying it on the black market were presented with certain dangers. He believed the prices were extraordinary. He believed the quality was poor. It was an act of compassion. He wanted to give it away without making any money."

The next facet of Serra's argument was that greedy, selfish individuals took advantage of Schafer's resources and good will, attempting to turn his activities into a commercial enterprise. The defense attorney alluded to evidence of violated trust and forged checks, both of which were discovered too late to save his client. "What my client will testify, and what he can say conclusively in retrospect, is that his intentions were betrayed by the people surrounding him, including his children. He did not have a firm grasp on the flow of money."

Serra told the jury that some of those who betrayed Schafer's intentions did so to receive leniency in their own criminal cases. According to Serra, these witnesses had agreed to testify for the government in exchange for a probable reduction in sentence. In characterizing the evolution of such deals, Serra impersonated an interrogator in heavy, exaggerated voice. "'We heard you sold lots and lots of plants – if that's true, we can make a deal—'"

The cartoonish representation may have hit a little too close to home for Pings, who promptly objected. Judge Damrell elected to forego the sidebar, and instead sent the jury from the courtroom. This time, things had gotten serious.

Once the door closed behind the last juror, Pings began explaining that Serra had "falsely mischaracterized" the circumstances of witness immunity. "The statute of limitations has expired," she told the judge. "These people smoked marijuana at some time in their past, and this interferes with their ability to remember, recall, relate. That's what the immunity was about."

Judge Damrell was at a new height of displeasure. "This has gone so far over the line, Mr. Serra – you know that! I have to make a curative instruction. I've got to rein you in. I have to cure the wrongs you've done."

"I've done no wrongs!" Serra exclaimed. "Now she says the immunity is for smoking pot. That's not what I understood."

As more details emerged, it became clear that the prosecution faxed a letter explaining the immunity to Serra's office in San Francisco on July 31st...precisely the time that he left to come stay in Sacramento for the trial. For a brief moment of resolution afterglow, things seemed to get downright chummy. "I think there was no bad faith here," Pings said amiably. "I think that's cleared up."

But the judge was uncomfortable about something else – the defense's incessant use of forbidden terms, in spite of objections and warnings from the bench. "I'm going to make a curative instruction.

I'm going to talk about the medical purpose of marijuana. I'm going to have to do that before we take evidence."

A proposed draft of the instruction was read, and it simply reminded jurors that, in spite of references to patients and medicine, marijuana is illegal under federal law. Serra appeared perplexed by the necessity of these statements. "I never said that federal law does allow it," he argued.

Judge Damrell was unconvinced. "It's my duty to make sure the jurors understand the law," he emphasized. "Right now, I think they have a misimpression of what the law is."

As the jury was being summoned back into the room, however, the judge was brushed by the feeling of increased benevolence, and he decided to wait until opening statements had concluded to make his instruction about federal marijuana law.

Serra then made one final point before giving the floor to Lichter. This point was aimed at getting the jury to scrutinize the role of law enforcement in these proceedings. "If you find that law enforcement has a political motive to destroy the state medical marijuana movement, you can take that into consideration when determining their motive for involvement," Serra said in conclusion. "If you find they have animosity towards state law, then you can take that into account – that taint, that bias – when ascertaining the credibility of those witnesses."

When Lichter took over, he introduced his client to the jury with pride. "It's an honor representing a female doctor," he said with convincing humility.

Continuing to sing Fry's praises, Lichter reached nearly two centuries into her family history and noted with admiration that she came from a line of medical doctors stretching back seven generations.

The defense attorney spoke at length about his client's predecessors and their achievements. Her grandfather, Francis Marion Pottinger, was a leading expert in the treatment of tuberculosis and was the creator of the charity Easter Seals. And, according to Lichter, there was something more to this forebear. "Mr. Pottinger was a very strange character," Lichter began, only to be cut off by an objection on grounds of relevance.

31

"She was born into a community who really cared about sick people," Lichter responded, justifying the diversion into his client's ancestry. "That cannot be taken out of it, cannot be considered irrelevant." But simply saying it did not make it so, and Lichter's oration on Fry's family tree was ended before jurors got to hear about the wackier side of Mr. Pottinger.

Instead, Lichter changed gears and told them about something far more sinister. The defense attorney started to explain that Fry had been molested by a neighbor at the age of two, and that she had developed kidney infections as a result. He had barely touched the subject before Pings objected, again questioning the relevance. In spite of the fact that Lichter claimed to have two witnesses who would be testifying on this subject, he was once again restrained after a sidebar discussion.

Laurence Lichter began the trial by detailing Dr. Fry's long family history in the practice of medicine. Sketch by Dr. Care.

The defense attorney then made a third try at launching his opening statement. This time, Lichter related how Fry was only ten years old when her mother died of breast cancer, and he got a couple sentences into describing the traumatic effects of this loss before he was again stopped short on a challenge of relevance.

A pattern had been established, with Lichter telling Fry's life story in tiny intervals broken up by frequent pauses for objections and sidebar conferences. It was a tedious way to tell a story, but the defense attorney took the interruptions good naturedly, and acted as though they were expected.

During his next go at it, Lichter got a good ways into describing Fry's education and training as a medical doctor, but stalled when he started talking about her philosophy of medicine. "She didn't like the changes in medicine," Lichter said of his client's attitude in the early 1990s. "She was unhappy with the emphasis in profit over care giving."

"Let's move along with this," Judge Damrell sighed. "Say what the evidence will show."

The judge's urging made little difference in Lichter's speech. The defense attorney was soon talking about Fry's battle with breast cancer, and consequently facing the same objections over state law that Serra handled. "She was put on chemotherapy," Lichter said gravely about his client. "The powerful drugs didn't just focus on the cancer cells – they made her so sick she didn't think it was worth it to go through with the treatment. Now, as you may know, before Proposition 215 was passed—"

Pings interrupted with an ardent objection. Lichter resumed, "Her doctor suggested she try a very powerful anti-emetic, cannabis. It also has an anti-inflammatory effect—"

The prosecutor's objection was uttered even more emphatically this time.

Judge Damrell was nearing the end of his rope. He gave the jurors a recess and then gave Lichter a piece of his mind after they had left the room. "I am tempted to give an instruction right now, rather than later," he alerted the attorney.

"I'm trying to follow all of your rulings, your honor," Lichter said.

"I wish you would!" the judge was exasperated. "And if you don't, I'm going to stop you and give a jury instruction right in the middle of your opening statement."

The jury reassembled and Lichter made another start. "Dr. Fry had no way to get this recommended substance. [Schafer] went to the black market. This made her nervous. She wanted to remain a doctor. They tried to learn the law—"

That was the breaking point. Apologizing to the jurors, Judge Damrell quickly sent them out of the room for a five-minute break. But if the judge thought he had five minutes' worth of outrage, he overestimated. His scolding of Lichter was forcefully uttered but remarkably brief.

"You are repeatedly violating the same topic," the judge said, leaning slightly over the bench. "I am going to instruct the jury right now. This has gone so far over the line!"

The curative instruction was nothing the jurors hadn't heard before, but they had no choice but to sit and listen to the lecture. "It is not a defense to federal charges regarding possession, manufacture and distribution of a controlled substance that a person did so for medical purposes," the judge explained once again. "I will not allow testimony on state law. This is a general intent statute – you don't have to show that they did it knowing they were breaking the law."

That done, Lichter simply found the place in Fry's biography where he had left off and commenced to put forward a few more sentences. "At some point, she felt well enough, and felt that her family was taken care of well enough, and she let it be known that other doctors could refer patients to her for consultation about a certain substance. Now, some witnesses will testify that this is not good medicine—"

After the familiar objection from the prosecution, the judge gave Lichter a harsh stare. "I already ruled there will be none of this testimony."

It didn't seem to matter much to Lichter – he was starting to wind down his speech. "My client did nothing beyond being a doctor," he declared. "She didn't cultivate, she didn't distribute. She didn't water a plant. She didn't take a bug off a plant."

All that was left was to re-state the major arguments, and Lichter got through it with no further objections. "She had an interest in getting the patients medicine cheaply, and she had an opinion on the people she thought were taking advantage of the patients...She voiced her criticism, but nothing more than that. Her interest was in publishing research, not dope dealing."

Once these declarations of Fry's innocence had been spoken, the opening statements were over. Jurors and courtroom spectators could now look forward to the presentation of witness testimony. But the courtroom's combative, restrictive atmosphere continued to spread to the audience area as well, with marshals hassling spectators about such innocuous stuff as bobbing their heads or possessing a water bottle in the courtroom.

For her part, radio host Christine Craft was shocked to learn about the way her on-air comments had been portrayed in court at the beginning of the day. On her next broadcast, she made an address about the matter. "If you're listening out there at the federal courthouse, I'm a lawyer and I would never tell anyone to disobey a judge." That disclaimer sufficiently issued, she addressed the other side of the issue, "But there's also a thing called jury nullification. If for any reason you think this law isn't right, if you think this law is ridiculous, you can say 'not guilty.'"

Craft's appeal had enough passion and potency to impress Serra himself, her revered on-air guest for the day. "We need you doing our closing argument," he joked.

It was all for giggles, though. The trial was still a long, wild ride away from its conclusion.

Paul Maggy, Part 1

Getting down to evidence, the prosecution made the bold move of leading with its most controversial witness – a young man named Paul Maggy whose disclosures had established the foundation of the government's case. Extensive cooperation with the feds had not won him many friends amongst the defendants' supporters, but it did win him a police escort to protect his movements. In all likelihood, Maggy faced nothing more than dirty looks from courtroom observers, but the fear of reprisal was still strong. This was the prosecution's star witness, and they weren't taking any chances.

As this Maggy took the stand, all eyes were fastened upon him, studying every detail. His suit appeared a bit too large for his slender figure, making the 35 year-old look boyish even beyond his naturally youthful good looks. His black hair was shaved short, and his dark eyes were framed by arching eyebrows. A thin goatee was sprouting along the jaw line of his tan face, completing the representation of a slick but slightly malicious look.

In spite of the intensive visual scrutiny, Maggy appeared calm and confident. He looked both Fry and Schafer unflinchingly in the eye as he pointed them out for the court record. If he had qualms of conscience about testifying against his former friends and employers, they didn't show in the least. To the contrary, Maggy displayed perfectly poised posture as he began his testimony.

Prosecutor Pings handled the direct examination, which revealed little more than the bare facts of the witness's involvement with the defendants. Maggy testified to meeting Fry and Schafer in the fall of

1999 during a seminar he attended in Lake Tahoe with his former girlfriend Traci Coggins. Maggy was already in trouble with the law at that time, fighting cultivation charges that he would ultimately resolve by providing information on Fry and Schafer in exchange for leniency. But the case against their new friends didn't raise a red flag for the doctor and lawyer, and instead the two couples hit it off right away. Coggins quickly became Fry's personal assistant, and shortly thereafter, Maggy was hired in the same capacity for Schafer. From this vantage point, the witness observed the activities of his employers close-up…and this is exactly what Pings was relying upon in her questioning.

Maggy described a flourishing business related to "marijuana recommendations," which began in the small town of Cool and quickly expanded to Oakland, Lake Tahoe, and various other locations where the defendants would rent space for the purpose of holding clinics. During his seven months of employment, Maggy reported, his bosses saw an estimated 100 customers per week.

But Pings was less interested in the patients who came for recommendations, and focused instead on questioning Maggy about other transactions he witnessed in the offices of the defendants. To this end, Maggy was happy to comply, and described a series of so-called "drug deals" arranged by Schafer.

The first of these occurred in February or March of 2000, at which time Maggy said that Schafer bought 3 pounds of high-grade marijuana at a price of $3700 per pound. According to the witness, Schafer then divided up the marijuana into smaller baggies and kept them in a blue duffel bag in his office so that he could sell them to the customers that visited him and his wife.

Maggy also claimed that Schafer deposited marijuana at the Tahoe home of Matt Egan, and that Schafer instructed Egan to deliver the marijuana to local customers at a price of $45 for an eighth of an ounce. In this arrangement, Maggy reported, Egan was allowed to keep $5 off the top and the remaining $40 went back to Schafer. A successful objection from the defense was the only thing that kept Maggy from stating how much money this arrangement would net Schafer per pound, leaving jurors and courtroom observers doing the math silently in their heads.

The beginning of the government's case consisted of testimony from the defendants' former friends. Sketch by Dr. Care.

Satisfied that she had produced evidence of the sale of processed marijuana, Pings moved on to address sales of what the prosecution referred to as "clones" or "starter plants." As she questioned Maggy, the witness detailed various areas of the defendants' home where he had seen marijuana growing: in a garage grow room, on a hill behind the house, and in a concrete room under the hill that was referred to as "the bunker." Maggy testified that Schafer told him the plants were for people who came into the office, but didn't specify whether they would be sold or given away. The plants growing at the defendants' home, according to Maggy, originally came from marijuana clones purchased elsewhere.

Maggy told the court that he was sent by Schafer to arrange such purchases and to inspect the facilities of those who would be supplying clones. One of these inspections, the witness said, was with a man named Donald Riniker, whose garden supplied a standing order of a hundred clones per week to Schafer. After that, Maggy recalled a specific order by Schafer to provide $1000 for the purchase of 100 clones from a couple in Calaveras County by the name of Rick and Sue Garner. Maggy also claimed to have knowledge of a transfer of 500 clones from the Garners to Schafer, but few details were supplied on this alleged sale, and it ultimately amounted to little more than a mention.

One of these clone exchanges, according to the witness, went in the reverse of the established order. Specifically, Maggy testified that he had seen Schafer give 40 clones to a glass-blower named Sean Cramblett and commonly known as "Nacho." In exchange for the clones, Maggy said, Schafer received a number of glass pipes.

It was then that the visual portion of the examination commenced, and jurors were given a slide-show presentation guided by the prosecutor's questioning. The content came from photos law enforcement officers had taken during their raid of Fry and Schafer's property in September 2001, and included views of the house, garage, hill and bunker room. Although Maggy had not been present on the day the pictures were taken, he described their contents meticulously, from the grow equipment in the garage and the bunker, to the plants growing on the hill. He was unable to give any guess about the amount of plants shown on the picture of the hill, but testified that they were, to his knowledge, marijuana plants. Aside from a close up on some of the buds, this hill shot was the only photo in this series that depicted plants. The rest featured only growing equipment, but a seemingly endless array of it: exhaust fans, lighting tubes, aerators, reflective insulation, plant nutrients, rock wool cubes, trays and flats. By the time the lights came back on in the courtroom, the audience had heard several tedious lists of these materials.

But the recitation of records had only just begun. The prosecutor's next focus was on lists of customer names that had been gathered at the Fry/Schafer office. These lists were sign-up sheets for a program called Home Health Horticulture Research (HHHR) that Maggy identified as an incarnation of Schafer's desire to help his customers grow marijuana for themselves. Maggy admitted to doing research for HHHR and developing the prototype for kits that facilitated indoor marijuana cultivation. The kits, he explained, cost $400 each and consisted of lights, plant nutrients and 6 marijuana clones ranging in height from 8 to 12 inches.

He continued by saying that customers would sign up for these kits after emerging from their consultations with Fry. At the end of each week, Maggy said, it had been his job to process the lists and divide the customers up by region in order to facilitate delivery of the requested grow kits. He referred to this process as "dispatching."

The direct examination had nearly ended at this point, but, in true fashion, Maggy would not be finished until he had implicated a few other individuals. To this effort, he named several people involved in the assembly and delivery of the kits: Schafer's semi-permanent houseguest Mike Harvey, Schafer's son Jeremy, and Randolph Gambourie, a former boyfriend of Schafer's daughter Heather.

Pings then wrapped up the loose ends, asking Maggy why he left Schafer's employment. "I was afraid – things were getting crazy," the witness said soberly. When asked how this was different from the marijuana club that he later set up on his own, Maggy began to state that a doctor ought not to be a provider of medicine. However, he tripped over himself in the middle of the thought, no doubt considering the court's restriction on using the terms "medical" and "medicine" when referring to marijuana. "I just didn't see writing a recommendation and then providing what the recommendation was for," was the explanation he finally settled upon.

And for the final happy ending, the audience was treated to a verbal snapshot of Maggy's current life – the witness described running a flooring business in Florida, where he's married and the proud father of twin babies. "I'm looking to move up," Maggy said with a cautious smile, before being turned over to Serra for cross-examination.

If Pings had navigated into the doldrums with her questioning, Serra was the perfect man to steer the proceedings back on course. Once the defense attorney took the floor, the conversation was instantly livelier, and the hotly contested objections soon began streaming in.

Serra's first triumph came as he redirected Maggy to the photograph of plants growing on the hill behind Fry and Schafer's house. "Is this photo similar to how it looked when you were there?" he asked the witness.

After Maggy affirmed the similarity, Serra had a new request. "Will you, in your expertise as an expert grower, point out what is a plant?"

"I'm not an expert grower," Maggy grumbled.

Undaunted by the witness's resistance, Serra moved right on with his strategy. Using a laser pointer, he circled one of the plants in the photo. "This looks like a plant," he said cheerfully. "Is it?"

Maggy agreed, following Serra through the same procedure for identifying all of the plants shown in the picture. At the end of the exercise, the defense attorney asked the witness to concur with a count of four or five plants, and Maggy obliged. Serra's tactic appeared to produce its intended effect of making the plant count seem rather trivial. This clearly defined count, topping off at a total of five,

During cross-examination, Tony Serra attempted to use government exhibits in his favor. Photo by Vanessa Nelson.

sounded far smaller in scale than the former portrayal of a whole hill of marijuana plants.

Continuing to diminish perceptions of the harvest yield, Serra scored from the witness a number of concessions regarding the large amount of unusable material in each marijuana plant. Adding in the ravages of a high mortality rate, Serra painted an extraordinarily bleak picture of his client's cultivation efforts. He questioned the witness about plagues of spider mites, epidemics of root-rot, lethal effects of over-watering, and feeding frenzies of deer and rodents. By the end of the series of inquiries, the defense attorney had created the impression that the survival of a marijuana plant in Schafer's garden was indeed a rare and miraculous event.

Maggy, however, was not entirely willing to go along with the assessment. Once the witness voiced his opposition, Serra got down to specifics. "While you were in the employ of Mr. Schafer, didn't a large number of plants suffer from over-watering?"

"I don't remember," Maggy replied. "I was just asked to come and look at them because they were turning yellow."

Serra, glowing with confidence, asked Maggy to recall an interview he had with Pings and another government agent. "Do you remember telling them on that occasion that you observed Riniker's marijuana plants at the defendants' house and recalled that most had died because they were over-watered?"

"I didn't say that," Maggy insisted defiantly.

Serra swung around to eye the prosecutor. "She told me you didn't lie," he said of Pings. "And I know it's not a lie – it's a police report!" There was more than a little sarcasm in Serra's quip, but the fact of the matter was that he produced the contested document in a flourish and put it squarely into the witness's hands. "Do you now concede that you told officers most had died because they were over-watered?" he asked after Maggy had looked over the report.

The witness admitted his error with an expression of defeat, but Serra was compelled to draw just a little more attention to Maggy's inaccuracy. "This is not a false police report, is it?"

"I don't believe so, no," Maggy said meekly, beginning to lose his footing.

Moving to another topic, Serra asked the witness if, following his debriefing that morning, he had spoken to anyone connected with the case. Maggy initially said that he had not done so, but when Coggins' name was mentioned, he affirmed that he had spoken to her earlier that day. In a similar pattern, Maggy at first denied that he had spoken about anything relating to his testimony, but once confronted with specific questioning, revealed that he had asked Coggins to refresh his memory about how much he earned and by whom he was paid while employed by Schafer. These were indeed matters Maggy had testified about on the stand, and his deceptive evasiveness under Serra's questioning contributed to the slow crumble of his credibility.

Remaining on the topic of collusion with Coggins, Serra began to address the patient lists and blank recommendation forms that were discovered in the couple's house. At first, Maggy tried repeatedly to deny that he had possessed these forms, coyly acting as though he had no idea what Serra was talking about. Eventually, however, the defense attorney established that these documents had been found in a home shared by Coggins and Maggy while they were living as fugitives, but even then, the witness tried to pin all responsibility on his ex-girlfriend.

"You had them because you took them from Dr. Fry and Dale Schafer," Serra uttered a typically ambiguous hybrid of a question and an accusation.

"I believe these were copies Traci had to keep with her everywhere she went," the witness attempted, playing on his former girlfriend's role as a notary. However, Maggy's claim deflated when faced with the fact that these documents were seized long after the couple left the employment of Fry and Schafer.

"Isn't it true that you spread a rumor all over northern California that Dr. Fry and Dale Schafer were no longer able to provide medical marijuana to people, and you were taking over the patient list, and you were soliciting for the possible transfer of marijuana to them!?" It was a mouthful of an allegation, but Serra managed to deliver it all skillfully in a tone of escalating outrage.

The witness denied it without comment, but the defense attorney had already made his point. Now it was time for him to use his incisors. "Isn't it true that you thought you would be arrested and so you split to Arizona, and you picked up a moral turpitude charge for theft because you took money for a bike and then you did not provide it back, either in money or in bicycle?"

Maggy admitted this, and also verified that he had been convicted on this charge. Serra then asked him if he had also been charged with a felony for impersonating his brother to a police officer, and Maggy again confirmed the truth of the description. "And, obviously, you're a felon, as you sit there," Serra said in summary.

"Yes." Whether sincere or simulated, the witness did an excellent job of sounding disheartened.

But the mention of Maggy's felonies was not meant merely to illustrate the details of his criminal past, but also to expose his motivations for cooperating with the government and for offering himself as an informant. To this end, the defense attorney brought Maggy's memory back to his testimony with the grand jury and to the meetings he had with the government after he decided to cooperate. Serra wanted to know how the witness had been restrained during these encounters, and so Maggy described being shackled the entire time in metal handcuffs, chains and leg irons.

Having circled a bit during the cross-examination, Serra finally went in for the kill. "You were facing a 5 year sentence – isn't that why you cooperated?" he asked pointedly.

The witness responded like a boy scout. "I cooperated because I wanted to put this behind me and accept responsibility for my part of this."

Serra poked at the façade of innocence. "But didn't you testify so you could get out of a mandatory minimum?"

"I just told you why," Maggy said, a hint of agitation showing through. "I wanted to put it behind me. I wanted to take responsibility for what I had done."

Watching a look of distress begin to emerge on her witness, Pings objected on grounds that the question had already been asked and answered. Judge Damrell appeared to agree, telling Serra flatly, "Counsel, he answered your question."

Tony Serra used provocative language to get under a witness's skin and express doubts to the jury. Photo by Vanessa Nelson.

"Ah, but from my perspective, that's wiggling out of a question," the defense attorney clarified, before turning right back to Maggy. "You're saying you cooperated out of patriotism, not to get out of a sentence?"

"I knew what I did was wrong," Maggy shot right back. "I was taking responsibility for it."

With growing exasperation, Pings made another objection, this time claiming harassment. The judge ordered Serra to move on, and this time there was the sound of a rattlesnake's tail in his tone. The defense attorney submitted, at least for the moment, addressing a few less relevant matters before eventually circling back to the issue of Maggy's motivation for testifying.

"So you've indicated that you weren't interested in a downward departure?" Serra asked the witness in a manner that was deceptively casual.

"I didn't say that I wasn't interested," Maggy tried to explain. "I said that isn't *why* I cooperated."

"But you didn't tell it that way to the jury, did you?" Serra asked, pouncing. "You said, 'Oh, I'm not doing this to reduce my sentence. I just want to get it behind me. I'm just *patriotic.*'"

As expected, Serra's cartoon-voiced ridicule of the witness's testimony was met with an objection and an interruption by the judge. The defense attorney then resumed, but from a different direction. "You walked when you were sentenced, didn't you?" he asked the witness.

Maggy admitted that this was true, and also verified that he had violated the terms of his supervised release on numerous occasions. By the defense attorney's account, after Maggy had tested positive for marijuana and gotten caught with marijuana in his car, he threw himself on the mercy of the court and begged for drug counseling. His request was granted, but he was quickly thrown out of rehab for developing an "inappropriate relationship" while in the program. The defense attorney extracted these tidbits, but focused most intensely on dramatizing Maggy's pleas for leniency. Serra said that Maggy had "violated a promise to the court to obey all laws and conform to the rules of supervised release," but was repeatedly given another chance. Mocking Maggy's request for drug counseling, Serra made the ceiling shake with his theatrical recreation of the feigned tearful appeal. "'I am a marijuana addict! Put me in rehab! I am so addicted to marijuana!'"

Pings, visibly annoyed, broke in, "Your honor, can we lower the decibel level in here?"

"Oh, that's my nature," Serra apologized with a humble lowering of his head. "I didn't mean to intimidate the witness."

It was a clever choice of words on Serra's part. The defense attorney played a card that stirred Maggy's machismo, and it worked like a charm. "I'm not intimidated," the witness declared.

"You don't look intimidated," Serra conceded amiably. Then the defense attorney began to skillfully play out his hand. "But you were scared when you were arrested, weren't you?"

"Yes," the witness answered cautiously.

Serra detailed the conditions of Maggy's experience: a young man, bound in handcuffs and leg irons, was interrogated persistently about crimes for which he faced years and years in prison. As he described each element of the situation, the drama of Serra's portrayal continued to rise. At its climax, he bellowed at the witness, "You were scared as *hell*, weren't you!?"

Maggy could give only a simple response. "Yes."

"And you did that because you were a coward and you didn't want to pay your own dues," Serra shouted, referencing Maggy's cooperation with the government. This time, the defense attorney was escalating his intensity at an even faster rate. "You would snitch out anyone – even your own mother!"

Maggy's denial was drowned out as Pings shouted back an objection, calling Serra's questioning argumentative.

Serra pushed his rhetoric forward immediately, not even pausing for the judge's decision. "But you snitched out your girlfriend, didn't you, to save your own skin?" he hissed at Maggy.

Pings was taken aback by Serra's relentlessness, this time reiterating her objection in tune with the frenetic energy of the room.

It was a dramatic moment to choose for the trial's first weekend break, but Judge Damrell demonstrated a fondness for cliffhanger endings and cut off the testimony at this suspenseful spot. With the instruction to discuss the case with no one and expose themselves to no related media, jurors went home for three days of reflection. Serra's accusations remained fresh in memory, his vivid images burned into the retina of the mind's eye and the tones of his theatrical voices echoing in the ear. Eager to hear more tales of a snitch who would rat out his own mother, courtroom observers salivated over the resumption of the cross-examination. Paul Maggy, no doubt, spent the weekend dreading it.

Paul Maggy, Part 2

When the trial resumed after the weekend break, it was clear that the defense had fresh tactics to employ in the cross-examination of the governent's lead witness. The "customers" referenced during the direct examination were rhetorically transformed into "patients," a linguistic strategy the government largely tolerated. Prosecutor Pings was not quite so tolerant of various other attempts to bring medical marijuana to the attention of the jury, however. What emerged was clearly a war of words, and the defense attorneys proved themselves quite innovative in the techniques of battle.

Serra's last sentences to the witness had accused him of snitching on his girlfriend and speculated that he would rat on his own mother. The tension of those statements eased during the three days of recess, and Serra approached the witness more gently when the cross-examination proceeded. "You testified that people left Dr. Fry's office with recommendations relating to marijuana and state law," the defense attorney began. "What is the difference between a recommendation and a prescription?"

"I don't know what the difference would be," Maggy replied, demonstrating a suspiciously low level of awareness for someone who had worked as the assistant for an attorney specializing in medical cannabis law. "I believe that throughout the time I was there, I was corrected on the term that was used."

Serra was on the trail of the scent. "Didn't you do research on the legality of—"

Pings chimed in with her first objection of the new week, claiming that the defense's question was asking for a legal opinion from the witness. Judge Damrell shifted his eyes carefully from one attorney to the other, "Overruled."

"I don't know where the term 'recommendation' came from," Maggy offered more glimpses at his supposed ignorance. "I just heard it used many times."

"And weren't there situations where people could get it for free?" Serra inquired about the recommendations.

"There were situations like that, yes," the witness admitted.

Serra then asked Maggy if there had been any stickers on the baggies of marijuana that he saw in the blue duffel bag in Schafer's office. The witness admitted they were marked "HHHR" for Schafer's Home Health Horticulture Research program. When pressed, Maggy revealed that the baggies had also been marked with a label that read "Medical Cannabis for the Ill."

Serra kept fishing, "Was marijuana given for free?"

"Sometimes," Maggy conceded.

With the prospect of free marijuana for patients in need, one would expect business to boom for Fry and Schafer. In spring of 2000, however, activities at the Cool offices appeared to, well, cool. Serra had a theory for this decline, and in presenting it he unveiled a new method of drawing attention to the medical nature of the marijuana in question.

He smiled at Maggy. "Wasn't this around the time you went on to create your own 'blank' marijuana project?"

It was astounding. For a single moment of bewilderment, all the players appeared to freeze and squint at what they had just heard. Upon consideration, it appeared that it was true – Serra had just succeeded at making the absence of a word infinitely more striking than its presence would have been.

Pings broke the spell and uttered an irritated objection, but Serra responded to the prosecutor's concern with eagerness. "Oh, can I say 'medical'?" he asked the judge in a chipper tone.

The prosecutor answered with her tattletale voice, "He's been violating the court order many times…"

The judge sighed, "You can convey these ideas – medical – to sell marijuana, right?"

"To dispense," Serra corrected.

"There you go," Judge Damrell said, but Serra had barely gotten into his next idea before the judge fell back into an old pattern of demanding the avoidance of the term 'medical marijuana.'

After bowing his head in accord, Serra proceeded onward with the point of his questioning – that when they left the employment of the defendants, Maggy and his girlfriend Traci Coggins had stolen patient records in order to start their own business. This theory explained why Maggy and Coggins were arrested in possession of various recommendations that had been signed by Fry…a fact that Maggy had previously tried to explain away by saying Coggins's capacity as a notary required her to possess the records.

Serra eyed the witness. "Isn't it fair to say that you knew the end was near with your tenure with Dr. Fry and Mr. Schafer, so you took – the more benign word – the recommendations for their patients so that you could make them your patients!?" The defense attorney was doing what he did best – escalating a question into an inflammatory claim.

Pings objected to the use of the word 'patients,' but the judge had other concerns. "These are compound questions, counsel," Judge Damrell observed.

The defense attorney was quick to simplify. "You ripped them off, didn't you?" Serra's voice had all the flourish of a magician who just succeeded in a visually stunning trick.

"No," the witness insisted, unflustered. "They signed up with me." Clearly, Maggy was referring to the patients, but was reluctant to refer to them in that terminology. He was the government's witness, after all, and he had a well-rehearsed sheen on his words.

Serra continued with an assortment of tactics to reinforce the medical nature of the marijuana. "When you were employed by Mr. Schafer," he asked Maggy in a slow lead-up, "were you told to be on the lookout for people who didn't look sick and might be defrauding the system?"

"I was told to be on the lookout for narcs," Maggy generalized.

"But how did you know?" Serra asked, his arms becoming increasingly animated as he talked. "You didn't see anyone with the word 'narc' written on their forehead, did you? They didn't come in and flash you a badge, did they?"

"No," Maggy gritted.

"So an indicator would be someone looking robust and strong, with no obvious illness?" the defense attorney was less in pursuit of an answer than the chance to stress some concepts…and he had ample opportunity.

"I was told to be on the lookout for narcs," Maggy repeated. He was continuing to avoid giving a direct answer, but this just gave the defense attorney yet another occasion to ask the question and put even more emphasis on words like "sick," "ill" and "obvious illness." Maggy's every evasion became Serra's additional advantage.

"You were told to be on the lookout for people who didn't look ill?" Serra ventured once again.

The answer was predictable, "I was just told to be on the lookout for narcs."

Maggy's calm had a hint of disruption, but it was Pings who broke in to voice her disapproval. "Objection, your honor – already asked and answered."

Serra moved on to questions that reinforced Maggy's involvement in leading the grow kit assembly and distribution process. Faced with these inquiries, the witness continued the finger-pointing at Schafer as well as the family houseguest and the two oldest Schafer children. In a strange twist of expectation, however, Maggy exonerated Fry, testifying unambiguously that the doctor had nothing to do with the assembly and delivery of the grow kits. It was a small victory for the defense.

After that detour, Serra wanted to know how many clones the witness would check for roots when he went on buying expeditions and garden examinations. Maggy testified that he checked about 10% of the clones, and all of those he checked had roots. Serra made sure, however, that the jury understood that the witness had not checked every clone...in fact, checking only 10% meant that an overwhelming majority of 90% went unchecked. Given the emphasis, the significance of the numbers could not have been lost on the listeners.

Numbers also helped Serra to demonstrate the extent of Maggy's involvement as an informant. Counting from the witness's multiple debriefing hearings, Serra came up with a total of 53 persons and groups on whom Maggy had provided information about criminal activity. This list, in all its enormity, was painstakingly read aloud to the courtroom as the witness shifted repeatedly in his seat. Once concluded, he had only vague denials to offer. "I don't believe I gave those names," Maggy shook his head. "They were taken off signature cards. I couldn't even remember that many names."

"You did that to save your own skin," Serra declared.

"I did it to tell the truth," Maggy echoed the lines of explanation he had used the week before. "It was in my best interest to tell the truth."

"You did it to clear your own conscience?" Serra asked in a dubious tone. "But you told law enforcement officers that Coggins said she was still smoking marijuana, but the quality was poor – it was purchased on the black market – and that her recommendation was no longer valid, and she was using teas and herbs to try to clean up her system for a drug test for pretrial release." Serra paused for a moment to let all the elements of the run-on sentence catch up with the listener, then turned back to Maggy with an expression of disdain. "You told them this about your girlfriend?!"

"She isn't my girlfriend," the witness said, amending the most trivial point of Serra's claim. "But I did say that."

"This is the person who wants to get it all behind him, purify himself?" the defense attorney asked incredulously. "You voluntarily sought to have her pretrial release revoked for marijuana use! That's what you were trying to do, weren't you?!"

"I answered truthfully to the questions that were asked," Maggy said with a cold calm.

"No further questions," Serra declared, smiling cheerfully as he gave the floor to colleague Laurence Lichter. There would be time for more character annihilation, but with Maggy, the target just seemed too easy. No amount of cover from the prosecution could keep this witness's criminal past and ulterior motives from showing, and there was little sport in exposing such egregious moral failings. But, as observers soon heard, Maggy claimed to have a rather shallow understanding of the vocabulary of ethics.

Laurence Lichter adeptly revealed the weaknesses of testimony from government witnesses. Photo by Vanessa Nelson.

"You used the word 'wrong,' not the word 'illegal,' when talking about what you were doing," Lichter observed, speaking about Maggy's characterization of his activities with Fry and Schafer. "Why did you use that word?"

"Because I was in custody," Maggy answered, "and I had a lot of time to read the law."

Whether on purpose or by honest mistake, the witness appeared to be missing the point. Lichter tried to reinforce the distinction he was making. "Did anyone tell you to say 'wrong' in your testimony?"

Maggy denied being instructed to say such a thing, so the defense attorney took the next logical step and inquired whether the witness truly believed his behavior had been unethical. The question was expected, but courtroom spectators were flabbergasted by the reply. "I don't know what that means," Maggy answered.

It should not have been surprising that this witness, who had acquired nicknames like "Maggot" and "Super-snitch" amongst the defendants' circle of friends, would need a lesson in the definition of morality. It was staggering, however, to have this admission laid plainly on the table with a sheen of honesty. The moment was too telling for some, as evidenced by their shared expressions of astonishment, but Lichter maintained expert composure and provided the necessary definitions.

"I didn't mean to do anything illegal," Maggy explained, showing little fatigue as his time on the stand began to reach the end of its second day. "Once I realized that it wasn't legal, I realized it was wrong."

The focus on morality was working to create some fascinating interplays. Maggy had been steadfastly claiming that his cooperation with the government was motivated by an enlightened need to confess wrongdoing. It was a characterization that Serra mockingly described as a drive for purification, heightening the religious symbolism. And through it all, Fry sat serenely, a large crucifix hanging around her neck and rosary beads moving through her fingers. The religious symbolism was swirling, and it was impossible to calculate what the jury would make of it. Would they buy the idea of snitching as a form of redemption, or would they see Maggy as the Judas handing his benefactors over to crucifixion?

Beyond the ambiguity of good and evil, however, it was undeniable that Maggy had been through tribulations of his own. Indeed, much of the defendant's misery was documented as objective fact, including the debilitating motorcycle accident that shattered several vertebrae and eventually led him to Fry's services as a doctor. Lichter illuminated this history during cross-examination, but he had only begun to target specifics before he slammed into a brick wall of objections.

The defense attorney began making inquiries about the accident. "How many vertebrae were broken?" he asked the witness.

Pings objected on grounds of relevance, and Judge Damrell sustained her objection.

"Were there five vertebrae broken?" Lichter tried again with this question, but it met the same fate as the last one. This time, however, the defense attorney began justifying his purpose. "Your honor, he looks healthy and yet he has a recommendation—"

Judge Damrell was infuriated. "He does, but it's irrelevant," the judge roared back, promptly sending the jury off on their afternoon break.

Once the jurors were out of earshot, the judge and attorneys then took the opportunity to intently discuss details of Maggy's health. Their objective was to settle whether questions regarding prescription medications and their effects could be asked during cross-examination. The defense was hoping to use these inquiries to impeach the witness, and Lichter submitted documents substantiating claims of misstatements the witness had made under oath on this subject.

The points seemed trivial to some ears, however, and Judge Damrell saw little use in quibbling over such concerns as whether Maggy was permanently disabled or had only a 10% disability. "I don't see a single thing that impeaches him here – not a word, not a sentence, not a thought," the judge declared after looking over Lichter's submissions. "And the danger is he could waive privileged information."

Pings wholeheartedly agreed. "It's irrelevant unless it affects his ability to perceive, recall and relate to the jury – that's all," the prosecutor proclaimed, echoing many statements the judge had made previously. "Since mentions of medical marijuana are not allowed, it would be inappropriate to ask the witness about his medical condition."

The judge nodded, and Pings went a little further. "I don't like all these references to 'patients,' but that's unwieldy and hard to control," she conceded.

"I made that ruling," Judge Damrell recalled, "but by continually referencing it, it could make too much emphasis on it. Mr. Lichter, you have a way of ignoring my rulings and doing whatever you want to do, and I don't want to see that happen in front of the jury."

Lichter's cross-examination on this subject would therefore be permitted to proceed as an audition, outside the presence of the jury. The defense attorney was limited to the issue of whether the use of any medications had impaired the witness's ability to observe or recall events that occurred while he was employed by the defendants.

It was revealed that Maggy had previously taken many types of muscle relaxers and painkillers, but that he had left off all prescription medications in favor of inversion therapy to extend his spine. Audience members exchanged knowing glances at this description – those who vilified Maggy had no trouble imagining him spending his free time hanging upside down in the posture of a classic vampire.

Lichter, however, didn't dally in metaphors. He got straight to his point. "Have you used sleeping aids?"

"Yes, but I had a hard time getting up in the morning," Maggy admitted. "I couldn't function properly."

Lichter fastened onto this last statement. "You couldn't function properly? What do you mean?"

Maggy's response provided no new information. "It was hard to get up."

Lichter then asked the witness if he still had pain and swelling, and the reply was solemn. "Yes, I'm going to be dealing with this for the rest of my life," Maggy said with gravity.

Judge Damrell was comfortable with the idea of the jurors hearing these questions, so he summoned them back to the courtroom and the proceedings got back underway. Once Lichter got beyond what had already been rehearsed, however, the cross-examination quickly heated up again.

"Did you take sleep aids while you were working for Mr. Schafer?" the defense attorney asked

Pings objected, calling the question irrelevant, but Lichter was undeterred. "Did you take sleep aids while giving information to the U.S. Attorney?" he pressed.

This inquiry elicited yet another objection, followed by a sidebar conference. When Lichter resumed, he had something new up his sleeve. "When was the last time you had insomnia?" he asked the witness.

"All the time," Maggy responded. "I sleep about five hours a night."

Lichter cocked his head, "How much did you sleep last night?"

The question seemed mild and harmless, but Maggy's answer raised eyebrows. "Seven hours," he said plainly.

There were smirks aplenty in the audience. It did not escape notice that the witness's insomnia seemed to have eased while giving testimony against his former friends. The mechanisms responsible for this phenomenon were likely complex, but on the surface it looked strange indeed. Spending multiple days on the witness stand is a distressing experience for most, but Maggy appeared more invigorated than disturbed. Either there was serenity to be gained in unburdening his soul, as he might have claimed, or he found a twisted satisfaction in betrayal. Whatever the opinions on Maggy, they were strong indeed amongst the courtroom observers.

Of course, Maggy had many reasons to sleep poorly at night, above and beyond the pain of a broken back. Whether his moral deficiencies were as severe as suggested in the cross-examination, he had much to fear apart from the ethical consequences of his behavior. If a troubled conscience was not the thing that made him toss and turn, certainly a fear of revenge would steal some slumber. It was undeniable that he had wronged many people, and this was the next theme addressed in Lichter's cross-examination.

The defense attorney detailed various thefts and treacheries associated with Maggy's run from the law, many of which related to his former bicycle shop. A checkered past now mapped out for the jury, Lichter laid into the witness. "Do you admit that you violated the trust of your employees?"

"Yes," came Maggy's serene reply.

"Do you admit that you violated the trust of your customers?" Lichter asked sharply.

The witness, unperturbed, answered again, "Yes."

Lichter went for more, "Do you admit that you violated the trust of your distributors?"

"Yes," Maggy replied.

The audience had been watching the exchange like a tennis match, and this volley seemed like it could go on forever. The witness played like a pro, coolly hitting whatever Lichter lobbed at him. But the pairing was an even one – the defense attorney clearly had at least as much endurance as the witness, and neither side appeared close to fatigue.

As the afternoon advanced, Judge Damrell finally lost his patience and intervened. "This is dragging on and on and on, and I don't know where it's going," he said to Lichter with increasing vexation. "I am going to ask you to move on to matters that are relevant."

Such a characterization could only demean Lichter's cross-examination, but the defense attorney continued nonetheless. Through questioning, he got Maggy to admit to selling marijuana to a long list of people whose contact information he had taken from the defendants at the end of his employment with them. The witness also testified to exchanges of small amounts of marijuana between himself and Fry.

"Not large amounts, like a conspiracy to distribute over a hundred plants?" Lichter suggested.

Pings stood up and made a successful objection, preventing the witness's answer. As soon as she bent her knees to take a seat, however, the cross-examination put her right back on her feet again.

"Were you aware of Dr. Fry's condition?" the defense attorney asked the witness.

"Objection, your honor!" Pings said urgently. Falling in with the pattern, her wish was granted.

Lichter turned back to the witness stand. "You testified that the only time you didn't have back spasms is when you were using marijuana?" he inquired.

Pings issued another earnest objection, with Judge Damrell coming in sternly behind her. "I'm not going to allow this questioning!" he insisted angrily.

Though his path had been blocked at nearly every turn he tried to take, Lichter's cross-examination had done much to provoke critical thought from the jurors. The battles that ensued over his questions served to highlight the significance of their content, and the appeal of the forbidden gave them additional emphasis. In this strategy, where answers are seldom permitted, the questions themselves become the most important rhetorical device, and Lichter fashioned them skillfully for this purpose. By the time he gave up the floor, he had given the jury great fodder for contemplation.

It wasn't the end of Maggy's time on the stand, however. The lead witness's marathon of testimony stretched out into a third day, and both sides got a last go at him before he was finally dismissed.

It was Pings's opportunity to counter some of the accusations and insinuations that had come up during the cross-examination. One by one, she addressed several controversial issues, speaking about them with an undertone of ridicule in her voice that made each one sound foolishly trivial.

"Was there anything about you being shackled that caused you to testify as you did?" Pings spoke as though an answer in the affirmative would have been laughably ludicrous. Obediently, Maggy denied that the shackles had influenced him in this way.

"And if you had simply been subpoenaed and come in like any other citizen, would you have testified any differently?" the prosecutor asked.

Maggy's answer was the expected one. "No, I would have testified the same as I did today," he said dutifully.

Having given his credibility that little boost, Pings then led her witness into admissions about seeing Fry and Coggins smoke marijuana during business hours at the medical office.

"Did you ever have any other job where you were allowed to hang out with your girlfriend and smoke marijuana?" There was more than a hint of derision in the prosecutor's voice.

"No," Maggy answered plainly.

Pings and her witness then discussed the clones he claimed to have approved for Schafer's purchase, and Maggy reiterated his statement that all of those he examined had roots and were therefore actual plants, by definition.

"You testified about the 100 plants from Mr. Riniker that 'most had died from overwatering,'" Pings said, glancing at her notes very quickly. "Were these amongst the 800 plants you once saw at the defendants' house?"

60

Maggy answered that this was true, and looked up pleasantly at Pings for the next question. "And how much room does a clone take up at its base?" the prosecutor asked.

"Basically none," Maggy said, shrugging slightly. Asked about the size of the rockwool cubes, he replied, "About one inch by one inch."

Pings paused for a second, appearing to consider whether the suggestion had been made strongly enough. The idea was not a complicated one – these plants took up so little room that even a tiny space could contain vast numbers of them, and this understanding headed off potential arguments that there was not adequate space in the defendants' grow areas for several hundred plants. After the moment of assessment, the prosecutor smiled with satisfaction. Her re-direct had been potent in its brevity and simplicity. "No further questions, your honor," she said, turning the witness over to the defense.

Serra's follow-up was also succinct, although some allotment was made for the defense attorney's notorious charisma. As Lichter had hoped to demonstrate about the effects of prescription sleep aids, Serra set out to show that Maggy's perception and recall were impaired during the time he worked with the defendants.

"At the time you got a recommendation from Dr. Fry, you were smoking marijuana for the same ailments you talked about – back pain and insomnia?" Serra began the questioning with his trademark auditory command of the courtroom, using a great range of inflection to draw the listener into his speech.

Maggy said that he had, and so the defense attorney proceeded to his next question. "At the same time, you were obtaining knowledge about marijuana?" he asked slowly and clearly.

Again, the witness confirmed this was true, allowing Serra to move forward. "And in that time, did you come across any statement that said marijuana affected memory?"

At this point, Maggy resisted, "I don't remember anything like that."

Serra then set out to determine the diameter of the bowl on Maggy's pipe, and the witness, appearing cautious of the direction of the questioning, stayed safely in the middle of the road. He replied, "Medium."

Serra's next inquiry got back to his point. "When you smoked marijuana, did that have any influence on your ability to think?"

Maggy gave a long "uh" and then asked for the question to be repeated. His hesitation may well have been a bid for more time to consider a strategy for his answer, but he came off looking comically confused.

Serra obliged and restated, "Did it cloud your mind, affect your ability to think?"

"No," Maggy answered confidently this time.

"Did you forget where you left your car?" the audience tittered with hushed laughter at the defense attorney's suggestion.

The giggles continued in response to Maggy's answer. "No, I don't recall that."

Serra kept up his questions. "So you would say that marijuana left your mind clear?"

Maggy said that it did, and shifted in his seat. Tiny hints of discomfort were finally starting to show in his demeanor.

"And would you say that's a common affect from marijuana, from your research?" the defense attorney asked.

"I didn't study stuff like that," Maggy said, but his assertion was guarded and unconvincing.

Though he maintained his composure, it was clear that the witness was somewhat distressed. He was wiggling where Serra had tried to corner him, and after the defense attorney ran through a detailed list of prior felony arrests, it was enough to leave Maggy a bit rattled. Grinning, Serra concluded and took his seat.

Lichter went next, using his follow-up questions to direct the jurors' attention to the issue that was always lurking in the shadows of the testimony in this case: the existence of state law permitting medical marijuana.

"You don't have any legal training, do you?" the defense attorney began.

"No," Maggy responded into the microphone.

"In fact, you majored in mortuary science and your family owns a string of funeral homes?" Lichter asked.

Maggy gave a simple affirmation, and in spite of the dark appeal of mortuaries, there was no further mention of funeral parlors. The defense attorney had objectives beyond such morbid titillations, and he pursued them with vigor. "But on the compassionate use certificate, isn't there one part that says: I understand that marijuana is illegal under federal law, I am a California resident, etc?"

The witness confirmed this was true, and Lichter pushed the notion forward into the next question. "And you believed that there was a conflict between state and federal law?"

Pings interrupted, objecting on grounds of relevance, and the judge decided to discuss the matter out of the presence of the jury. It was an interplay that had become a tedious pattern early in the trial, but there was a surprise in the outcome this time – in spite of the judge's sternness on evidence regarding state law, he made the rare move of over-ruling one of the prosecutor's objections.

"They made everyone sign this," Pings said of Fry and Schafer's patient declaration forms. "I assume so they wouldn't get sued."

"I think the question is relevant," the judge pronounced. "If it brings up some hearsay, we'll deal with that. I understand that Mr. Schafer gave advice about whether it was legal or not, but I won't get into legality of case law at the time."

"Your honor decides the law in this case, I understand that," Lichter said, suddenly obsequious.

With that, the jury re-entered, and, in an unusual turn of events, the defense was allowed to proceed with its questioning after an objection.

"You signed the patient declaration?" asked Lichter.

"Yes," Maggy admitted without hesitation.

"And you signed a contrary one on a later date?" the defense attorney prodded.

The witness, however, blocked him entirely. "No," Maggy replied.

"You didn't sign one that said it was legal?" Lichter asked, demonstrating surprise.

Pings cut in abruptly, objecting. "It's been asked and answered, your honor," she said of the defense attorney's question. "May we approach?"

Lichter cringed at the request. "Do we have to go to sidebar?"

With a glance of ominous intensity, Judge Damrell gestured for Lichter to come to his bench. The attorneys all obeyed, and white noise came over the courtroom speakers. As the muted conference progressed, it became increasingly apparent that the defense's luck had been short-lived. The sidebar crushed Lichter's line of questioning this time around, and Maggy's testimony ended up concluding with a whimper rather than a bang.

After three days on the stand, Maggy was finally dismissed. It was a lengthy span of testimony by any measure, during which he had born the burdens of being the prosecution's lead witness and had withstood cross-examination by a pair of extraordinarily clever defense attorneys. And in doing so, he had spent so much time on the stand that it would be no surprise if the seat had molded into a distinct impression of his buttocks, leaving the next witness with the challenge of reshaping the sitting area.

Michael Harvey, Part 1

After countless hours spent scrutinizing the prosecution's first witness, courtroom observers were ready for something different. What they got, however, was more of the same – another witness whose testimony spanned multiple days in a prolonged effort to incriminate the defendants in every way permitted…and even some that weren't. But the revelations of this next witness lacked much of the clarity and consistency of his predecessor, pushing the rhetoric to the brink of humor and to the boundaries of tolerance.

Mike Harvey proved to be a difficult witness for both sides during trial. Sketch by Peter Keyes.

Even before cross-examination began, Mike Harvey had already shown himself to be utterly unreliable in his testimony. And by the end of his two-day stretch on the stand, it was doubtful that he added anything to the case but headaches, tense laughter, and agonized confusion.

Harvey presented as a gaunt, dark-haired man of middle age, and had a decidedly haggard look about him. He appeared to have attempted to clean himself up, but his dress shirt was wrinkled and hung awkwardly loose on his frame. His movements betrayed discomfort, not the least of which was shown in his constant fidgeting.

Perhaps to explain this conspicuous nervousness, the prosecution started out the direct questioning of Harvey by establishing that he didn't want to be there on the stand. Pings proceeded with attempts to reduce his anxiety, explaining that immunity had been granted for his testimony. In spite of her efforts, the prosecutor didn't get very far at putting her witness at ease, so she turned instead to testimony about the background of his involvement with the case.

Harvey's story started out in the army, where he worked at a missile site. He was honorably discharged from service twice, and went on to a foundry in Ohio as well as to landscaping work. Ultimately, he was introduced to Fry and Schafer through his niece, who was an employee of the defendants. When he first arrived at the Fry/Schafer home, he lived inside the house with the family, but eventually he moved into a trailer that sat on their property. He worked for the defendants while living with them, doing handyman tasks, feeding the animals, driving the children around to their extra-curricular activities, and helping to grow marijuana.

Once she got to the subject, Pings had plenty of questions about marijuana. According to Harvey, he didn't use marijuana when he arrived at the Fry/Schafer home, but began smoking it within three weeks of moving in. He said he saw both defendants smoke marijuana daily, and that both defendants asked him to do tasks related to marijuana cultivation. He started out with twenty plants grown from seed within his own living quarters, then later transferred these to the greenhouse on the Fry/Schafer property.

In spite of the tone of his rhetoric, it came out during cross-examination that Harvey was much more familiar with marijuana than he initially suggested on the stand. By saying that he didn't use marijuana when he arrived at the defendants' home, Harvey was referring only to a short period of abstinence. The statement was phrased in such a way, however, that it could easily be interpreted as meaning that Harvey did not initiate marijuana use until he came to live with Fry and Schafer. Though his words had been technically true, they were misleading and had an undercurrent that hinted that the defendants had a corrupting influence. In fact, Serra later got Harvey to admit that he had been smoking marijuana for 25 years prior to meeting Fry and Schafer. But even before that admission was made, it was clear that Harvey was no novice. All during the course of the direct examination, he claimed that he didn't need any instruction on how to grow marijuana plants.

Pings asked Harvey about one of his first tasks in setting up the grow room – covering the walls in reflective foil. According to the witness, both defendants had told him to do this job, but he insisted that he didn't need the reason for it explained to him. "I knew what the purpose was," he responded snidely.

Harvey made the same claims about the other tasks he performed in the grow room – watering the plants, giving them nutrients, installing lights and taking measures to ensure climate control. According to his testimony, he didn't even need to be instructed about the use of the timer or how to dry the harvested plants. Of course, he wasn't terribly good at describing these processes, and often made blundering mistakes when talking about the tasks and equipment. At times it seemed he couldn't get the right words out of his mouth to save his life.

The failures of communication began subtly, such as when Harvey repeatedly referred to the defendants' "drying room" in a way that sounded to Pings as though he was saying "drawing room." After a few encounters with this language, the prosecutor decided to straighten out the matter for good. "Some old-fashioned people on the east coast use the term 'drawing room' to refer to their living room," she explained. "That's not what we're talking about, is it?"

While Harvey appeared oblivious to the concept of a 'drawing room,' he eventually came to understand the distinction he was being asked to make. Obligingly, he described a room where marijuana was dried after harvest, as "whole plants were hung from the ceiling to let the THC drain down to the buds."

Most of the misunderstandings that occurred while Harvey was on the stand were minor and somewhat humorous. They were the type of shaky communication that people might have immediately upon meeting, while getting used to the particularities of each other's conversational style. But the difficulties never quite worked themselves out, and it was as though an impenetrable wall of verbal opacity hung between the prosecutor and her witness.

When Pings asked Harvey about the size of the lights in the grow room, he repeatedly insisted they were twelve feet long. He said it so many times, and with such assurance, that the prosecutor seemed unsure about how to coach him to a more appropriate answer. Finally, Pings got her witness to approximate the size of the lights in comparison to a normal household object. "Like a good loaf of bread," he responded, appearing weary of the subject. "Twelve feet long." He held up his hands and approximated a one-foot space between them.

"Okay, a loaf of bread is *not* twelve feet long," Pings clarified, eliciting smiles and giggles from the audience.

"Oh, I meant twelve inches," Harvey said after scrunching his face into a moment of thought.

As the courtroom of spectators watched, they let out a collective sigh. This was going to be a lengthy witness, and likely a frustrating one too. He was obstinate with the prosecutor, often using a condescending tone to insist on wildly inaccurate and inconsistent statements. But Pings stuck with it – no matter how agitated and difficult he seemed, Harvey was, after all, *her* witness.

The prosecutor tried again to get down to specifics. "What was the most plants you saw growing on the hill when you were working for the defendants?"

"Approximately 150," Harvey responded.

The prosecutor's reaction suggested that the answer was not quite what she had expected, and she pressed, "Does that include plants in the ground and in buckets?"

"Yes," Harvey said plainly.

Pings tried again to elicit a more specific response before ditching the subject altogether, "And *when* did you see 150 plants?"

But Harvey stuck to his answer. "At harvest time."

When asked about the intended recipients for the plants, Harvey said with assurance that he was growing "for the patients." Later, he clarified that this term referred to people with doctor's recommendations. And for these people, Harvey said, he was instructed by the defendants to make home deliveries of marijuana. The prosecution had already promised that their witness would describe this process as being similar to pizza delivery, but on the stand, Harvey drew a blank on the analogy. Pings had to try twice before finally coaxing it out of him, using questions like, "But didn't you say it was *similar* to something?" and, "Didn't you say it was *just like* something else?"

Pings then addressed the duration and the frequency of the deliveries. "How long did you make deliveries?" she asked the witness.

"Three months," was his simple response.

But the prosecutor had reached a limit with Harvey's inconsistencies, and she couldn't bear to let another one slip by. "Didn't you tell the grand jury that it was for a *year*?"

Serra knew when his territory was being infringed upon, and he interrupted with a tone of disbelief. "Objection," he called out to the judge. "She's impeaching her own witness!"

Judge Damrell barely looked up at the exchange. "Overruled," he mumbled.

Harvey struggled to rectify his response. "It was intensive for three months, and slow the rest of the time."

"How often did you make deliveries during the intensive period?" Pings asked.

Harvey contorted his face, as though the process of invoking memory was a physically painful one. "Five or six times a day, for 10 hours a day," he finally answered. He also told the prosecutor that he made deliveries within a wide range of geographical areas, between Vallejo and the south shore of Lake Tahoe, based on orders that came down through Fry's office.

At some point, however, Harvey got tired of all the driving and opted to take an ill-fated shortcut. He went to a mailing center and tried to send the marijuana packages through the United Parcel Service. Employees became suspicious of the packages and turned them over to federal agents, thus sparking the criminal investigation of Fry and Schafer. But, on the stand, Harvey's recall about these packages was predictably flawed.

At first he told Pings that he only sent five of these parcels, but when evidence was presented of seven seized packages, Harvey changed his answer. One thing he consistently maintained, however, was that the defendants were the ones that provided the marijuana and the orders to deliver it.

"Who gave you the marijuana to send?" Pings asked her witness.

"Mrs. Schafer," Harvey responded.

Pings clarified, "Do you mean *Dr. Fry*?"

"Yeah," Harvey agreed.

"And who would weigh out the marijuana?" the prosecutor ventured.

"Dr. Fry would do it," Harvey answered, "in her bedroom."

Pings pressed, "What did she use to weigh it?"

Harvey's response was quick, confident. "A triple-beam scale."

Pings was on her first roll with her witness, every answer coming back as expected. The prosecutor pushed her luck. "What is a triple-beam scale?"

"It's like the scales of justice," Harvey answered.

Pings took a half-step backwards, suppressing a sigh of disappointment. "Doesn't that technically have *two* beams?"

Things weren't getting much better for the prosecutor, so she advanced her questioning to address the end of Harvey's relationship with Fry and Schafer. "Did there come a time when you had spider mite problems with the plants?"

Harvey admitted that this was true, telling Pings that the infected plants had consisted of between twenty and thirty mature plants and two to three trays of clones.

"Did someone hold you responsible for that?" the prosecutor queried.

"They didn't say that, but they had someone else take care of the plants after that," Harvey answered. "I left right after that."

"When did you leave?" Pings asked.

Harvey didn't hesitate in his answer. "November 2001."

Pings paused, giving Harvey a chance to catch his own mistake. But, like every other time this scene played out, Harvey was either unaware or unconcerned about the errors in his testimony. "Are you sure about that?" Pings finally gave in and asked the question outright. "Were you there for the serving of the search warrant on September 28th, 2001?"

"No," Harvey answered Pings with a tone of annoyance, as though she had failed to do her own arithmetic. "I had been gone for two months," he added, acting like the answer should be obvious. This put Harvey's month of departure at July 2001, but this estimate didn't even last for the rest of his direct examination. After discussing the seized UPS packages one more time, he decided that he had actually left in February 2001 and amended his statement. By the time the judge sent the jury off to a break, things in his courtroom had become quite confused and confusing.

But there were other matters to sort out, one of which involved a question that had been sent to the judge by one of the jurors. Paper in hand, Judge Damrell frowned down at the handwritten inquiry before reading it out loud to the parties in the courtroom, "'When was the bunker built? Who built the bunker?'"

It appeared that at least one juror was considering the significance of whether the defendants constructed the safe-house on their property, and, presumably, whether they had done so with the ulterior motive of using it to stealthily grow marijuana. Judge Damrell suggested that the witnesses ought to be questioned more thoroughly on the issue, but Lichter was confident that the matter would be fully elucidated without additional focus. "I think it will become clear that the bunker was a fallout shelter and was built before the defendants arrived," Lichter said with assurance.

Sighing, the judge decided he would inform the jurors that their questions would go unanswered, at least for now. His instruction would be for them to let the trial take its course, and to ask questions only after hearing all the witness testimony. It was a simple enough solution, but resolving this issue left the parties facing another, more

71

complicated matter. While continuing to question Harvey, the prosecutor was preparing to present to the jury a series of photographs that the defense did not want shown.

These pictures depicted Fry and Schafer's young children playing and posing in the midst of marijuana plants, ostensibly while a reporter from *High Times* magazine covered a harvest on the defendants' property. The images were later published on a website, which is where federal investigators found them, but it was unclear whether Fry and Schafer objected to the presence of the photos on the internet. "They didn't give permission, but they also didn't take action to have it taken down," the prosecutor said of the defendants.

Whatever attitude Fry and Schafer had taken about the pictures being online, they felt strongly about the idea of the prosecution presenting these images to the jury. The defense attorneys had successfully prevented this from happening, forcing Pings to withdraw the photos initially. But the prosecutor changed her mind at the last minute and decided she wanted to use the pictures after all. "I don't mean to take back what I graciously offered before," she said, justifying her sudden change of plans. "But I think that's what I'd like to do."

This announcement stunned the defense, but Serra was quick to oppose the move. "Each of these photos shows minors, and that will potentially inflame the jury. It will do irrevocable damage," he declared. "Children next to marijuana plants, children touching marijuana plants, children seemingly frolicking in a marijuana area…[the prosecutors] want it because it shows marijuana and it shows some big buds."

Pings didn't argue with this claim. Instead, she referenced a photo of the defendants' daughter Caroline, who was nine years old at the time, holding what the prosecutor described as "a large and quite fruitful cola." The size was the important thing to convey here, according to Pings. "This contradicts the defense's assertion that they were not very good at growing," she concluded. The other photos, she explained, were important because they showed the number of plants in buckets on the defendants' property.

For Serra, these points certainly didn't justify the use of the photographs. "None of the reasons for producing these photos require the presence of the children," he maintained. "They are surplusage. They can be masked, covered up, marked over, etcetera, to keep out the inflammatory nature of having children there at a marijuana harvest."

But showing that there were children at the harvest was precisely what Pings wanted, and she made no apologies for her intentions. "This shows that he's handling his kids in such a cavalier way," the prosecutor said about Schafer. "This goes against the contention that he ran only a strictly professional, responsible business based on charity."

Serra turned to the judge, suggesting that Pings was being greedy on this issue. "She wants her cake and to eat it too," he said of the prosecutor. "These pictures were there because the defendants believed one hundred percent that what they were doing was legal. But, we can't say that to the jury. And the jury could be so prejudiced by these photos that there could be no prospect of us raising reasonable doubt."

Judge Damrell, however, was not about to let the photographs be seen by the jury without first having the images of the children removed. He listened carefully to Serra's speech, after which the parties began debating how and what to redact from the pictures. The defense insisted on bodies as well as faces being blurred out, but consented when the judge decided to leave in arms.

When the images were finally returned by the prosecution, they looked quite odd. Bright white glows stood in place of the children in the photographs, giving an eerie, paranormal quality to the figures. These 'ghosts' fenced with branches from marijuana plants, held up large buds, and sat on a pickup truck loaded with marijuana, waving indistinctly at the camera. It was a strange sight indeed, but both the defense and the prosecution approved the alterations, and the judge proceeded to set down the rules regarding their use. Harvey would be allowed to see the unaltered images, privately from a binder on the witness stand, but he was instructed not to refer to any of the identities of the blurred-out persons. The jury, of course, would only be permitted to see the photos in their altered form.

Harvey resumed the stand once the jurors were back in the box, and Pings had full use of all the redacted pictures. But Harvey's memory problems only continued to increase, making him a difficult witness even for the basic task of identifying items in photographs. He was unwilling to estimate when the photos had been taken, saying only that harvest was done "when the plants were ready to harvest." It was just one of the many redundancies in Harvey's speech.

In the picture with plants in buckets, Harvey gave his count as a mere eight plants, which hardly sounded like a condemnation. But Pings used the photo series to get as close as she could to suggesting that the defendants' minor children had helped with the cultivation and distribution of marijuana. In Exhibit 167, she displayed a photo of Schafer and Harvey in the living room of the defendants' home, trimming marijuana plants. "The individuals in this redacted area, are they participating in this activity?" Pings asked, pointing to the blurry, whited-out figures in the picture.

Harvey glanced between the courtroom projector screen and the binder on the witness stand. "Yes," he answered, unambiguously.

Other answers were harder to summon, however. There were many times in the remainder of the direct examination when he would be unable to remember any details at all, like what the letters in Fry and Schafer's "HHHR" organization stood for. "I don't know what they all meant," he snapped at the prosecutor, appearing to resent that the question was asked.

He was equally indignant when he failed to recall the names of Fry and Schafer's kids, the very children whose care he had undertaken. "I'm just really nervous at this time," he said in a huff, glaring over the microphone on the witness stand.

A lack of memory was one thing, of course, but inconsistent recall was another matter entirely, and sorting out Harvey's varying answers ate up a significant amount of time during both the direct questioning and the cross-examination. The process seemed unending – Harvey would insist devotedly on an answer that would later be shown to be factually incorrect, at which time he would simply give a new answer and insist upon it with similar devotion. It was a maddening cycle indeed, inspiring expressions of deep frustration on the faces of the jurors.

When Serra finally began his cross-examination, there was ample material for attack. As his first major inquiry, the defense attorney chose to focus on the issue of when Harvey stopped residing at the defendants' home. "Was it November 2001 or February 2001?" Serra asked simply. "When did you leave? You answered both ways."

"November 2001," Harvey replied without hesitation.

Serra challenged the witness. "So you were present for the search warrant?"

"No – you have me really upset," Harvey sneered. "No, I wasn't present."

Serra persisted, "Isn't November after September?" When Harvey admitted that this was true, the defense attorney hit him with the next logical question. "So you *would* be there?"

"Yes," Harvey said, beginning to look seriously pained.

"But you *weren't*, were you?" Serra asked, prodding.

Harvey hit his limit at that moment, his temper boiling over in a hiss. "I just don't remember *everything*," he insisted, his small eyes blazing. "You have me rattled. You're good. That's my story and I'm sticking to it."

Of course, claiming difficulty with his memory didn't let Harvey off the hook – it just gave Serra a new hook to put him on. "You testified for the grand jury that you weren't good with dates," the defense attorney reminded the witness.

"I may forget things, but I don't fill in the blanks," Harvey said, attempting to defend himself. "Everyone forgets things."

Serra got to the point. "Do you forget things?"

Harvey shot the question right back, adding a tone of irritation. "Do *you* forget things?"

Judge Damrell broke in, instructing the witness to answer rather than argue, and Serra asked his question once again. "Do you forget things?"

"Yes," Harvey admitted.

Finally gaining ground, Serra pressed for more. "Is there any infirmity to your memory?"

Harvey acquiesced. "Yes."

"Your recommendation says that you're disabled, that you have memory loss, headaches, alcohol abuse," Serra said, listing off the conditions.

But Harvey became stubborn again. "Just headaches," he said firmly.

Serra insisted, "You have a bad memory caused by 30 years of alcoholism – is that true?"

"No," Harvey said, denying the description flatly.

Serra was buoyant. "Did you say that to Dr. Fry during your evaluation?"

"I don't remember saying that," Harvey was muttering now, almost like a gruff whisper to himself.

"Do you want to see it?" Serra asked, offering to show the document.

Harvey refused, narrowing his eyes. "If it's there, it's there," he conceded.

Serra continued, "On the form, you said you were fired from two jobs because of emotional problems and poor memory."

"I don't recall that," Harvey said obstinately.

Pings objected to the line of questioning, and after a relatively brief sidebar, Serra restated his inquiry. "I referred to a diagnosis," he clarified to the witness. "Were you aware you were diagnosed by Dr. Fry as—"

The prosecutor broke in again, objecting frantically this time and calling Serra's claims hearsay. "It's foundational," the defense attorney assured the judge before turning back to the witness. "When you came to Dr. Fry and Dale's Schafer's premises, do you recall saying you needed time to dry out?"

As he did with all the other suggestions of alcoholism, Harvey resisted this characterization. "I don't recall," he said plainly.

Judge Damrell was skeptical. "Is this foundational?" he asked before allowing the defense attorney to continue.

Serra explained, his signature confidence shining. "It's about memory loss," he told the judge matter-of-factly, then returned to the witness. "Do alcoholics have gaps in memory?"

"Everybody has gaps in memory," Harvey said vaguely. It was evident that the witness felt more comfortable with generalizations than with inquiries about himself.

But Serra insisted on keeping it personal and specific. "Do you?"

"Yes," Harvey said, then echoed his last answer. "Everybody does."

Serra began extending now. "Delirium tremens?" he asked. Harvey denied it.

"Blackouts?" the defense attorney queried. The witness wouldn't even acknowledge the possibility.

Blocked, Serra went back to the discussion of impaired memory. "How long did you suffer from memory loss before arriving at my client's premises?"

But instead of answering, Harvey balked at the barrage of questions. "Am *I* on trial, sir?" he demanded of the defense attorney.

Serra just gave back a kindly smile and repeated his efforts. "How long did you suffer from memory loss before arriving at my client's premises?"

"I don't know," Harvey said grudgingly.

"Longer than 10 years?" Serra nudged the witness.

"I don't know," Harvey repeated, starting to steam up again.

"Why not?" the defense attorney pressed.

"I just said I didn't know!" Harvey exclaimed, nearing a full yelling tone.

Serra took full advantage of the emotional intensity initiated by the witness, and began laying into him with a tone of righteousness. "The defendants took you into their family...they gave you a place to sleep...you sat at the family table...they paid you a salary, gave you room and board...you went with them to church every Sunday...they gave you presents on Christmas, and you got healthy and strong under their care..." Serra's voice rose with each description, like a sermon approaching a climax of glory. He paced, looking around the courtroom as he made a list of the intimacies between Harvey and the defendants. Then, in a snap, he turned back to the witness to hurl the accusation, "And then you went and became an informant behind their backs!"

Pings issued a resounding objection to Serra's terminology, but it was a problem that was not so easily fixed. The parties tried out terms like "cooperating witness" and "testifier" before they finally settled in agreement on an acceptable term, but the witness already had the idea of what was meant.

"I was approached by the DEA," Harvey admitted to Serra.

"Were you scared?" the defense attorney asked.

"No, I was *happy*," Harvey's voice was drenched in sarcasm.

Pings objected, claiming that Serra was badgering the witness. "Yes, you are," Judge Damrell agreed frankly, asking the defense attorney to move on.

Serra kept the fire-and-brimstone vibe as he moved on with the witness. "Isn't it true that Dr. Fry and Mr. Schafer paid you a social visit six months ago and they asked you if you were testifying, and you *lied* to them?!" He made heavy eye contact with Harvey as he concluded. "These good people took you in and you looked in their face and *lied to them*!"

Harvey swallowed. "I am looking you in the face right now and telling you the truth," was the response he managed.

Serra smirked. "You understand your status as you sit there, don't you?"

"Status?" Harvey asked, perplexed.

Serra shot the answer back fast and loud. "You're a RAT!"

Judge Damrell was aghast. "Oh, counsel…this dramatization…oh," he floundered, caught in a state of shock and dismay before finally ordering the jury to recess. Once all jurors had left the courtroom, the judge turned back to the defense attorney and addressed him with equal parts of pleading and outrage. "Mr. Serra, calling a witness a rat is going way too far. I know you love the dramatics and the theatrics, but there are rules of the courtroom to abide by. You're going way over the edge this time. I don't know how your clients are helped by your conduct."

Tony Serra's decibel level and character descriptions pushed the boundaries of courtroom decorum. Photo by Vanessa Nelson.

Serra shrugged, at first standing by his call, "That is his milieu, your honor." Pressed, however, the defense attorney relented, "Okay, I won't use the term again."

In a move that left watchers flabbergasted, Judge Damrell simply stood up and exited the courtroom. His body language spoke loud and clear –proceedings had concluded for the day, and there would be hell to pay tomorrow.

Michael Harvey, Part 2

Mike Harvey's second day on the witness stand began with drama, picking right up where it had left off the previous afternoon. When Judge Damrell entered the courtroom and walked toward his bench shortly after 9am, he moved with a greater heaviness than ever before. This case, it appeared, had begun weighing on him.

He looked down at the participants with a stony expression, surveying them carefully before beginning. The hesitation gave his authoritative disapproval a moment to sink in, and it did so with gravity. When he finally spoke, he went straight to the point.

"Court ended early yesterday because things had gone over the line," Judge Damrell said. "Mr. Serra, I've given you latitude. You're a lawyer and you're passionate about this subject, but what you say is not evidence and the jury will be told that. When a trial focuses on the lawyers, it's focusing on the wrong people."

"I apologize, your honor," Serra responded, his voice bold but sincere as he explained that he was helpless in his reactions to informants. "For me, it's Pavlovian."

"Well, you better keep that dog under control," Judge Damrell snapped back, showing that his outrage did not impair his wit. "You've got more experience in the courtroom and you know exactly what you're doing. Pavlovian doesn't cover it."

But Judge Damrell had more than one item on his list of grievances.

The prosecutor stepped forward to inform the judge that the defendants' family had been spotted on the 11th floor of the court building, which is where the U.S. Attorney's office is housed. Pings reported this sighting with a pitch of such indignation that it perplexed the watchers who were packed into the gallery seats. "So what?" one observer whispered, only to get looks of incredulity from his companions.

As it turned out, the person who had committed this misdeed was Heather Schafer, the oldest daughter of the defendants' brood. Heather, who suffers from lupus, later explained that she had become ill that afternoon and was taking the elevator down to the ground floor in order to use the bathroom. She said she thought she had made it there when the elevator stopped on the 11th floor, and, nauseous, she rushed out to get to the bathroom. Quickly realizing her mistake, she turned around to re-board the elevator...but not without escaping the notice of government employees.

"It's inappropriate," Pings stressed in court, trying to express her shock to the judge.

Courtroom observers, however, continued to exchange looks of disbelief. It seemed strange that a young woman who got off on the wrong floor would be held in such high suspicion of spying, and stranger still that the prosecutor who conveyed these suspicions had built her own case on witnesses who had done a great deal of covert surveillance on the defendants, and who had falsified personal information in an effort to gain access to their clinics. As she reported the incident in dramatic tones, it seemed clear that Pings was appalled by the very thought of spying...unless, of course, it was done by law enforcement officers.

Serra, however, was quick to defuse the situation, telling the judge that he had spoken to the defendants' family members and they had agreed to stay away from the 11th floor. It imparted an aura of the ominous to what was otherwise just a number on the elevator journey down from Judge Damrell's 15th story courtroom, evoking feelings of the dangerous woods and mysterious locked chambers of fairy tale lore. But the solution was clear – whatever the 11th floor held that was so risky, the Fry/Schafer family had pledged to avoid the temptation of the forbidden elevator stop.

Pings appeared pacified by the concession. Her lair was now secure, but getting to it safely was another matter of concern and anxiety. As she described it, the defendants' supporters had "formed a horseshoe around the door and hissed" at her and her witnesses as they left the courtroom the previous day. Once again, she spoke with the tone of one greatly affronted, and, this time, she won words of dismay from the judge.

"I understand that there has been a large group of people here, and they are very interested in this case, but if there's stuff like that going on, I'll have to remove supporters from the courtroom or cite them for contempt if there's any intimidation," he scolded sternly. "This is a court of law."

The admonition continued once the jury had been brought in and seated in the box. Explaining to them the reason the proceedings had ended early the day before, he added, "This is not an argument on the street corner or the schoolyard. This is a court of law." Reinforcing his point, the judge advised, "What the lawyers say is not evidence. You must listen to the testimony."

Serra then stepped towards the jury box with his words of penitence. "I apologize to everyone for my outburst," he said with a sensitive smile. "We will proceed henceforth with dulce voce – that is, sweet voice."

If things seemed back on track, however, it was only because they had fallen back into a familiar pattern. As soon as Harvey was back on the stand, the ballet of resistance and insistence continued between him and the defense attorneys. And, as before, the testimony was plagued by the witness's imperfection of recall.

Starting in, Serra referred to statements Harvey had given to the prosecutor. "You said you made 5-6 deliveries per week," the defense attorney noted. "How long did you do that?"

"On and off for a 6 month period," Harvey answered, his eyelids already crumpled into a distrustful squint.

"Isn't that the same time you were the gardener, doing the watering?" Serra asked.

"Yes," Harvey responded pointedly.

Serra raised his eyebrows in astonishment. "So how could you be gone 5-6 days per week, for 10 hours a day, and still do everything you needed to do to maintain this huge grow?"

"How?" Harvey asked back, conveying his confusion.

"You're not a split personality, are you?" Serra shot back.

Judge Damrell interrupted, reminding Serra firmly that the witness had described his delivery schedule as being "on and off." But the judge's assistance did not reassure the witness, who was beginning to transform his apprehension into self-shielding cynicism once again.

"Do you have houseplants, sir?" Harvey demanded of the defense attorney. Do you water your plants all day?"

Serra looked back at the witness with a bemused smile. "I get to ask the questions," he informed Harvey good-naturedly.

Judge Damrell chimed in, growing weary of the dance already. "Let the lawyers ask the questions," he told Harvey with a sigh, settling in for what promised to be a long and heated cross-examination.

Serra kept with the theme of questioning Harvey on what he had previously told Pings. "On redirect yesterday, she asked you how many times you delivered clones and you said ten times, but at the grand jury, you said you didn't recall."

"I can't really say," Harvey mumbled, scowling.

"Your memory is not like a fine wine that gets better with time, is it?" Serra inquired, warming up to the full heat of accusational questioning.

"I'm not a doctor," the witness returned. "I can't really say."

Serra persisted. "Your memory fades with time, doesn't it?"

"Doesn't everybody's?" Harvey, when not angry, was conspicuously evasive.

Serra edged closer to his objective. "So wouldn't the grand jury testimony in 2003 have been better for your memory, since it was closer in time to the event?"

"I can't say," Harvey responded, visibly vexed. "Sir, I was so busy at the time, I didn't know how many clones I delivered."

Serra put his palms up. "Then why would you testify that you'd done it 10 times?"

Lack of recollection was this witness's perpetual refrain. "I don't have the exact memory," he offered again.

When questioned about outdoor marijuana plants that were allegedly grown on Fry and Schafer's property, Harvey gave a repeat performance. There was already confusion over the plant count when the defense started cross-examining the witness…and more inquiries just made for more confusion.

Serra again referred to Harvey's prior testimony. "You just testified that the most plants you saw on the hill was 150 plants growing?"

"Yes," Harvey answered solidly.

"But when you testified for the grand jury," Serra noted, "you said that 250 was the most plants you saw on the hill at any one time."

"I wasn't in charge of the numbers," the witness shrugged. It was a perplexing response.

Perplexity, however, didn't deter Serra – rather, it ignited him. "But how do you explain the discrepancy?" the defense attorney asked.

"They were different times and dates," Harvey said slowly and loudly, as though being made to explain something painfully obvious.

The defense attorney had a look of concentration. "So you were there for two harvests?"

"Yes, I was," Harvey insisted, claiming he had seen 150 plants on the hill in August 2000 and 250 plants in October 2001. It was an odd answer, given that the plants had been confiscated by law enforcement on September 28th, 2001.

"So in August 2000, how many plants did you see?" Serra asked. When Harvey hesitated, the defense attorney nudged him. "Did you see 150? Or 250? Or less than 20?"

"Did I say less than 20?" Harvey hissed, confusion bringing out his temper.

"I'm saying the space could only accommodate that many," Serra said quickly, trying to slip the comment under the prosecutor's radar. "How many plants did you see?"

Harvey was obstinate. "I already said."

"Did you leave in February of 2000 or 2001?" Serra asked, attempting to bring the witness's error to his attention.

"Is this a trick question?" Harvey said with heated suspicion. "I left in February 2001."

When the defense attorney asked the witness how many harvests he had witnessed on the defendants' property, Harvey said he had only seen one. "How is it, then, that you saw two different numbers of plants?" Serra wondered. "Did you sneak back later and count?"

"No, I flew over in an airplane," Harvey barked back facetiously. Observers in the gallery flashed quizzical looks at each other, no doubt pondering whether the witness had been on flyover surveillance with law enforcement. "At one point, there were over 250 plants," Harvey clarified. "125 were brought in buckets, for me to watch, and then they were gone."

"You exaggerated when you said 250 plants," Serra declared, his voice rising. "That was pretty sly of you—"

Pings objected on the grounds that Serra was badgering the witness, forcing the defense attorney into a different question. "Were you there more than one time when officers counted the plants?"

Harvey replied that he was not.

Serra inquired further, "Did you count with them?"

"No," Harvey admitted.

"Did they tell you that they counted all the plants?" Serra asked, only to be thwarted by an objection from the prosecutor.

"It calls for a hearsay response," Pings said, on her feet.

Judge Damrell agreed. "What does he know? That's what you have to find out," the judge said to the defense attorney. "Ask him what he knows."

Serra immediately turned to the witness and asked in a booming voice, "What do you know?!"

"Your honor!" Pings tried desperately to interject. "The decibel level!"

But Serra wasn't listening. He was too busy preaching to the witness, his voice still projecting to great heights. "On each occasion, there were less than 50 plants—"

"Mr. Serra, stop yelling at the witness!" Judge Damrell shouted, clearly exasperated. "We can all hear you very well. You're only 20 feet away!"

Under the mightiness of Serra's voice, Harvey's facial expressions had twisted into those of outrage. "If I say I don't remember, then I'm an idiot," he said, summing up the public perception of his testimony. "So, I'll say I don't know."

"That's not what I'm asking you," Serra corrected, then tried again. "Isn't it true that the police count was less than 50 plants both times you were there?"

Pings objected that the question had already been asked and answered. It was an opinion the judge shared.

Serra tried another tactic, asking the witness, "So you told the grand jury what they wanted to hear?"

Harvey, as usual, appeared to resent the traps being laid for him. "I always tell the truth," he asserted sharply.

Serra moved on to reference a series of receipts that had been displayed earlier by Pings during a dull series of overhead projections that lulled the gallery, quite literally, to sleep. These receipts were, as Harvey had testified, for marijuana deliveries he had made while employed by the defendants. The prosecutor's slow, tedious sideshow had the effect of magnifying the perception that many deliveries had been made…which was, most likely, her intent.

The defense attorney, however, focused on one particular aspect of the receipts. Nearly all of these documents referenced something written as "sample #" and Serra was anxious to clarify what this meant. Harvey informed him that each plant was numbered, and when they sold marijuana from that plant, they listed its number in the "sample #" column of the receipt. Accepting this, Serra pointed out that, in all the receipts that were shown, the figure listed in this column never rose above 35. It was a quite expected number, given that this was the approximate number of plants seized when the property was raided.

"We didn't see, for instance, number 105?" Serra asked.

"No," Harvey admitted.

The defense attorney continued, "120?"

Harvey obliged, "No."

Serra had made his point abundantly clear by now, but he kept sailing on the smoothness of the questioning. "150?"

"No," Harvey confirmed.

It was the easiest exchange the pair accomplished. Serra didn't expound on the subject, leaving the jury to draw its own conclusions about the significance of these low plant numbers, and gave the floor to Lichter for cross-examination.

For his part, Lichter employed several lines of questioning that danced around issues involving federal law and DEA policy. "Did you ever have any discussion about taking care that less than a hundred pounds would be distributed?"

Tony Serra and Laurence Lichter debated the details of their legal strategy. Photo by Vanessa Nelson.

"Pounds?!" Serra broke back in, having barely settled back into his seat at the defense table. He then engaged in a short, whispered side conversation with his colleague.

Lichter returned to address the witness, amending his question. "Did you ever have any discussion that deliveries should not exceed a hundred plants?"

Harvey admitted he had, and Lichter pressed forward. "Wasn't there an event you went to in Berkeley where you met a gentleman and had a discussion—"

Pings was right on cue, objecting on the grounds that the defense attorney was eliciting hearsay. But Lichter was adamant about continuing, "Let me finish my question!"

"This is hearsay," Judge Damrell said rigidly.

Lichter protested, "For a conspiracy charge—"

Judge Damrell cut in again, his tone coming close to scolding this time. "You're a lawyer. I'm a judge. I make the rulings. Don't put words in his mouth that are going to be objectionable."

Thus thwarted, Lichter moved on with the cross-examination. "Wasn't the office for Dr. Fry and Dale Schafer right next to the post office?" he asked. When the witness affirmed this fact, Lichter made an inquiry about the marijuana deliveries Harvey had sent through UPS. "Why didn't you use the post office to mail the packages?"

"Because I'm not an idiot!" Harvey retorted.

Lichter questioned the witness with quiet calm. "Do you mean because it's against U.S. federal law to use the mail to send marijuana?"

Harvey was prickling, but he answered nonetheless. "Yes."

"Then why did you use UPS?" the defense attorney asked.

Harvey had a quick response. "It's not a federal agency."

"You were concerned because you didn't want to break federal law?" Lichter presumed.

"Yes," the witness agreed, his exhaustion beginning to show.

Lichter had the witness back on track now. "Wasn't this a concern of the people around you, Dr. Fry and Mr. Schafer, to not break federal law?"

"It was a concern," Harvey said carefully.

"Does this help you remember a discussion about a hundred pounds or a hundred plants?" Lichter asked, jumping on the opportunity.

Harvey paused, then tried to sidestep. "I've already answered that question."

This time, however, Judge Damrell wouldn't let Harvey dodge the question so easily. "Answer it again," the judge instructed.

But Harvey was dead-set on evasion. "My answer hasn't changed," he said petulantly.

Judge Damrell had to guess. "The answer was that you don't know or can't remember?" he asked. Harvey said this was true.

Lichter had only dipped his toe into the waters of forbidden evidence, and now he began easing in more assuredly. "Did you deliver to people with doctor's recommendations?"

Harvey was terse. "Yes."

"Did you deliver to people without doctor's recommendations?" Lichter asked.

Harvey seemed appalled, "Absolutely not!"

Lichter seized on the witness's dismay, "Why not?"

Pings had been watching carefully as the defense attorney walked the boundary lines, and she finally objected at this point. It was a vaguely worded objection, as she didn't want to call too much attention to the fact that evidence was being restricted, but she had a strong tone of warning in her voice. "Move on," the judge urged Lichter simply.

"Was the idea of using UPS your idea?" Lichter asked the witness.

Harvey denied it with a plain, "No."

Lichter challenged him. "But you said that you did it because you weren't an idiot."

"I said that," Harvey acknowledged. "Yes, I did."

Further questioning did little more to elucidate who made managerial decisions, and it took a long time to establish who Harvey's boss had been during his time with Fry and Schafer.

"Did your instructions from the office come from Mr. Maggy?" Lichter asked.

"Sometimes," Harvey responded, apprehensively aloof.

The defense attorney pressed to establish the specific chain of command. "Was he your boss?"

"No," Harvey said, rejecting the portrayal.

Lichter tried again. "Was Traci Coggins your boss?"

"Who?" Harvey asked, baffled. When Traci was described to him, however, his memory was jogged and he answered. "No."

Even though demands were occasionally given through third parties, it eventually became clear that Harvey considered Fry to be his boss. He had testified that she was in charge of the orders regarding the UPS packages, but also admitted that all the checks for these orders were written to Dale Schafer. According to Harvey, he would know that the check was for a delivery because it would come to him in an envelope with 'Attn: Mike' written on it.

"Did it say anything else?" Lichter inquired, only to receive blank stares from Harvey. "Cool Madness? HHHR?" The defense attorney suggested.

"I don't recall," the witness said, playing the memory card again.

Lichter pushed for some kind of disclosure. "Was there anything else inside the envelope?"

"It didn't have a birthday card in it, if that's what you mean," Harvey sniffed, his manner defiant once again.

Clearly, Harvey was putting up another show of insubordination, and Lichter was not as intent as his colleague in breaking down those blocks – he was more adept at working around them. In spite of the rhetorical skills of these expert defense attorneys, however, it soon became apparent that Harvey's stubbornness had great endurance. When he didn't want to be moved, he simply couldn't be.

"Was there a time when police came over without a warrant and wanted to look around?" the defense attorney asked.

"Yes," Harvey disclosed.

"And Mr. Schafer let them?" Lichter suggested.

The witness agreed, "Yes."

Lichter continued to inquire about this encounter. "Did you show law enforcement the bunker and the hill?"

"Yes." Harvey's answers had all become tight monosyllables.

"Was there ever an incident where you were told the police were coming and to get rid of the marijuana plants?" Lichter asked.

Harvey shook his head and said, "No."

"You testified that Dr. Fry said to always tell the truth?" Lichter was questioning the witness on his prior testimony.

"Yes," Harvey said, his voice softening just a bit.

The defense attorney focused in on this point. "In the time you knew Dr. Fry, did she always tell the truth?"

"I trust her," Harvey grumbled. Fry watched him with beatified eyes, her hands clasped on her rosary, but Harvey refused to meet her gaze.

"Did you ever know her to lie?" Lichter asked.

Dr. Fry smiled serenely as former friends testified against her in court. Photo by Vanessa Nelson.

The prosecutor objected, but Lichter was content enough to end the cross-examination on an upbeat note. "Nothing further," he said, taking his seat.

But before the defense concluded its questioning officially, Serra rose and went towards the witness stand with a document in his hand. "This was your doctor's recommendation for marijuana?" he asked Harvey.

The witness barely glanced at the paper. "Yes," he said. "Isn't it obvious?"

Serra then asked if Harvey had suffered from the conditions that were listed on the recommendation. The witness admitted to having lower back pain and muscle spasms, but when it came to the issue of alcohol abuse, he denied it vehemently.

The defense attorney wanted to be clear. "Did you have alcohol abuse?"

"No," Harvey answered stridently.

"Did you ever go back to Dr. Fry and say 'My God, this is the first thing you wrote on this certificate, and it's wrong'?" Serra asked with growing intensity. "Did you do that?"

Harvey was relentless in the denials. "No," he insisted again.

"No further questions," Serra said, relinquishing the witness.

Pings had nothing more to extract from Harvey, permitting him to climb down from the witness stand for good this time. The ordeal appeared to have drained him, and he seemed all too eager to get out of the courtroom.

What the prosecution gained from this witness was anyone's guess. The decision to put him on the stand was either a catastrophic disaster, or it was a mysteriously brilliant tactic whose fruits were not immediately visible. In the alchemy of legal strategy, it is notoriously difficult to discern the nature of each transmutation, let alone its ultimate result. With a bit of confusion and agitation now in the atmosphere, the courtroom welcomed its next witness.

Sgt. Robert Ashworth

The claim of entrapment by local law enforcement was always a central part of Fry and Schafer's defense. From the very beginning of their case, the defendants have maintained that they were visited at their home multiple times by sheriffs who observed their plants and assured them that their cultivation was legal. According to Fry and Schafer, these visits lulled them into a false sense of security, just as the deceptively friendly sheriffs were cooperating with a federal investigation of the couple.

Robert "Bobby" Ashworth of the El Dorado County Sheriff's Department was vital to this operation, and when the unassuming sergeant took the stand to testify, observers saw a hollow-looking man. Ashworth looked as bland as the gray suit he was wearing, his dark hair starting to fade to white and his solemn face punctuated only by small round eyes. He answered questions with calm disengagement, as though speaking from a distance, but when the prosecutor played an audio tape of his undercover phone calls to Fry and Schafer's office, the courtroom heard a whole different personality from Ashworth. The seemingly reserved man became suddenly upbeat and gregarious on tape, a transformation that finally gave some insight into how the defendants could be so easily fooled by his confident assurances.

"Hi, I need to get some information on the Saturday seminar," Ashworth's voice was the opener on the undercover recording, undeniably cheery and sociable. Office assistant Jamie Daniels responded by giving him the number for Cool Madness, Schafer's hydroponics business. The undercover cop then made another request. "Hey, I heard we could purchase clones there?" Ashworth asked, his

95

affability still shining. Daniels verified the availability of clones at the seminar, advising him to bring his certificate with him.

The receptionist was clearly in a rush, but Ashworth wanted one more thing, and it was hard to deny such a charming fellow. Daniels politely answered his question about prices, telling him that clones would be sold for $5 apiece. The short conversation concluded with Ashworth's jovial gratitude and a pleasant goodbye from Daniels, and that was the end of the undercover phone recording.

The courtroom then turned its attention back to the sergeant himself, and the difference between live and Memorex couldn't have been more striking.   During his direct examination with prosecutor Pings, Ashworth seemed dreary and dull. It was a night-and-day contrast with what was heard on the tape.

The sergeant testified to visiting the defendants' home on two occasions, along with his partner, Detective McNulty. Ashworth described being shown around the property by a groundskeeper on July 25th, 1999, at which time he observed 21 marijuana plants growing. An additional visit was made on August 17th, 2000, when he reportedly saw 43 marijuana plants and was escorted through the grounds by one of the defendants. Under questioning, Ashworth maintained that he was not shown the bunker, the garage grow room or the drying room during these visits.

At some point that was not crisp in the sergeant's memory, he began cooperating with the federal investigation of the defendants. It was clear, however, that he got to participate in flyover surveillance of the property on September 26th, 2001, and he remembered that experience distinctly. After all, it must have been a lot more fun for Ashworth to be flying around in a plane and taking aerial photographs than to act in the capacity of a sergeant. As a local cop, all he got to do was trod around to take a gander at a couple dozen plants before meekly leaving. Of course, the aerial photos didn't show much other than the top of the house and garage, and an undefined view of a fenced-in garden area. Still, Ashworth was involved in something bigger when he joined up with the feds, and he followed it through to the raid itself.

Pings began her questioning on a shaky foot. "On September 28th, 2000, did you participate with the DEA in the execution of a search warrant at [the defendants' home] in Greenwood, California?"

"Yes," Ashworth said confidently.

"Oops – I meant September 28th, *2001*," Pings corrected herself.

"Yes," the sergeant replied again, his answer unchanged.

Ashworth then verified that he was in charge of outdoor seizures during this operation, and he detailed the marijuana plants that were found in each location. His testimony on each seizure was guided and complemented by photos Pings displayed on the courtroom projector. First, the sergeant described to the jury seizing two marijuana plants from the greenhouse, which had been irrigated with hoses that drew from a nearby creek. According to Ashworth, both of these plants were approximately nine feet tall.

On the hill, where the fenced-in garden area was located, the sergeant reported finding a total of ten plants. All of them, he said, were flowering. Of these, seven were in the ground, measuring about six feet high, and another three smaller plants were contained in pots.

Several members of the audience, most notably Sacramento Bee contributor Denny Walsh, had been lulled to sleep by the soft tones of the witness's voice and the low lighting necessary for the projected photographs. Walsh's comically loud snoring made an impressive play on the acoustics of the courtroom, and at its height seemed to create a surround sound phenomenon. Judge Damrell appeared mystified by the noise, twice

Denny Walsh, who covered the trial for the Sacramento Bee, took a snooze in the courtroom. Sketch by Dr. Care.

looking up and around the room at all sides to determine its source. But in spite of Walsh's snorts and sputtering, the curious judge never solved the mystery. While embarking on her next question, Pings delivered a sudden, explosive sneeze directly into the microphone, and the jarring burst of sound rocked the courtroom to full alertness. Alternating apologies with helpless giggles, the prosecutor finally managed to move on to her intended inquiries, and when she did, she had the full attention of everyone in attendance. It was, however, just more documentation of the search operation at the defendants' home.

The final seizures took place behind the trailer where handyman Michael Harvey formerly lived. There, Ashworth claimed, agents found 22 marijuana plants measuring between one and three feet in height, all contained in buckets. These plants were rooted, according to the sergeant, who proudly pointed out a photo that displayed 22 small plants lying on their sides with their rootballs all exposed in unison. After making these seizures, Ashworth testified, he met with DEA Special Agent Brian Keefe so that he could take samples of the plants for lab testing. The final photo displayed during direct examination was a pick-up truck whose bed appeared to be loaded with marijuana, ready to be driven over to Keefe.

Serra began the cross-examination swiftly, asking the sergeant about the genesis of his relationship with the defendants. Ashworth described making his first visit to the Greenwood residence in response to a phone call Fry made to the sheriff's office in 1999. According to the witness, Fry had been "calling to tell us she was growing marijuana." Serra, quite predictably, asked Ashworth if he knew at that time that the defendants had doctors' recommendations for marijuana. The sergeant replied in the negative, and the defense attorney asked if he *ever* became aware that the defendants had recommendations. A quick objection from Pings killed the line of questioning before Ashworth could respond.

When Serra asked if Ashworth had been cross-deputized as a federal agent prior to Fry's phone call in 1999, Pings made another objection and halted the questioning again. The prosecutor wanted to discuss the issue at a sidebar, but she couldn't lure Serra over to the judge's bench this time. Instead, the defense attorney voluntarily abandoned the subject, saying he would rather forfeit the question than spend ten minutes at sidebar only to be denied. "It's not worth it to me," he said simply, and proceeded instead to establish the extent of the witness's encounters with the defendant.

Ashworth had, according to his testimony, visited with the defendants at their home, been to their office, and spoken to them on the phone, all on multiple occasions. He agreed that the visits had been friendly and cordial, but disagreed when Serra described the defendants' attitude as "candid, open, honest and unguarded." Nonetheless, he had gotten friendly enough with the defendants that he still referred to them as "Dale and Mollie," and had to be reminded on the stand to call them "Mr. Schafer and Dr. Fry." But calling them by their first names was such an ingrained habit that Ashworth ended up slipping multiple times during his testimony.

In return, Serra confirmed, the defendants often addressed Ashworth casually, referring to him as "Bobby." Ashworth claimed that he did not make the visits in an undercover capacity – though he was casually dressed in jeans and a t-shirt when he came to the Fry/Schafer home, he insisted that he represented himself as a law enforcement officer. By contrast, Ashworth *did* consider himself to be acting in an undercover role when he made the recorded phone call to talk about the grow seminar. When Serra asked what misrepresentations were made during that call, Ashworth shrugged and resorted to the hypothetical. "If I was asked for a name, I would have given a false one," he speculated.

Serra focused on the point that Ashworth did not make it known during the call that the conversation was being recorded. At the same time, the defense attorney emphasized the fact that law enforcement officers are permitted to perform such acts of deception. When Serra asked Ashworth if he knew the penalties private citizens would face if they performed similar actions, an objection from Pings cut him short. Serra surrendered the subject without hesitation, moving on instead to a more important question: when the word "certificate" was used during the recorded conversation, did that refer to a recommendation for medical marijuana issued by a licensed physician? Ashworth admitted that it did.

An official tally was taken of all the marijuana plants observed during each visit to the home, but Ashworth couldn't remember whether he had done the plant count or whether it was done by his partner, Detective McNulty. This was Ashworth's excuse for not being able to independently recollect how many plants were observed in the greenhouse and how many were observed in the vegetable garden. He also could not recall whether it was he or McNulty who went into the greenhouse, and although he admitted to seeing dwarf citrus trees inside that structure, he could not estimate what percentage of the space they took up. Serra's questioning about the greenhouse appeared to be going nowhere, but the defense attorney had a trick up his sleeve. If Ashworth saw the greenhouse, he would have seen the medical use documentation that hung at its entrance, and Serra was determined to get this tidbit across to the jury.

Putting Exhibit 117 on the courtroom projector, the defense attorney presented a photo of the greenhouse. It was a picture that had already been shown, and as such the jury and the audience waited expectantly to have its significance revealed. And wait they did, as Serra bumbled with the projection technology in an endearing show of technological ineptitude, trying to enlarge a portion of the photo. Getting the hint about his intentions, Pings made an objection and a request for a sidebar. "I want that blown up," Serra protested, gesturing towards the projection screen. "It's in evidence."

Judge Damrell accepted the sidebar, and it appeared to go favorably for the defense. Directly afterwards, one of the prosecutor's assistants was instructed to help Serra with the enlargement task, and the pair finally got the desired section of the picture selected. But the demonstration was a disappointment – blown up to the size of the projection screen, the image of the signs by the door of the greenhouse had blurred out hopelessly. At this point, Pings again announced to Judge Damrell that she objected to the content. Another, more lengthy sidebar followed, after which Serra dropped the subject and continued the cross-examination with other questions.

The defense attorney established that Ashworth did not recall the size of the plants he observed during his visits to the defendants' home in 1999 and 2000, and that no measurements had been taken of those plants. Serra then began to ask another question about Ashworth's knowledge during those visits, "Were you advised that the defendants were caregivers for—"

Pings chimed in, her voice full of outrage and urgency. "Objection, your honor!"

"I was just going to say, 'approximately 40 people,'" Serra said to Judge Damrell, slipping in the rest of his question as a barely-disguised explanation. This tactic did not impress the judge, who firmly sustained the objection and then instructed the jury to disregard the question altogether.

Next, Serra moved on to address the search operation on September 28th, 2001. Ashworth testified that at least ten officers participated, both male and female, and that Pings herself was also present. The prosecutor shifted her weight as she listened intently to the questioning, ready to jump to her feet for an objection. It was an action she could manage in a split-second, since she seemed to never fully sit down during the cross-examination. Instead, she appeared to hover expectantly over her chair while Serra spoke, perpetually prepared to make an objection. This time, however, the defense attorney's questioning departed from the usual sly theatrics and swerved into bizarre and irresistible humor.

While discussing the two 9-foot tall plants agents reportedly found in the greenhouse, Serra drove home the point that, no matter what their height, these were only *two* plants and legally counted as such. He also established that, during the seizure, Ashworth did not check any of the plants for signs of infestation. The sergeant readily admitted that he did not use microscopic or other means to examine the leaves, stalks, or stems. As Serra suggested, the witness had instead been fixated on another part of the plant.

"Based on your photos, you were intrigued by rootballs," the defense attorney observed.

Ashworth was hesitant, unable to detect the motive for the questioning. "That's how you tell if it's a plant," he said cautiously.

"On a clone, maybe...but on a 9-foot plant you know very well it has roots," Serra told the witness.

Ashworth was caught off guard, and managed only to convey a vague affirmation. But if he thought this answer would satisfy Serra on this topic, he was quite mistaken. The defense attorney had much more to say on the subject of rootballs, confusing Ashworth even further. "You've probably never had rootball soup, have you?"

"No," the sergeant replied, uttering the word slowly.

"So your fascination does not extend to that menu item?" Serra continued.

"No," Ashworth appeared conflicted here, as if unsure whether his answer validated the idea that he did indeed have a rootball fetish.

"Well, if you have asthma, it will help you," Serra inserted the comment glibly, bringing Pings to her feet once again.

Responding to the prosecutor's objection, Judge Damrell looked squarely down at the defense attorney. "Counsel, don't give medical advice," he cautioned.

Serra threw up his hands in an apologetic gesture, surrendering the subject of rootballs. Instead, he began ridiculing the size of the police operation that was used to seize a mere three dozen plants from the defendants on September 28th, 2001. "Here we have twelve grown up police officers raiding the big marijuana garden, and 'oh boy, we've got 36 plants—'"

Pings issued another objection, appearing increasingly exasperated. "Your honor, this is badgering," she claimed.

"I wonder if that's what my kids thought all these years," Serra mused with an impish smile. He then turned back to Ashworth and asked if the raid had been an "insulting, disappointing waste of resources." After the witness replied in the negative, Serra gave the floor to his fellow defense attorney.

Though Lichter's cross-examination was relatively short, it was not without its many points of controversy. It appeared that the defense attorney's primary interest was trying to reveal when and how Ashworth had presented his reports on the defendants to federal investigators. Lichter eventually got Ashworth to reveal that feds had approached him to gain information on Fry and Schafer in 2001, and that the first contact had occurred in relation to an investigation about "marijuana sent through the mail." Ashworth also denied that he was formally deputized as a DEA agent, but all of these admissions were hard-won. The cross-examination inspired ten objections from Pings in a span of less than five minutes of testimony.

"Did you ever take the information to prosecutors and see if there were grounds for charges?" Lichter asked Ashworth, referencing the marijuana plants witnessed during friendly visits to the Fry/Schafer home.

Pings objected, claiming that the defense attorney was making an improper inquiry about state prosecutions. "I was talking about all prosecutors," Lichter insisted. "She's objecting to half the question."

This comment made fertile ground for puns, given the fact that a medical condition had been impeding Lichter's speech and causing him to repeatedly excuse himself by saying, "I'm sorry your honor, but I can only talk with half a mouth."

But Pings saw no humor in Lichter's response, and insisted on the objection. "There's a door opening here."

After a sidebar, Lichter refined his questioning, asking if Ashworth had taken information to *federal* prosecutors. He responded that he had done so, and the defense attorney began a series of guesses about when this collaboration began. Finally, the sergeant revealed that he started sharing information with federal agents about a year and a half after meeting Fry and Schafer, which gave him the opportunity to observe two grow cycles at the defendants' home.

"You were invited over to inspect it any time you wished?" Lichter asked.

"Pretty much," was Ashworth's casual response.

Lichter then mentioned phone calls that were made between Schafer and Ashworth at this time. "And you had many conversations with Mr. Schafer – you were told many times that he was keeping his wife out of this because she was just a doctor?"

"Objection, your honor!" Pings broke in. "This is self-serving hearsay."

The judge agreed, forcing Lichter to try another issue. "Did you suggest to them that they were endangering life and liberty by breaking federal law?"

Pings was suddenly standing again. "Objection! Relevance, your honor. This goes to the court's ruling."

Lichter tried to explain to the judge that he was asking about *federal* law, when the ruling the prosecutor referenced was against mentioning *state* law. Judge Damrell didn't accept the defense's rationale, and Lichter tried a different question…only to be met with the very same consequences.

"Are you familiar with the concept of entrapment—" he began, eliciting a familiar response from Pings.

"Objection, your honor!" the prosecutor interrupted, looking at the judge for support. Her voice conveyed a sense of disbelief, as though she couldn't quite reconcile her expectations with the reality of the questions she was hearing.

Judge Damrell also appeared incredulous, astounded that the defense attorney would go so far. "I've ruled on that," he said, echoing his previous warnings.

But Lichter just ruffled the judge's feathers even more. "I'm not sure you did, your honor," he said. It was calm, polite defiance, but it was defiance nonetheless. The defense attorney was suddenly doing more than questioning the *witness* – he was questioning *authority*, and the judge was overtly displeased.

"Oh yes I did!" Judge Damrell boomed down at Lichter. "I did. Go back and read your notes, and you'll *see* I did!"

Lichter turned back to the witness, but only got out nine words before he was stopped again, "Did you seek out the DEA or federal prosecutors—"

Pings objected, but Lichter successfully argued that his question was relevant. "It's about motive," he stressed. Permitted this time, he asked his question in full. "Did you seek them out to get Dr. Fry and Mr. Schafer in trouble?"

"No, sir," Ashworth denied the characterization with emphasis. He made more definitive denials when asked if he had been formally cross-designated as a DEA agent, and also in response to a suggestion that he had initiated the contact with the federal government about this case. After accepting all of these responses, Lichter once again started inquiring about the conversations between Ashworth and the defendants.

104

"Did you and Mr. Schafer discuss ways physical safety could be ensured for people growing marijuana?" the defense attorney probed.

"Objection, your honor," Pings said, cutting in. "The answer calls for self-serving hearsay."

"Did you suggest he grow *indoors*?" Lichter ventured, asking the witness about his conversations with Schafer.

"Objection," Pings said, her eyes widening with exasperation. "Relevance, your honor."

The judge's patience had long been waning as well, but he continued to endure the near-constant stream of objections. "Sustained," he announced. "It's *not* relevant."

Lichter wrapped up his questioning rather abruptly, handing the witness back to Pings. On redirect, the prosecutor had just a couple points to cover with the sergeant.

"Did you have a role in whether there was a prosecution or not?" Pings asked, only to be met by a quick objection from the defense.

"It's beyond the scope," Serra declared. "It's not in evidence."

Lichter also chimed in, challenging the relevance of the inquiry and its answer.

Pings blamed the defense attorneys, indicating they had opened the door with their own questions on the subject. "They asked about it," she said of Serra and Lichter.

A sidebar conference ensued, after which Pings returned and rephrased her question just a touch. "Did you have any role in decision-making about whether the defendants would be arrested or not?"

The sergeant said that he did not, at which time the prosecutor asked him to explain the benefits of the type of undercover investigation he performed on the defendants. "What better role than to develop a relationship, rather than to go undercover and live a lie that I'm not?"

It was an odd soliloquy, especially given his previous testimony that he *had* acted in an undercover capacity for part of the investigation in this case. Nevertheless, Pings accepted the speech and confidently continued her redirect. After an over-ruled objection from the defense, the prosecutor once again extracted testimony from Ashworth that he was never shown the bunker, the garage, or the drying room during his pre-raid visits to the property.

"That's all," she said. "No further questions."

Ashworth was then dismissed from the witness stand and made his way across the courtroom to the exit. Many El Dorado County residents had seated themselves in the gallery to watch, and their eyes had been on the witness unceasingly during his testimony. This scrutiny continued up until the moment of his exit, ending only when the court's double doors shut fully behind Sergeant Bobby Ashworth.

John Nolan

Before DEA Special Agent John Nolan took the witness stand, he sat in the courtroom with a female companion and watched as everyone returned from the lunch break. When Fry entered and took her seat, Nolan was watching her with interest. "She's put on a lot of weight," he commented glibly to his companion. The matter got little further discussion, and the pair went on to chat on other superficial topics as they waited. Neither one seemed to consider that, at the time the defendants were investigated, Fry had only recently been recovering from chemotherapy and a double mastectomy. Her increased robustness should have been no surprise, in light of those circumstances, but Nolan gave no mention of such a thought. Instead, the grown man came off sounding like a catty schoolgirl dishing out dirt on her rivals.

But Nolan was not there to just to gossip and make insensitive comments. The purpose of his testimony was to describe his undercover participation in a seminar on marijuana products hosted by Cool Madness, Schafer's hydroponics business. Although neither of the defendants attended this event, Nolan testified that their daughter Heather Schafer functioned as one of the instructors and spoke profusely about her father's activities.

In fact, it was one of those remarks that allegedly motivated the agents to accelerate the process of obtaining and serving a search warrant on the defendants' home and offices. According to Nolan, Heather made a comment that the family was cleaning out the house due to her father's campaign for El Dorado County District Attorney, and investigators got scared that evidence might disappear before they had a chance to seize it.

That was the practical concern that inspired the sudden push for the warrant, but there were other, more subtle factors contributing to the rush. The defense claimed that there were political purposes to the timing, and that Schafer's well-connected opponents were intent on derailing his campaign. In addition to this, Nolan's testimony revealed that something specific happened during the seminar that made the matter frighteningly personal for him – for the first

The U.S. Attorney considered charging Heather Schafer alongside her parents, but ultimately decided against it. Photo by Vanessa Nelson.

time in his life, he found himself under the influence of marijuana. Or so he claimed.

The seminar, which was held at the Garden Valley Grange on September 22nd, 2001, required an entry fee as well as photo ID and a doctor's recommendation. Nolan testified that he paid $30 at the door, flashed a Costco card that bore his picture, and submitted a forged recommendation.

"What was the ailment listed on the recommendation?" Pings asked her witness eagerly.

"Muscle spasms," Nolan answered.

"And in 2001, do you look the same as you do now?" Pings inquired, seeming to hint that the seminar instructors would have been fools not to guess that the robust-looking agent was a fraud.

"Yes," Nolan answered, then quipped, "but maybe a few pounds lighter."

Once he was successfully inside the seminar, he said, Heather Schafer moderated discussion and led the group through a series of workshops with different instructors: a tutorial on trimming buds, a demonstration on extracting oil from the plant, and, finally, a segment about how to cook with marijuana products. According to Nolan, the instructors made a tincture that they also used in making Rice Krispie treats, which were passed around to the group as free samples once they were completed.

Pings then produced Government Exhibit 200, and the witness identified the evidence as the Rice Krispie treats he obtained from the seminar that day. Nolan held up for the jury's view a large plastic bag containing several individually-wrapped confections.

"Even after all this time, they still look like Rice Krispie treats, don't they?" Pings mused to her witness.

"With a greenish tint, yes," Nolan replied.

Pings then played the portion of the undercover tape where Heather Schafer made her infamous comment about the family cleaning out the house. The mention was part of a refusal of Nolan's request for clones, which were absent from the seminar in spite of earlier undercover phone calls that had established that clones would be available for purchase at that time. In consolation, Heather instructed the agent to call and leave a voice mail message for her, so that she could arrange the provision of clones in the future. She also warned Nolan that, unless he had a doctor's verification of his required amount, he should be careful to not grow more than six plants at a time to stay within his county's guidelines. This was the final exchange Nolan had with the seminar instructors before leaving the event.

"And how did you feel when you left the seminar?" Pings asked.

"I believed I was under the influence of marijuana," the agent replied, citing the cooking segment as the portion that exposed him to intoxicants. The exact mechanism of exposure, however, was still unclear.

"Did you do anything but stand there?" Pings inquired of her witness.

"No," Nolan maintained.

"Did you partake in anything else that would have put you under the influence?" It was the prosecutor's last question for her witness.

"No," he answered definitively.

The agent was then turned over to the defense attorneys for cross-examination, for which Serra took the lead. The charismatic lawyer paid little mind to Nolan's claims of intoxication, leaving that subject to be further illuminated by later questioning from his colleague. Instead, Serra focused on the details of Nolan's infiltration of the seminar.

"Did you have any weaponry?" the defense attorney asked.

Nolan revealed that he had a handgun on his person, and that it was concealed.

"Was it loaded?" came Serra's next question.

Pings objected, but not quickly enough to prevent an answer.

"Yes," the agent admitted.

Judge Damrell looked over at the jury and instructed them simply, "Disregard that last answer on whether it was loaded or not."

As the cross-examination continued, Nolan revealed that he forged his recommendation by finding one that was lying around the office, then obliterating the original name and adding his own. When asked about his cover story, Nolan said that the recommendation listed muscle spasms as the ailment, so it was an easy decision to simply claim muscle spasms as his own condition.

"But you don't have muscle spasms, do you?" Serra asked pointedly.

Nolan acknowledged that he did not.

"Creating your cover story, it's almost like preparing for a performance, isn't it?" The defense attorney gesticulated as he made his point.

"No," the agent rejected the characterization.

"Except your purpose is not really to entertain, but to deceive," Serra clarified.

Nolan finally admitted to the applicability of this analogy, and the defense attorney, satisfied, went on to question him about other details of the seminar he infiltrated.

"Didn't Heather Schafer say, 'Call the number and leave a message and let *me* know you need clones?'" Serra asked the witness, referencing the undercover audio recording.

"I believe so," Nolan replied.

"I'm emphasizing the pronoun," the defense attorney continued. "She said 'me,' not 'my mom' or 'my dad'?"

The witness agreed with Serra's assessment, and the questions continued. "Was Dale Schafer even there?" Serra asked.

"Not that I'm aware of," Nolan responded.

"How many patients were there?" the defense attorney inquired. "Exclude yourself."

Pings, reacting like a shot to the word 'patients,' made a swift objection. The judge, again turning to the jurors, told them to ignore the phrase. Serra, complying, amended his question. "Okay, then. Persons. Persons with recommendations. How many of those were there?"

"There were four or five others," Nolan recalled.

"And did the recipients of the instruction manifest any illnesses, any symptoms of sickness?" the defense attorney continued.

Pings let out another objection, and the judge responded, calling Serra's question irrelevant. The defense attorney, accepting the block, turned instead to another topic. "Was pest control addressed during the seminar?"

"Yes," Nolan replied.

"And its devastating effects on young clones?"

"No," the agent said. "It was just brought up as being a nuisance."

The defense attorney gave the witness a skeptical look. "Did you take notes?"

Nolan confessed that he had not, and Serra went on to ask, "Isn't it true that it's hard to remember from way back then?"

"Yes," the agent admitted.

Serra then quickly wrapped up his cross-examination and handed the floor over to an eager-looking Lichter. The questioning soon became centered on Nolan's sense of intoxication following the distribution of Rice Krispie treats made with a marijuana tincture.

"Someone said, 'Don't consume these here unless you're very comfortable,'" Nolan related to the defense attorney. "They said, 'Just consume them at home,' and they passed out baggies."

"That's a safety concern," Lichter commented. "Did you drive?"

"Yes, to the prearranged meeting place," Nolan admitted. "But I didn't feel comfortable driving, so I asked another agent to drive me home."

The defense attorney, however, was looking for other potential intoxicants. "Did you partake in any other psychoactive substances, like alcohol in the tincture or the sugar?"

Nolan seemed unaware of what the defense attorney was asking, possibly confused by the description of sugar as psychoactive. Lichter made his requests more particular. "How did you know you were under the influence?"

"I felt sort of lightheaded," Nolan explained.

"Were you giggling?" Lichter asked.

The agent gave a simple reply, "No."

The defense attorney continued his inquiries. "Had you ever experienced marijuana before?"

"This was my first time," Nolan declared firmly.

Lichter probed, "Your first and only time?"

"I encountered it in other undercover operations since then," the agent explained. "It's similar to being drunk – it's the same sort of feeling."

"Have you ever been drunk?" Lichter asked.

The agent confirmed that he had been drunk, and the defense attorney went on to inquire about the seminar itself. He wanted to know whether the instructors had discussed methods of delivery other than smoking and oral ingestion. "Did you talk about topical application?"

"Yes," Nolan said.

Lichter put forth another question. "And what would topical be good for?"

Pings objected, feeling the cross-examination moving uncomfortably close to talk about medical uses. The judge sustained her objection, and then looked up at Lichter to see if he had any further questions. The defense attorney had nearly concluded, but he had just one more matter he wanted to bring up.

Lichter turned back to the witness. "The forged notes – were they from Dr. Mikuriya?"

"Yes," Nolan answered. "I believe so."

"And do you know who he is?" Lichter asked.

"A doctor who writes recommendations," came the commonsense response.

Lichter sounded surprised. "You didn't read his obituary in the New York Times?"

Pings objected at this point, to which Lichter shrugged and said, "He *just* died." The judge paid the comment no mind, sustaining the objection.

Lichter tried another tactic, asking pointedly. "Did you ever tell Dr. Mikuriya that you used his name this way?"

"No," Nolan replied.

On the verge of another objection from Pings, the defense attorney concluded his questioning and the witness was dismissed from the stand. Nolan was not free to leave the courtroom, however, and he took a seat at the prosecution's table instead. As it turned out, Pings had pegged him for some heavy lifting chores involving the transportation of evidence, and these would take up the rest of the afternoon.

Brian Keefe

DEA Special Agent Brian Keefe had been at the prosecution's table during the entire trial, sitting attentively at Pings's side. He served as the prosecutor's little helper at all times, wheeling carts of evidence around, escorting witnesses in and out of the courtroom, and assisting with document retrieval.

Throughout the trial, DEA Special Agent Brian Keefe was on hand to provide assistance to the prosecutors. Sketch by Dr. Care.

'Little helper' was of course a figure of speech – on the contrary, Keefe had an impressive build, his height given additional severity by his shaved bald head and robust physique. The agent even maintained what might be called an air of intimidation, which held strong until the moment he took the stand and opened his mouth. At that point, it was quickly revealed that Keefe had a high nasal voice full of sniffles that made him sound rather like a kindergartener. As was soon demonstrated, the agent's range of vocabulary and consistency of recall were similarly undeveloped.

In spite of these shortcomings, the first portion of Keefe's testimony was undeniably engrossing...but this was probably due to the fact that he was not actually speaking. Instead, the court listened to a surveillance tape he had recorded of another agent posing as a customer for Fry and Schafer. It was just one of many undercover stings where officers misrepresented their medical histories and forged documents in hopes of obtaining a medical marijuana recommendation from Fry.

This time, the undercover agent was successful, and he was given his recommendation on February 15th, 2001. Audience members exchanged knowing glances when they heard that detail of the operation. Its numerical date is 2/15, which corresponds with the proposition number of the initiative that legalized medical marijuana in California. Since the passage of the law, activist groups have staged Medical Marijuana Week on February 15th of each year. Given the increasing awareness of this event and its meaning, those observing the Fry/Schafer case were left to wonder whether it was random that the most significant sting of the medical practice occurred on that particular date.

The big undercover operation was certainly planned, after all, and the infiltrating officer was John Landahl a.k.a. John Elmore. On his hidden wire, he transmitted audio of his conversations back to the receiving station where Keefe recorded it. The portion of that recording that was played for the jury began with Landahl informing Fry that he wanted to be able to grow his own marijuana. The agents had studied their subjects well – it turned out to be the perfect bait.

Fry practically squealed with approval on the gritty audio recording. "That's what we encourage people to do – grow your own," she said pleasantly. "My husband has a business – actually, it's a service – where we're trying to help people set up tiny little co-ops," she explained. The goal was to stay small enough to avoid a federal bust, but still be able to produce an adequate supply of low-cost medicine.

But there were pitfalls, of course, and one of the difficulties was safely obtaining growing materials. "Do not go to Greenfire," Fry warned sternly on the tape. "Greenfire is staked out by the narcs. They take down your license number, then wait two months and raid you." It was a spiel that might have sounded paranoid were it not an objective description of the procedures used during a very real and very invasive law enforcement sting at that establishment.

In addition, Fry told Landahl to be careful about infestation. She detailed the procedures of her own grow operation, admitting that she had four cultivation areas at her home: a room for mother plants and a room for clones, as well as inside and outside grow areas for budding plants. Guarding against cross-infection between rooms was crucial, according to Fry, but even the highest degree of vigilance is no guarantee of success. Describing her own ordeal, she told the undercover officer about a down-on-his-luck friend she hired to tend her plants…only to later discover his ineptitude when he allowed spider-mites to destroy her entire crop of 45 plants. "They had their claws in the leaves, there were webs all over the place, they had gone all yellow," Fry said of her lost plants. "It was awful."

Fry continued, describing an ambitious plan, "We want to get the price of marijuana down to $100 a pound." That was a challenge, the doctor admitted – she said she had tried to grow for 45 people, but ran out in three months and was only able to get the cost down to $80 per ounce. There were shortcuts to try, however, and she suggested purchasing a $400 grow kit from her husband's service. It was a comprehensive package, including everything from marijuana clones to hydroponics equipment to consultation services. Fry identified the customizing expert as "Sam" and described him as "so incredibly awesome."

Another cost-cutting method was obtaining a discount from your electricity provider, citing medical marijuana cultivation as the reason for the price break. Fry bragged that she had personally just negotiated a 15% discount from Pacific Gas & Electric.

"That's great!" the undercover officer said in a gush of exuberance right before the tape cut off. The selection had largely been Fry's monologue, but Landahl managed to get in an occasional bit of cheerleading. The tape itself revealed nothing of the agent's cover story, nor did it demonstrate any facts about the visit. In his cross-examination, however, Serra got right to work filling in the blanks.

The defense attorney first asked about the background story the agent had invented for his undercover work on this operation. "The cover story was the DEA agent was a pot patient with ailments who was seeking a marijuana recommendation and wanted to use marijuana for his ailments?"

"He was from WENET, not the DEA," Keefe responded, referencing a joint agency task force called the Western El Dorado Narcotics Enforcement Team.

The defense attorney got more to the point. "But this wasn't true, was it? He was not a prospective patient?"

"No," Keefe admitted.

"And he didn't have these ailments?" Serra questioned.

At this point, however, the witness maintained that he didn't know, forcing the defense attorney to get more specific. "But he didn't intend to use marijuana medically for these ailments?" Serra asked.

"No," Keefe said.

"And that's lawful," Serra summarized. "These agents can lie to their targets, and they can do that?"

Keefe agreed, "Yes, they can."

Serra went on. "And when Dr. Fry says, 'I lost my whole crop – I lost 45 plants,' did you—"

"Objection!" Pings interrupted. "Your honor, it speaks for itself."

Judge Damrell looked down from his bench. "It says what it says – she lost all 45 plants."

"I want to know his professional take," Serra explained. "Did you go up and count the dead plants that day?"

Keefe said that he had not done so, but the defense attorney kept pursuing the subject. "She said it's a service, and they're losing money by doing it," Serra referenced back to the audio recording, "Did you do anything to ascertain whether that was untrue that day?"

"No," Keefe responded. "I don't recall."

Serra then directed Keefe's attention to the recommendation that had been obtained by the undercover agent. Made out to the alias John Elmore, the recommendation was signed by the agent below a few lines

118

that Serra pointed out to the witness. "Look at that sentence: 'I declare the above to be true and correct under the penalty of perjury.'" The defense attorney used a loud declaratory voice when reading the sentence, then lowered it for his next question. "He perjured himself, but he's immune, so he can do that?"

The idea he discreetly implied was that, at any time, a law enforcement officer could be legally perjuring himself...even the agent who was giving testimony at that very moment. It was a nuance that might have escaped the jury's attention, were it not for Serra's masterful linguistic emphasis.

"Yes," Keefe responded simply.

Serra smiled, "No further questions, your honor."

The cross-examination was now in Lichter's hands, and the defense attorney began questioning the witness on the mechanisms responsible for the poor quality and accelerated recording speed on the audio exhibit. Keefe denied technical difficulties, but admitted the recording was not representative of real-time sound. "This is sped up, isn't it?" Lichter asked. "Dr. Fry and Dale Schafer don't normally sound like Chipmunks, do they?"

"No," Keefe admitted. "That's adjusted."

After that, Lichter picked up right where Serra left off and colored in a few of his colleague's more subtle implications. "Does an officer get any training on when it's okay to commit perjury and when it's not?"

Keefe said he didn't know.

Lichter went deeper. "Did the timing of the raid have anything to do with Mr. Schafer's campaign for D.A.?"

"Yes," Keefe admitted plainly.

"Was there a personal interest in Schafer running for D.A.?" the defense attorney inquired.

Now, Keefe began to back off and deny. "No," he insisted.

"Then why raid *then*?" Lichter asked, referring to the fact that the search warrant was served just prior to the election.

Keefe's response was vague. "Because she said they were cleaning out the house."

The defense attorney questioned the agent about who and what he was referring to, and Keefe revealed that he was referencing a comment made by Heather Schafer during an undercover operation by agent John Nolan.

"Was that your only evidence of that?" Lichter asked.

"Of the removal of plants, yes," Keefe clarified.

"Did you have a bias against Mr. Schafer one way or another with regard to federal law on marijuana?" Lichter attempted.

"Objection," Pings interjected. "There's no bias."

The judge agreed with the prosecutor. "Counsel, you know that's improper."

Lichter tried again, substituting the name of the defendant this time. "Did you have a bias against *Dr. Fry* one way or another with regard to federal law on marijuana?"

The judge broke in this time, exasperated. "Mr. Lichter, you know my rulings on this, but you proceed anyway." Judge Damrell seemed get more agitated as he spoke, as though saying the words reminded him of his anger. "This is contemptuous conduct!"

"No further questions," Lichter said. As he was returning to the defense table, he muttered the aside, "I can't ask any of my questions."

This only infuriated Judge Damrell further. "You can ask any question you want, as long as it's proper, but that was inappropriate," the judge lectured. "I am following the law as best I can. I have made rulings on this and I am following them, and I expect you to do the same, without whining."

"It was for the record, your honor," Lichter said, explaining his side comment.

"No it wasn't," Judge Damrell insisted. "It was a complaint." As may be expected in such situations, the judge had the last word on the subject, and the proceedings moved on to address other matters.

Once the origins of the witness's involvement were established, the prosecutor quickly moved on to discuss interviews Keefe had conducted with Fry's former patients. The agent testified that he became part of the investigation on January 12th, 2001, when the security office in Rocklin, CA, seized seven UPS packages containing marijuana and he booked the evidence into custody. The origins of his involvement established, the prosecutor quickly moved on to discuss interviews Keefe had conducted with Fry's former patients.

As soon as this questioning began, however, it ran into problems. It turned out that Keefe had a very poor memory of the results of these interviews, and was all too willing to put confident guesses in the place of fact.

Pings first confirmed that Keefe interviewed Jody Bollinger on June 28th, 2004, and then asked if Bollinger had identified the photo of a man who sold her marijuana. The agent answered that this was true, and said with assurance that the picture that was identified had been of Michael Harvey. Growing slightly uncomfortable, Pings reminded her witness that he was being asked about his interview with Bollinger, but Keefe simply repeated the answer he had previously given. Harvey, he insisted, was the suspect Bollinger had identified as the seller of marijuana. Pings was forced to ask her witness if he needed to review documentation in order to refresh his memory. Keefe timidly consented and began a lengthy perusal of written reports.

Lichter broke in with an objection, "I think it's clear the question was about Ms. Bollinger."

Judge Damrell lifted his gaze to the attorney. "What's your objection, counsel?"

"Asked and answered," Lichter suggested.

The judge huffed a quick denial. "Overruled."

The miscellaneous shuffling and coughing noises of a quiet courtroom dominated for the next few minutes. Finally, Keefe looked up from the papers, and it seemed that everything was ready to proceed.

"Do you believe you were mistaken?" Pings asked. Once the witness agreed that he had been in the wrong with his previous answer, the prosecutor went on to correct the error. "Whose photo did you show to Ms. Bollinger?"

Keefe had only a blank look in response – an inferior reward for the patience Pings was struggling to sustain. "Just a minute, please," he offered before delving back into the documents that still sat on the stand in front of him.

The clock continued to tick away the remaining time of the afternoon session, but the agent just flipped through page after page without any sign of enlightenment or clarification. This time, it was Serra who broke the silence. "I object on 403, your honor," he declared with a smile. "Too much time."

The resulting laughter did a bit to erode the boredom, but even Pings began to get a little antsy as Keefe continued to lose himself in the paperwork. The prosecutor continued to try to direct him to a more accurate answer, offering other reports until finally the agent indicated his readiness. When asked again about whose photo had been identified by Bollinger, he replied with a far different name than before. "Jeremy Schafer," he responded, giving the name of the defendants' oldest son.

Extracting this small piece of information had been awkwardly laborious, and it appeared that it was going to become a trend when Pings asked about the results of the next interview. "May I have something to refresh my memory?" he requested.

As the agent put his sloped nose back into his papers, Serra raised his objection again. "This is undue consumption of time," he put forth.

It wasn't humorous this time, and not meant to be. Even the judge had grown weary enough to attempt circumventing this portion of the examination. "How many more of these questions will you have, counsel?" he asked with a tone of annoyance.

"Hopefully not many," Pings responded. It was not just a pleasantry or an excuse – the prosecutor sounded like she *really* meant it.

The judge sighed, and the pattern of long lapses between answers continued. Keefe finally gave a correct account of Harvey being identified by an interviewee, after which Pings decided to leave off further inquiries on this subject and move on to questions about the locations of several seized items.

Serra, however, was quick to return to the matter in his cross-examination. In fact, the defense attorney had some serious criticisms about the procedures used by the agent in his interviews, and he voiced them with due gravity. First, however, he established Keefe's inexperience – the agent, it was revealed, had less than two years of DEA experience under his belt at the time he began investigating the defendants.

"Therefore, in 2001, you were a neophyte," Serra declared.

Keefe was lost, "I don't understand that term."

"You were a little bit green," the defense attorney offered a string of definitions. "You were a young, budding DEA agent."

"I was a junior officer," Keefe said simply. He then gave a short account of the progression of his career, concluding with a description of his transfer to New York and his current position there.

Serra accepted the characterization, but pried a little further into the agent's understanding of DEA policy at the beginning of his employment. "Didn't the DEA, in your tenure out here, have policies with regard—"

"Objection," Pings cut in.

Serra paid the prosecutor no mind and completed his question without a pause. "—to state legal marijuana?" The question was finished without giving the prosecutor even the acknowledgement of hesitation.

"Objection, your honor!" Pings repeated with insistence, outrage in her voice.

Serra was not a man to be interrupted, and he didn't even wait for the judge's response before he rephrased. "Wasn't it the DEA policy in 2001-"

"Objection, your honor – relevance!" Pings shouted over the defense attorney, frantic that he was pushing forward with such brute force. "May we approach?"

But the prosecutor was met with Serra's firm opposition yet again. "No!" he said, boldly defiant.

"Finish the question, and then we'll have a sidebar," Judge Damrell ordered.

"I'm sure we will, because we always seem to—"

This time, it was the judge who interrupted. "Just ask the question, Mr. Serra!"

The defense attorney complied, resuming with his inquiry. "Wasn't it the DEA policy in 2001 that if the grow was under a hundred plants, you guys wouldn't be involved?" As soon as it was uttered, the parties were whisked away to the predicted sidebar conference, during which the matter was noticeably obliterated.

Serra faced the witness again, looking every bit his cheerful, resilient self. "Moving on to another subject," he said, "You showed to both Ms. Bollinger and Mr. Langley a *single* photograph to obtain an identification?"

"Yes," Keefe answered.

"Do you know what a photo spread is?" the defense attorney asked. However, he simply went on to define the term himself, characterizing it as the procedure of presenting multiple photos of possible suspects and then having the witness try to ascertain the perpetrator by memory

"That's correct," Keefe affirmed.

"And haven't you been taught that to present a single photo is considered unduly suggestive and prohibited by law?!" Serra concluded in his triumphant, accusatory tone.

"Objection, your honor!" Pings said, her urgency renewed.

The defense attorney amended the question before the judge could make his ruling. "That to do so is not appropriate," Serra rephrased his inquiry about the practice of showing a single photo to interviewees.

"Not to my knowledge, no," Keefe said.

Following the agent's testimony on the interviews, the prosecutor moved on to the livelier portion of the afternoon – the presentation of the physical evidence.

124

While the jury was on break, carts and carts of materials were wheeled into the courtroom. The procession consisted mostly of boxes, but several large lighting fixtures and dusty hoods were also conspicuous. As the carts were unloaded, the defense was given the opportunity to witness the opening of the boxes and examine the evidence prior to testimony about it. Lawyers on both sides followed the lead of the officers and snapped on latex gloves for the exhumation, and the defendants shuffled over to the prosecution's side to get a glimpse of items they hadn't seen in six years.

Of course, Fry and Schafer were not the only ones peering in for a look. Courtroom observers, held back only by a thigh-high wooden gate, flocked over to the edge of the barricade to get a peek into the mysterious boxes. Eyes bright like kids on Christmas, the crowd leaned forward from the front row of seats and watched with eager amazement.

Pings was troubled by the intense observation. "This isn't about *you*," she hissed to the two conspicuously nosey onlookers in front of her. Turning to the marshals guarding the doorway, she pled for some intervention. "Can you, uh, get them away…?" But the marshals just smiled – no one raised a finger to get the pesky spectators out of the prosecutor's hair. It appeared that she would have to cope with the scrutiny, unaided.

Dr. Fry expressed surprise when reviewing the evidence seized during the raid. Photo by Vanessa Nelson.

In the meantime, the defendants combed through bag after bag of green leafy substance and marveled at the bulk. "Did you guys dry this?" Fry asked Keefe incredulously. "We didn't have *this* much stuff at our house."

Schafer hushed his wife promptly. "Shhhh – we'll get our chance," he assured her.

When the defendants gave the sign they were ready, the jurors were summoned to the courtroom and the testimony about the physical evidence began. Keefe gave long lists confirming the identity of each exhibit, verifying the location where it was seized and declaring that DEA lab testing revealed the plant material was marijuana. A series of Ziploc bags were held up for the view of the jury, and boxes containing loose vegetation were tilted forward for a view within.

Special Agent Nolan was enlisted for the job of lifting the light hoods to the eye level of the jury. The strapping narc strained at the weight, wincing as he heaved it up. "I didn't know I was going to be doing manual labor," he muttered comically as he returned to his seat and reclaimed his suit jacket.

A slideshow of interesting photographs followed, all of them portraying evidence that was taken on the day of the raid. One scene was from the living room of the Fry/Schafer home, and it depicted four paper grocery bags sitting on the floor next to a sofa. Keefe testified that the bags contained marijuana, but they did not appear full in the least. Two of them looked crumpled over in collapse, and one of them had a couple sticks poking out haphazardly over the top of the bag.

Another picture showed a large plant mass that Keefe claimed was discovered in the master bedroom of the residence. The picture was such a close-up that the plant filled most of the shot and there was little in the background to use as a point of reference for determining scale.

"You wouldn't call this a tree, would you?" Pings asked her witness.

"No," Keefe replied, gazing up at the screen.

"Why not?" the prosecutor prodded.

"There's no real central rooting system," Keefe explained. "This is a large marijuana branch."

Ample contrast came in the display of Government Exhibit 180, a profoundly pathetic display of plant cuttings that had been placed optimistically in rockwool cubes. Pings asked the witness whether these were clones with roots, but Keefe told her that he didn't know. To the eye, these cuttings were no more than a series of tiny sticks, weathered and largely bare. The fortunate few had a miniscule, shriveled leaf still clinging on for hope, but most were bent over at the top in a quite dejected posture. It was one of the bleakest images of marijuana cultivation that this author has ever encountered.

The defense also had concerns relating to this exhibit, and Serra took the lead with cross-examining on this matter. "You know that these items are not plants, right?" Serra said, gesturing at the photo displayed on the screen. The agent seemed to hesitate, but Serra was happy to clarify. "No root, no plant – fair?"

"Yes," Keefe said, "but I didn't know that at the time."

"Do you know that now?" the defense attorney asked. The agent verified that he did have such knowledge.

Serra drove his point home one more time, giving it extra dramatic emphasis this time. "And they were dead as doornails when you seized them, right?" the defense attorney gave the assessment, only to encounter another pause from Keefe. "They're dead cuttings?" Serra tried again.

The agent responded with a denial, and so the defense attorney went back into definitions again. "These are cuttings?" He received an affirmation from the witness. "And 'dead' means 'not alive.' And 'alive' means 'has roots.' Fair?"

"Yes," Keefe gave in. "I know that now."

As for the agent's further knowledge abut marijuana cultivation, Serra was unable to extract much more. Keefe testified that he wasn't really sure whether stems and stalks were a usable part of the plant, and had to be talked through the analysis. "Maybe you can use them in twine or hemp clothing or paper," Serra mused, "but stems and stalks are not marijuana products that are smoked or eaten, right?" Keefe eventually came around and agreed.

The agent also pled clueless about the ratio of wet to dry plant weight, a concept that had to be explained to him initially. "I have no idea what the breakdown is," Keefe shrugged, going on to deny any particular knowledge about fungus and pesticides. It was a state of claimed ignorance that seemed measureless, but Serra tested its depth nonetheless. The defense attorney concluding his questioning by asking Keefe about his understanding of the phenomenon of the 'contact high.'

"You sat in close proximity to the marijuana exhibits," Serra noted, looking over at the boxes and bags of plant material still sitting in the courtroom. "Did you, like your predecessor John Nolan, experience what I'll call a *contact high?*"

"I wore gloves when I contacted it," Keefe explained. If he was playing dumb, it was quite an act, and audience members rolled their eyes at the comment.

"Do you understand what's meant by a contact high?" The defense attorney had good reason to doubt the agent's comprehension.

"Yes," he responded.

"So you understand that it has a very significant subjective component?" Serra spoke slowly, but Keefe still didn't understand the terminology. Since the defense attorney couldn't seem to lay off the four-syllable words, communication with the DEA officer was becoming impossible.

"Huh?" Keefe could barely articulate.

"That you manifest the symptoms of intoxication," Serra attempted to explain. "That it's an empathetic response you can't control."

"Objection," Pings broke in, claiming that the defense counsel was testifying.

"I'm trying to ask a question, " Serra maintained.

"That's the idea," Judge Damrell said snippily. "You ask questions, he answers. You don't make speeches."

If they wanted questions, then Serra would give them questions. He turned back to the witness with renewed enthusiasm. "You don't, as you sit up there on the stand, feel more *aesthetically oriented?*"

The witness denied such an experience.

"You don't feel more *spiritually oriented*, do you?" Serra asked, lilting his voice to near histrionics.

"No," Keefe said simply.

"And you don't, say, feel more compassion for brotherhood or sisterhood?" the defense attorney was getting into his true element now, the thespian in him shining.

"Not with respect to marijuana, no," was the agent's curious response.

"Objection," Pings shot out, trying to stifle laughter. With the whole courtroom in excited giggles, it was impossible to choke down all effects of the mirth, but the prosecutor made a valiant effort nonetheless.

The defense attorney, of course, kept going. "And you don't feel more creative, do you?"

"No," Keefe replied, his body language betraying his discomfort.

Pings tried an objection again, but the courtroom was in an uproar that only Serra could control. And control it he did, bringing the line of questioning to a perfect finale.

With a tone of ceremony, Serra bellowed the proclamation, "I pronounce you *un-stoned*!"

It was as good a place as any to end the cross-examination, but the comic diagnosis also turned out to be the finale for the prosecution's law enforcement witnesses. Although Pings had anticipated more expert testimony for her case in chief, the length of Paul Maggy's stint on the witness stand inspired predictions that the trial would stretch into September. Feeling that he would be breaking a promise, the judge had dreaded telling the jurors that the time-line for the trial would be extended, and he had developed a daily habit of asking the attorneys anxious questions about the scheduling. In a moment of amity, however, the prosecution and the defense came together to make a list of agreements – the defense would stipulate to a series of facts that would eliminate the need for several government witnesses. When Pings announced the decision, it was as though she was presenting a surprise gift to the judge.

Soaring on the rare moment of benevolence, Serra asked Judge Damrell to officially praise the attorneys for speeding up the trial. It was a move he hoped would balance the repeated blame on the defense for slowing the trial down. "I hope you will publicly congratulate the attorneys for accelerating the process," Serra asked the judge with a bow of his head.

Pings, however, made it clear that she wanted specific credit for the surprise gift. "Well, congratulate those who *contributed* to accelerating the process," she said, amending Serra's request.

The goodwill between the two sides was apparently lacking in strength or permanence, but it had nonetheless accomplished its intended job. Judge Damrell seemed pleased with the outcome, and the jurors went home for the day with smiles on their faces.

Sean "Nacho" Cramblett

Sean Cramblett was supposed to be the prosecution's witness. As a matter of reciprocity, the government had every reason to expect him to testify in a way that benefited its case. After all, he had already been rewarded with freedom for his role in this prosecution – in exchange for his cooperation, a simple phone call from Anne Pings had gotten Cramblett cleared of a slew of marijuana-related charges that had been pending against him in Lake Tahoe, California. Whether the government got its due share in return, however, is more debatable. Cramblett testified in the grand jury proceedings that secured a federal indictment against Fry and Schafer, but, at trial, his performance was woefully weak.

The problem was not that Cramblett was a renegade witness. He certainly gave every appearance of attempting to serve the government well. Try as he might, however, the young witness was hopelessly outmatched by two very clever defense attorneys. During a lively cross-examination, Serra efficiently trounced the witness, then gave the floor to Lichter, who delivered a resounding smack of insult to the injury. The defense attorneys also appropriated the witness, using him as a tool to present to the jury numerous mentions of medical marijuana and state law.

When Cramblett walked up to the witness stand, observers saw a fair-complected young man in his 20s, built tall and thin, with deep-set eyes and a shaved head. From the starting gate, he showed a tremulous quality that gave him the look of vulnerable prey. His ears only enhanced this perception, protruding conspicuously as though alerting to danger.

Pings started out her direct examination by having Cramblett air a few details of the charges he had faced in Lake Tahoe, and in doing so, the witness set a tone of blame. Cramblett claimed that the plants from his bust had been given to him by the defendants, and that he had been hired to cultivate for them. After getting these accusations out of her witness, Pings asked him to explain how he became acquainted with the defendants in the first place.

As it turned out, Cramblett had been a good friend of the government's lead witness Paul Maggy several years ago. Both in their early 20s at the time, the two young men were snowboarding buddies who also smoked marijuana together. Maggy had become acquainted with Fry and Schafer in 1999, the year his girlfriend began working in their office.

At that time, Fry had been in need of custom-made glass pipes and Cramblett was a glassblower who wanted a doctor's recommendation...so it seemed only natural that Maggy would do some match-making in this situation. In the winter of 1999, therefore, Maggy introduced his friend to the defendants at a clinic they were holding at the Embassy Suites in Lake Tahoe.

At this point, Pings asked her witness to identify the defendants from where they were sitting in court and what they were wearing. Such moments often get dramatized in television and film depictions of trials, but Cramblett's fingering had none of the emotional climax of those media portrayals.

In fact, Cramblett's identifications had the opposite effect, and ended up adding a little touch of lighthearted humor. When he was pointing out Schafer, the witness said simply, "He's wearing a suit."

Since there were suits galore in the courtroom, Cramblett's description was comically inadequate. Amongst assorted giggles, Pings gave her own laughingly wry smile. "You're in federal court," she informed her witness. "I think you have to be a little more specific." And so Cramblett complied, giving a more detailed portrayal of Schafer's appearance.

Once identities were established, Cramblett continued with his recollections about meeting the defendants at the Embassy Suites. He explained that his motivation for going to the clinic was to get a recommendation for marijuana.

"And that's a piece of paper that can help you to not get arrested under state law?" Pings asked.

"Yes," Cramblett said, yielding to the prosecutor's phrasing. He also acknowledged that he succeeded in getting a recommendation that day, following his consultation with Fry.

As she questioned her witness, Pings made sure to put emphasis on two facts: that Cramblett has asthma, and that Fry had given approval for an asthmatic to smoke marijuana. The prosecutor was implying reckless negligence of the part of the doctor, but these accusations stayed simmering on the government's back burner for the time being. Pings was focused on getting more substantial admissions from her witness.

When asked if he got anything other than a recommendation from Fry that day, Cramblett testified that he had also received marijuana. According to what he told the prosecutor, he hadn't asked about marijuana, but during the consultation Fry pulled out a quarter-ounce bag of it nonetheless and asked Cramblett if he wanted some. The marijuana wasn't meant as merely a gift, however. Cramblett maintained that Fry wanted compensation for any pot she gave out.

"What did you tell her?" Pings asked.

"That I didn't have money, but I could trade glass pipes," Cramblett recalled. As he remembered it, Fry had been receptive to the idea, but wouldn't do the trade right then and there. Instead, Cramblett claimed that the doctor arranged a meeting later that day at his friend's house. At that rendezvous, Cramblett testified, he met with Schafer and traded five glass pipes for a bag of marijuana.

While assessing the financial values at work in this barter, Pings had a few questions. "How much do your pipes sell for?"

Cramblett spent a moment in thought before coming up with a vague figure. "Twenty dollars and up," he replied.

"And aren't marijuana pipes works of art in addition to their purpose?" Pings asked.

133

Cramblett replied simply, "Yes."

Pings was also interested in how the relationship between Cramblett and the defendants developed beyond this initial encounter. As the witness described it, the next meeting happened a few weeks later at Fry's office in Cool, and he had come because the defendants wanted to purchase marijuana pipes that they could then sell out of their office. Cramblett could not, however, recall whether he had met with Schafer or Fry at this time, but he leaned towards the belief that it had been the latter.

Lichter spoke up from the defense table, saying the witness was speculating, but he was quickly silenced when the judge overruled the objection.

As for the results of this sales meeting in Cool, Cramblett explained that he left some glass pipes on consignment at the office, where they were sold in a display case along with other accoutrements for marijuana smoking. The name for this paraphernalia-sales operation, the witness revealed, was Cool Madness.

Cramblett then began talking about a later visit he made to the defendants' house, and Pings appeared to get much more enthusiastic about examining her witness at this point.

The story that emerged was about a visit to the Fry/Schafer home for a Sunday brunch, attended by Cramblett, Maggy, the defendants and their minor children, Heather Schafer and her boyfriend, and the family's accountant. Cramblett testified that he went upstairs after the meal and smoked marijuana with Maggy and Fry, and that Schafer asked Maggy if he wanted some morphine for his back pain...an offer Maggy reportedly refused.

According to Cramblett, the accountant joined the group upstairs and business negotiations ensued, resulting in the defendants loaning Cramblett $8500. There had been, according to the witness, talks about his desire to start a glass-blowing business, and also discussions about him growing marijuana for the defendants to sell. Cramblett may have meant to convey that these plans were interwoven, and that the defendants would not have loaned him money unless he agreed to cultivate, but this was not clarified on the stand. It's also unclear how enthusiastic Cramblett was about the suggestion that he grow marijuana

134

plants, although he did explicitly mention the *defendants'* enthusiasms – that they were eager for him make pipes with Fry's logo on the side, and that they were so keen for him to cultivate that they had a set of clones to give him right away.

This handover happened later that day, Cramblett recalled, after going to the bunker and seeing that it was being used as a grow room. He said he observed mature plants in pots under grow lights, and he put the quantity in a range between twenty and fifty. The defendants' garage, Cramblett testified, had an area partitioned off to be a room for cloning, in which there were fluorescent lights and small plants on a table. According to Cramblett, Schafer gave him a tray of forty of these clones, a portion that was only a small percentage of the plants that were there.

The witness was insistent on the issue of the clones being rooted, and, since this was what made them officially plants rather than mere cuttings, the prosecutor was also earnest about emphasizing the point. "Did you pick them up and see [the roots]?" Pings asked.

"Yes," Cramblett said with certainty.

Pings sought to give the declaration further credence. "Would you want to take them if they weren't rooted?"

"No," Cramblett answered, "because they would die."

Even though he maintained that the $8500 loan was made in order to help him get the marijuana grow started, Cramblett also testified that he paid the defendants $400 for the clones he took home that day. It was not an entirely rational arrangement, but the witness stuck to this story despite the fact that he couldn't remember how he paid this sum.

Once the clones were in his possession, Cramblett recalled taking them home and then going out to put his newly-acquired funds to use. Right away, he spent a thousand dollars at a hydroponics supply store called The Phat Farm, buying grow lights and nutrients for the plants. After that, Cramblett described making another forty clones from his original forty clones, and he then proceeded with his efforts to grow a crop for Schafer and Fry.

As for why the defendants wanted him to grow marijuana for them so badly, Cramblett could only offer a simplistic statement. "Mollie said she wanted to get the price down for 'her people,'" he told Pings.

The way Cramblett explained the arrangement, he was supposed to give the harvested marijuana to the defendants in exchange for $2000 per pound. Fry's plan, Cramblett claimed, was to sell that marijuana to other people for $6 per gram. At this point, Pings scribbled some calculations, concluding that Fry would realize a profit of $700 per pound through these deals.

Of course, there was still the matter of re-paying the loan, and expectations were well-documented on this matter. The loan agreement was signed by all parties as well as a witness, and it included an articulated payment schedule. But Cramblett testified that he only made two payments on the loan, explaining that he was arrested for marijuana cultivation shortly after receiving the clones.

A falling out with the defendants then ensued, and Cramblett described the tension culminating in a hallway of the county courthouse where he was arraigned on his charges. There, he said, Fry demanded that Cramblett give her back *her* plants. No plants were returned, however, and the loan was never fully re-paid.

"Is it possible they think you still owe them money?" Pings inquired about the defendants.

"Yes," Cramblett admitted.

The prosecutor continued, coaxing. "But who were you growing marijuana plants for?"

"For Mollie's people," the witness replied.

"Are you making things up about these defendants so you don't have to pay them back?" Pings asked.

"No," Cramblett answered.

"Objection!" Tony Serra cut in, his voice loud and clear. "It's argumentative."

Judge Damrell shot a quick glance over at the defense table. "Overruled."

This denial seemed not to matter, however, given the logistics of the proceedings. That is to say, Serra was not silenced for very long at all. He gained the floor soon afterwards and quickly got to work on a zealous cross-examination.

Tony Serra skillfully conveyed his skepticism about government witnesses and their motives.
Photo by Vanessa Nelson.

To watch Serra with a witness is like watching a surgeon who operates skillfully and gracefully but without anesthetic, and, in this instance, the defense attorney made his incision by going over the witness's Lake Tahoe bust.

As Serra recounted, Cramblett had been arrested on May 5th, 2000, and was shortly thereafter arraigned on three charges: felony counts for cultivation of marijuana and possession of marijuana for sale, as well as a misdemeanor count for the destruction of evidence. The charges indicated 85 plants, but Cramblett could explain all of them easily – five of them belonged to his roommate, and the other eighty were the aforementioned forty clones plus the forty cloned clones. The trouble, however, was that Serra wasn't buying the timeline of this account.

Over the prosecutor's objections, Serra showed the witness a document indicating the receipt of forty clones from Dale Schafer on April 16th, 2000. The receipt had not been in evidence, but Serra was nonetheless determined to interrogate Cramblett about the dates.

"You received the clones on April 16th, and you were arrested on May 5th," the defense attorney summarized. "You're not saying you could make forty clones in two weeks?"

Cramblett asserted he had done precisely that, and also claimed that he didn't recognize the receipt.

Undeterred, Serra continued, his eyes wide with incredulity. "You can double your clones in a month?"

"*I* did," Cramblett said simply.

What blossomed then was a minor debate about the length of the growing cycle, which was resolved when Cramblett revealed he had taken cuttings from his original forty clones almost immediately after receiving them.

"So you cloned *immature* plants?" Serra clarified.

Cramblett confirmed this, trying to defend the logic of his process. "My system held eighty, so we cut them up to make eighty," he explained.

It was not necessarily a prudent decision, and Cramblett realized this. "The grow had troubles," he stated straightforwardly. "It was my first time."

Serra went back to figures. "So you spent $1000 of the $8500 on the grow equipment?"

Cramblett admitted this, "Yes."

"And what did you do with the rest?" the defense attorney asked, raising his eyebrows.

"It went into my glass business," Cramblett told him.

Serra then began making expansive gestures with his arms out, rotating them upwards at the shoulder as though expressing abundance. He paced around the front of the witness stand as he gestured, circling his victim like a smiling shark. "And this was legal...and they sell well...and they are *beau-ti-ful*," he said of the glass pipes, stretching out his last word as long and loud as it would allow.

The witness acquiesced, "Yes."

"So why didn't you pay Dale back?!" Serra asked, whirling around to face the witness, his demand loud and adamant.

Cramblett talked about the cost of his Lake Tahoe case, muttering about lawyer's fees and such. But Serra simply used this opportunity to point out that Fry and her husband had gone out of their way to come to Cramblett's aid when he was in court. Serra's argument, in addition, gave him a medium for a few sly references to medical marijuana.

"They came to court and said, 'This is medical marijuana! This is legal! He's under our auspices!'" Serra said, painting a vivid picture of the defendants' rescue effort. "They were righteous when they were there, and [Fry] said, 'This was legal because this was for patients,' or whatever she said."

"But the police just laughed at me, and they didn't even look at my paper," Cramblett recalled. "The bust didn't go down like they said it would," he added, referring to the defendants.

His tone turning suddenly casual, Serra affected what sounded like a switch into benign smalltalk. "How's your glass-blowing business?" He asked the question as though he were catching up with a friend over coffee.

"It's doing okay," Cramblet shrugged.

The defense attorney was quick and sharp. "So where's Dale's money?!"

When he finally began to open up about his failure to re-pay the loan, Cramblett revealed his bitterness and hard feelings. "Basically, I was upset," he divulged, his eyes flashing bright in their deep sockets. "I feel that I was misguided."

Serra had done it – excavated from Cramblett an admission of resentment towards the defendants. Grudges and revenge motives erode a witness's credibility on their own, but Serra kept scraping away at Cramblett's validity with new tactics.

Next, the defense attorney made a pensive pause, his tone sliding back into the casual. "You used to have dredlocks, didn't you?" Cramblett denied this idea outright, so Serra quickly modified his question. "Long hair?"

The witness was evasive. "Possibly."

"Hippified?" Serra asked, conjuring a term that received grins from the gallery.

"You could say that," Cramblett confessed obliquely. "I was in Tahoe."

Though the witness's reply was not wholehearted, Serra seized upon the admission of hippie-ness when going through Cramblett's description of his Sunday brunch at the Fry/Schafer home.

"In that time frame, were you smoking pot?" Serra asked.

Cramblett had already testified to this, and he re-affirmed it effortlessly.

But it was just the beginning of the inquisition about that day's marijuana use. Serra was relentless about the specifics, trying to pin down time-frames and amounts…and, finally, potency. "Were you smoking *strong* pot?"

The witness answered slowly, "Probably." He seemed to sense the need for caution without fully grasping the reason why it was necessary.

There was not long to wonder, however, as Serra quickly revealed his intentions for the queries. "When you were making the tour, would it be fair to say that you were under the influence of marijuana medicine?"

Pings immediately protested the terminology, presumably dissatisfied with the use of the word "medicine," and her objection was sustained. Nonetheless, the defense attorney's language became increasingly heated.

"—that you were under the influence of marijuana?" Serra amended, slicing off the tip of his previous question and thereby calling more attention to its absence.

"Yes," Cramblett granted.

"Would you say that you were stoned *out of your mind*?!" the defense attorney was exuberantly dramatic again, hurling the question as a strident accusation.

Cramblett refused the suggestion flatly. "No."

The witness's denial gave Serra the opportunity to play his next card with flourish. "But back when you were a hippie, weren't you *always* stoned out of your mind?"

"Objection!" Pings said, asserting that Serra's questioning was argumentative.

Serra receded at that point, pulling away from the witness stand and bringing his rhetoric backwards for just a moment. He paced back and forth over a small area as he constructed the scene of the brunch. "It's a convivial mood... You're getting $8500... You smoked a little pot... You had some food... You're walking around smiling."

"Yes," Cramblett said at the first substantial pause, unsure whether comments had ended and questions had begun.

"You weren't taking notes like a student?" Serra asked.

Cramblett gave the expected answer. "No."

The defense attorney then brought up the plants Cramblett had testified to seeing in the bunker, recalling that he had given no indication of plant quantity other than a wide range of possible numbers. "Couldn't it have been *one* plant that was taking up all that space?"

"It's possible," Cramblett admitted, but not without injecting doubt. "But I do remember seeing more than one."

"I'm saying it was about a dozen plants," Serra pitched. "Can you go with that?"

The witness gave a tentative agreement, but Pings was clearly distressed by the negotiation and interrupted with an appalled frown. "That is not an appropriate question."

Serra ignored the prosecutor. "Would you say there were twelve?" he asked the witness.

"Objection," Pings said, her dismay quickly becoming outrage. "Asked and answered." The judge agreed.

"You're not certain you saw twenty to fifty plants, are you?" the defense attorney was focused tightly on Cramblett.

"Objection," Pings repeated. "Asked and answered."

"Not with *certain*," Serra argued.

Judge Damrell was not persuaded. "Sustained," he declared, looking as though he had just begun to detect a foul odor.

The defense attorney, of course, furnished plenty of other opportunities for the judge to have his sensibilities offended.

"Even though there was a state law, you were in a county that was marijuana unfriendly," Serra reflected. "You probably thought 99 was the Oakland standard and you had less than that –"

"Objection!" Pings prickled as Serra skirted the borderlands of the forbidden topic.

"Sustained," Judge Damrell said, his ruling quick and stern.

But Serra didn't back off the boundary lines. "Didn't you join Mr. Maggy's new co-op in order to have a defense?"

Pings objected, but Serra pushed her protests aside and rephrased his question in even more contentious language. "Didn't you pretend to be part of Mr. Maggy's co-op to have a legal defense in your state case?" he asked the witness.

"No," Cramblett insisted.

But the defense attorney had proof, and he wasn't backing off the question. "Do you remember speaking with law enforcement on April 4th, 2002, here in Sacramento, with Ms. Pings present and Mr. Brock present?"

Cramblett admitted that he recalled the interview, at which point Serra produced the written report of that session and brandished it. But in the enthusiasm of his gestures, he dropped the document before getting it up to the witness stand for Cramblett to view. Glancing down at the document on the floor momentarily, Serra enlisted the assistance of his co-counsel.

"I have two titanium hips, so, Larry, would you help me pick that up?" he asked, beaming appreciatively at Lichter as he scurried to help.

The report finally made it in front of Cramblett, but the witness looked at it with disbelief. "I don't remember saying that, but it's there."

Sean "Nacho" Cramblett

Serra pushed to gain more territory, getting closer to his point. "And you accept that you must have said it if it's there?"

Cramblett allowed the encroachment. "Yes."

"Assuming that it's true," Serra proposed, "then you were seeking to defend yourself by deceit?"

The witness tried to deny the accusation, but Serra had him crammed into a difficult spot. The inference was that defending oneself by deceit could easily translate into testifying deceitfully as a witness, but the defense attorney was also using the line of questioning to get more references to "legal marijuana cooperatives" into the jurors' ears.

"Your state case was dismissed because of your cooperation in this case?" Serra followed up.

"Partly," Cramblett acknowledged. "Not right away."

"I understand that," Serra said, his tone amiable. Turning away, he announced, "Nothing further."

As usual, Serra's multi-climactic performance was a tough act to follow, and when Lichter finally got the floor, there was little left to cover. His cross-examination, therefore, was short and focused almost entirely on one subject: Cramblett's insistence on blaming the defendants for his Lake Tahoe bust.

Lichter's initial questions were designed to characterize the relationship that had developed. According to Cramblett, the defendants had allowed him to barter in order to pay for a recommendation and for marijuana, invited him into their home and fed him, and even gave him $8500.

"You must have thought they were nice?" Lichter asked the witness.

"Yes," Cramblett agreed.

But kindness had little to do with Cramblett's expectation that the defendants could have somehow prevented his arrest. After all, they had no knowledge, and no control, over how many plants Cramblett was growing with his roommate in their home. It was quite a presumption to believe that the defendants could somehow guarantee protection from a bust.

Lichter, of course, was quick to suggest this point. "Dr. Fry and Mr. Schafer didn't know you were cutting into double clones, did they?" he asked the witness.

"No," Cramblett admitted.

"They knew what?" Lichter speculated, giving a perplexed expression. "That you were patients, growing for patients?"

"Objection," Pings cut in. She gave the judge a knowing look and explained simply, "Terminology."

Judge Damrell responded by instructing the defense attorney to "avoid the use of those terms."

Lichter then asked the witness various questions about what strategies he had explored and attempted as part of his defense in the Lake Tahoe case. The impression Lichter created was that Cramblett had done little to fight his charges, and instead had merely looked for ways to dodge them…ways that involved, of course, an agreement with the U.S. Attorney to testify against Fry and Dale Schafer.

Lichter pressed Cramblett on this agreement. "So it was your idea to cooperate to get the charges dropped rather than finding out what was legal and right?"

It was a suggestion that Cramblett denied, claiming that the option of cooperating with the government had been raised by his attorney. But, to Lichter, this fact did not explain or justify the decision. He continued this line of questioning, his eyes fixed intently on the witness. "But weren't you charged in *state* court, not *federal* court?"

"Yes," Cramblett conceded.

"But what you chose to do – you had a guaranteed dismissal if you went along and didn't fight," Lichter observed, shaking his head.

"No," Cramblett answered, tightening his thin mouth. As he testified earlier, there had been no guarantee of dismissal. Nonetheless, there was an assurance of the likelihood that the charges would be dropped if he agreed to testify for the government, and, predictably, that likelihood had become a reality.

Lichter had one last question. "Did Dr. Fry and Mr. Schafer deal dishonestly with you?" he asked the witness, his voice low and serious.

"No…just the fact that I got arrested and I went to jail, and they said that wouldn't happen," Cramblett answered, attempting to substantiate the reasons for his grudge. Then, softly and thoughtfully, he acknowledged, "Otherwise, they were fine people."

Lichter, looking contented, left it at that. With nothing more of substance from the prosecutor, Cramblett was excused from the witness stand. He had been a relatively minor witness, but his testimony nonetheless marked a turning point in the government's case.

The marathon-length witnesses were done, and it looked like the rest of the prosecution's showing would be winding down with a whimper. Although their testimony had been far from perfect, the law enforcement officers had been the prosecution's real strength. The defense punctured the veneer of their credibility at various points, but nonetheless, these witnesses had held up well during the enormous strain of cross-examination. After all, they were professionals.

Under similar pressure, Mike Harvey had succumbed to confused anger. Paul Maggy had employed various evasions. For his part, Cramblett appeared to merely shut down and crumble to the greater force of power. Pings, as expected, kept a stiff upper lip during this minor downturn in her case, leaving observers to wonder if she was at all disappointed. But how much could she have reasonably expected from a boy nicknamed Nacho?

Michael Langley

As the government continued to bring witnesses to the stand, those who were called to give testimony were beginning to look remarkably reluctant. While it was an anomaly that an individual appeared to truly relish the time spent on the stand, the witnesses who had testified so far seemed to have some degree of disapproval or some instance of bad blood regarding the defendants. Michael Langley gave no indications of either condition, and when he entered the courtroom to testify, he looked to have the aura of the regretful.

It was either that, of course, or a slight sunburn, an extended blush, mild rosacea, or a reflection from his pink shirt. Whatever the cause, the middle-aged Langley exhibited a ruddy skin tone that remained unchanged during his short stint on the witness stand. Augmented by silvering hair and a pleasantly-rounded physique, Langley's complexion might have imparted a feeling of jolliness were it not for the aforementioned mood of regret. After being sworn in, he took his seat with a sigh, waiting for the prosecutor to approach.

But Anne Pings, who had handled most of the government's witnesses thus far, remained seated. Instead of rising, she gave a nod of deference to freshly-hatched prosecutor Sean Flynn. The dynamic between Pings and her apprentice, although a standard mentoring relationship, was nevertheless intriguing. Peculiarly enough, to watch the fostering of a young prosecutor evoked none of the archetypal images of nurturing, nor did it have any such sentimentality. That is to say, it was not like the sight of a loving mother feeding or bathing a newborn baby. It was more like a mama tiger teaching her cub to hunt.

To say this is not to dehumanize the prosecutors, but rather to note that, in spite of the intellectual gravity of their jobs, there was also something distinctly primal at work in the training process. Of course, such metaphors are colored by the high level of contrasts between the two sides at trial. Painting a rigidly contrasted picture of courtroom battles is a temptation to be avoided, but the defense's dramatic appeals were so emotional that some degree of polarization was indeed occurring. Up against the strong tides of unfettered zeal and passionate rhetoric from the defense, the prosecution had been playing it cool and cunning so far. Emotion was not part of the government's strategy, and when used, it served only as a minor boost to the potency of the factual evidence. As Pings nodded at her predecessor to begin the questioning, it was with a look of calculated efficiency rather than ardor or pride. Under her watchful eye, Flynn would handle the examination of the remainder of the government's witnesses.

The youthful prosecutor started out by asking Langley about when he met the defendants. It was a routine way to begin examining a witness, but Flynn ran into a problem nonetheless.

"On October 9th, 2000," Langley said confidently, "when I went to obtain a certificate for medical marijuana."

Flynn tried not to flinch, remaining casual in the face of the forbidden term. "You're talking about a recommendation you thought would allow you to purchase marijuana?" he asked.

"Yes," Langley answered congenially, nodding his head. As the prosecutor began to smile back at him, however, he quickly added, "For medical purposes."

Flynn's smile faltered, but he kept it up nonetheless. There was a brief exchange of whispers with Pings as he retrieved a piece of evidence from the prosecution's table, and then Flynn came back to the witness stand with a document. "What is Exhibit 18?" he asked the witness cheerfully.

"My certificate," Langley replied, "for medical marijuana."

Things were not going well for Flynn. The witness in front of him seemed affable and gave every appearance of being compliant. But just a few minutes into his testimony, Langley had already managed to

148

reinforce the concept of medical marijuana...and to do so *three times*. The prosecutor decided to leave the matter alone – trying to correct the witness only gave the topic more emphasis. Flynn simply jumped ahead to questions about what had happened *after* the witness got his certificate.

Langley testified that when he spoke to Fry about obtaining marijuana, she agreed to arrange it – he was told to stay in the waiting room until a Jeep arrived in the parking lot, then go out and introduce himself. After a half hour later had passed, Langley recalled, he got concerned and complained to the receptionist, who simply told him "to be patient." Although he had been eager for the Jeep to arrive, a glimpse at the unshaven, shaggy-haired driver reportedly made Langley nervous...but not too nervous to go out and introduce himself.

According to Langley, the driver was Mike Harvey, but he wasn't there to make a delivery – he wanted Langley to get in the Jeep. "I did get in," Langley testified. "He advised me the transaction couldn't happen on the premises, so we drove to the parking lot of a strip mall." Once they had stopped, Langley recalled that Harvey pulled out a brown paper bag that contained a half-ounce of marijuana and gave it to Langley in exchange for $50 in cash.

"Did you seek marijuana from him again?" Flynn asked.

"Yes," Langley admitted. "After a month, I called – or *attempted* to call – Mr. Harvey to obtain a refill, and got his voicemail two or three times." After Harvey's voicemail filled up, Langley stated that he tried to establish contact by completing and mailing in a survey Harvey had given him. This tactic supposedly worked, as Harvey finally responded and then drove out to Langley's residence in Roseville. "[Mr. Harvey] arrived with a brown paper bag with a half-ounce of marijuana in it, which he sold to me for $60 in cash," Langley revealed about the visit. The extra ten dollars, he said, was for the delivery fee.

Despite the shaky start, Flynn's direct examination had gone smoothly. He had elicited from the witness the narrative of a hand-to-hand marijuana sale allegedly arranged through Fry, without any further mention of medical marijuana. "No further questions," Flynn said pleasantly, turning Langley over to the defense.

Serra stood up and then, with an amiable smile, declined cross-examination and sat back down in his chair. Lichter, however, was not willing to forfeit the opportunity to question the witness. In fact, he had so much to address that he started out his cross-examination with a sidebar conference regarding documents he had submitted about the witness. But in spite of this preliminary chat at the judge's bench, there was little agreement on the proper course of questioning. Lichter's cross-examination was heavily punctuated by objections from the government.

In fact, Lichter only got one answer from the witness before the objections began. After establishing that Langley had brought medical records with him to his appointment at Fry's office, he asked, "Did you bring the test results from your magnetic resonance –"

"Objection," Flynn broke in.

"Sustained," Judge Damrell determined, watching the exchange with careful scrutiny.

The defense attorney quickly switched the topic, questioning Langley about a video he

Laurence Lichter didn't shy away from pushing his points during cross-examination. Photo by Vanessa Nelson.

recalled seeing directly before his consultation with Dale Schafer. "Do you remember the content of the video?" Lichter asked.

"Vaguely," Langley replied, adopting a contemplative expression while he summoned his memory. "It went over the law or the proposition that was passed–"

"Objection," Flynn announced, interrupting the witness.

Judge Damrell was more perturbed about this topic than he had been about the reference to the medical records. "That is clearly objectionable, counsel," he rumbled, admonishing Lichter. The judge then turned to the jury box and more cordially told the jurors, "I instruct you to disregard that answer."

Lichter turned next to Langley's testimony about contacting Harvey through the mail, and had this correspondence entered into evidence. They had been sent to the "California Medical Research Center" and marked "Attn: Michael." There were two items included in this exhibit – the survey Langley had previously mentioned, as well as a short note he had written. It was this note that Lichter asked the witness to read aloud, and the request was followed good-naturedly.

The letter was written to Mike Harvey, but also acknowledged Fry and Schafer, and started out with Langley gushing about how good it had been to see all of them recently at a medical marijuana festival in Berkeley. "Man, hearing Country Joe took me back 35 years," Langley had reminisced charmingly in the note.

The letter also apologized for Langley's delay in completing the questionnaire. "I'm sorry it's taken me a month to get to the survey," Langley penned, adding, "It was very effective."

But the note concluded by getting down to business. "I am ready to have another prescription filled," Langley wrote. "How can we arrange this?" Before ending the letter, Langley had suggested times that would be convenient for him – he would be settling up his child support payments on the second of the month, he mentioned, and it would be opportune if a meeting could be arranged after that.

Lichter then directed the witness's attention to the questionnaire and inquired about its nature. "It was to assess the effectiveness of medical marijuana in several areas," Langley described. As it turned out, the survey listed a series of conditions and Langley had reported how much marijuana had helped him in those particular areas, using a numerical scale in which ten indicated the maximum benefit.

In spite of the government's qualms, Langley was permitted to recite the conditions as well as his corresponding numerical assessments of marijuana's benefit. "Insomnia" had gotten a 9, as had the "Insight" and "Muscle Spasms" categories. "Anger" and "Nausea" received impressive scores of 10, but "Appetite" was rated with a 7, the lowest mark Langley had given. "Mood Elevation" and "Pain Relief" each earned an 8, while "Anxiety" ranked slightly higher with an 8+.

151

Flynn looked at his folded hands while the witness went through the list, while Pings, sitting at the prosecution's table, tapped her hand soundlessly on the papers in front of her.

It was a somewhat abstract way of conveying the idea, but the survey results still managed to reinforce to the jury the medical uses of marijuana. The questionnaire had even, quite succinctly, described many of the specific areas in which patients received the health benefits. This was a small victory, but Lichter won the battle nonetheless, and, satisfied with the tiny triumph, he had little more to ask the witness. When Langley was excused, he smiled graciously and appeared quite relieved to vacate the witness stand.

Jody Bollinger

Another seemingly-reluctant witness came in the form of Jody Ann Bollinger, who was escorted into the courtroom and then walked to the witness stand with an apprehensive slowness. She was a middle-aged woman with long, dark hair and a round face that didn't offer a single smile. In fact, her features were astonishingly inexpressive while she testified, frozen in torpor and inscrutable. But her voice was even more difficult to interpret – soft, timid and prone to choking up on itself. The emotions and circumstances that lay beneath her mannerisms would remain a mystery, but from a distant perspective, Bollinger presented as a tortured soul.

Whatever the explanation for her demeanor, there would be little time for those in the gallery to study Bollinger's pained countenance. Her spell on the stand, as it turned out, would be remarkably and mercifully brief.

Flynn approached the witness with a typical opening, asking her questions about how she knew the defendants. Bollinger testified to meeting Fry on November 9th, 1999, during an appointment to "obtain a physician's prescription for marijuana." Although she said that this service cost $150, Bollinger couldn't remember how much she paid that day. She could, however, vividly recall the doctor and her appearance. As Bollinger described her, Fry had long-hair and wore a gauze shirt. When the witness used the description "hippie-like," however, it was unclear whether she was referring to the apparel or to the doctor herself. The distinction mattered very little, of course, and the prosecutor did not pause to clarify.

*Dr. Fry is known for taking an empathetic approach with her patients.
Photo by Vanessa Nelson.*

Instead, Flynn showed the witness a record of her recommendation, which had been issued for "vertigo and severe menses." Bollinger confirmed this, but the prosecutor's interest was not in the medical evaluation itself. Flynn wanted to know what happened after the appointment with Fry, and through gentle questioning, he drew out the details of the witness's story.

Bollinger testified that she received a phone call from the defendants' daughter Heather Schafer after the appointment with Fry. The purpose of Heather's call, according to Bollinger, was to ask if she was interested in purchasing marijuana.

154

"What did you say?" Flynn asked.

"That I was," Bollinger answered simply. She said she later called the number Heather gave her and left a message, after which her call was returned by the defendants' son Jeremy Schafer and a delivery date was arranged. According to Bollinger, Jeremy came to her house that week, bringing with him an "18-inch backpack" containing marijuana.

"He took out an ounce of marijuana packaged in sandwich bags into eighths," Bollinger said of Jeremy. She reported that, after examining what Jeremy brought, she purchased two of the baggies with a $90 check.

Flynn showed the check to the witness, who confirmed it was the one she used to pay Jeremy that day. The prosecutor immediately moved it into evidence, and then questioned Bollinger about a particular detail on the check: it was made out to Dale Schafer. When asked why, the witness explained that she was instructed to do so. "Jeremy said to make it out to Dale so if there were any questions, they could say it was for legal fees," she claimed.

Bollinger also described having an interview with the DEA about her visit to Fry's office and the subsequent marijuana delivery. During this interview, she said she identified Jeremy Schafer by photograph as the man who had sold her the marijuana. These admissions were satisfactory to Flynn, who ended his direct examination there and left the witness to be questioned by the defense.

Serra, flashing a disarming smile, stood up only long enough to announce, "Everyone will be delighted that I have no cross." Apparently, it would be Lichter's job to handle the witness. His cross-examination would, however, bring him more objections than answers.

"What did you talk to Mr. Schafer about?" Lichter asked, starting out.

Bollinger's answer was terse. "The law."

But when Lichter wanted her to clarify her response, he was stopped in his tracks. The prosecutor made a general objection, which the judge sustained without comment. It was the pattern that would prevail during the entire questioning.

The defense attorney tried another approach. "Did you talk to Dr. Fry about having Ménière's Disease?"

The witness began to say that she had, but the prosecutor simultaneously issued an objection. Judge Damrell, with a blank nod, sustained the objection.

Ménière's Disease, as it turns out, is an inner ear condition that disturbs balance and involves the progressive loss of hearing. If Bollinger did indeed have this condition, it would certainly explain the episodes of vertigo that her recommendation had noted. Nonetheless, the jury would hear none of it.

"What is this disease?" Lichter inquired.

Flynn was quick. "Objection."

"Sustained," Judge Damrell said, casting a quick eye over at the jury box.

The defense attorney persisted. "Did you try using marijuana for your condition before getting your recommendation?"

Bollinger never answered. Instead, the question was killed as the judge upheld the prosecutor's protest.

Lichter began firing off his questions more quickly now, giving them a sense of urgency. "Did you try other medications for your condition?"

The witness had developed the habit of glancing at Flynn before replying. And this time, as usual, she stayed mute as the prosecutor put forth another successful objection.

"Had you taken Valium prior to meeting with Dr. Fry?" Lichter asked.

Flynn responded in pattern, as though returning a shot in a casual game of badminton. "Objection."

"Sustained," the judge muttered.

"Had you taken Motrin prior to meeting with Dr. Fry?" the defense attorney queried.

156

The volley was getting faster, but Flynn interrupted on cue. "Objection."

Judge Damrell didn't look up. "Sustained." He had long since begun sounding automatic.

"Is it true that you are allergic to Vicodin?" Lichter asked in a flash.

"*Ob*-jection!" Flynn declared, emphasizing the first syllable and betraying a hint of annoyance.

Judge Damrell only sighed. "Sustained."

Lichter slowed down the pace a little, changing gears. "When you met with Dr. Fry, did she offer to sell you marijuana?"

Bollinger's eyes lingered on the prosecutor for a few moments. When he didn't make his usual move, she turned back to Lichter. "No," she replied softly.

"Did the receptionist offer to sell you marijuana?" Lichter asked the witness.

Again deferring to the prosecutor, Bollinger gave Flynn the customary span of silence before responding. She answered in a near-whisper, "No."

Lichter then asked the witness about two aliases of hers, but there was seemingly nothing sinister about these other identities – they consisted only of two different surnames, most likely gained through marriages. When Bollinger said that she had no criminal record under those names, Lichter did not challenge her or present evidence to the contrary.

The defense attorney did, however, want to know why her marijuana purchases had ceased. "Is there a reason you didn't buy more marijuana from Jeremy Schafer?"

"No," Bollinger answered. She had made only a second's pause, giving Flynn a shorter window of opportunity than before.

"Did you stop using marijuana after that?" Lichter asked, his voice and gestures becoming more animated. "Were you *cured*?"

"Objection!" Flynn cut in, adamant this time.

Judge Damrell was getting stern now. "Sustained," he asserted, frowning. But the judge's expression loosened once he heard Lichter's next statement.

"No further questions," the defense attorney announced, giving the witness a slight bow of the head and returning to his seat.

It had been the shortest cross-examination so far, and, as Bollinger was excused from the witness stand, the trial appeared to finally gain momentum.

Jeffrey Teshera

When Jeffrey Teshera entered the courtroom, he came with a *presence*. He was a tall, muscularly-built man with a shaved bald head and a beard that increasingly lost its pigmentation as it went farther down his face. He gave the impression of being in his finest dress and on his best behavior, but no amount of grooming could downplay his fierce eyes. If anything, they stood out in contrast to the appearance of pleasantry he was trying to cultivate.

As he did with all the other minor witnesses, Flynn handled the direct examination of Teshera. Like his mentor in this case, Flynn began the questioning by casually airing his witness's flaws while also being careful not to emphasize them. For Teshera, these flaws seemed to be his priors – conviction and incarceration on counts of robbery and theft.

Largely, the young prosecutor succeeded in acknowledging the criminal record without suggesting scandal. With the priors aside, Flynn got down to business and directed the witness to describe his involvement with the current case. Teshera testified that he first met Fry in August of 2000, when he accompanied his wife to get her "license to smoke marijuana." The couple paid with a check made out to Dale Schafer, which Flynn promptly brought into evidence.

A "license to smoke marijuana" wasn't much use without any marijuana to smoke, so the couple asked Fry if she could supply some. She agreed, according to Teshera, but because she was paranoid about police officers being nearby, Fry wouldn't hand over any marijuana then and there. Instead, Teshera said, she gave him the phone number for Mike Harvey, a "horticulturalist" who made home deliveries of marijuana.

The witness described Harvey arriving with a "regular-sized blue backpack" full of baggies of marijuana, out of which Teshera's wife received a half-ounce and paid $40 in cash. Allegedly, Harvey was forthcoming about his source – he explained that he grew the marijuana himself on Fry's property, in greenhouses and in a barn. And, as Teshera reported, Harvey had to depart promptly because he had many more deliveries to make that day on a circuit that took him through several counties.

This description echoed Harvey's own testimony about maintaining a grueling distribution schedule, and also explained the motivation for the eventual change in the method of delivery. Teshera testified to getting five home deliveries from Harvey before the system was modified – rather than being handed over during house calls, the marijuana was now sent through the United Parcel Service to those who mailed payment to the defendants' office. Teshera recalled that his wife received a half-ounce of marijuana through UPS several times, and Flynn supplied the documentation that supported this claim – three checks the couple made out to Dale Schafer on various dates in October 2000. Two of these were for $40 and included the memo field notations of "personal" and "Rx," Teshera explained, while the third included an extra $10 fee that had been added to compensate for delivery costs.

The witness then testified about the second time he saw Fry, which occurred when he came to her office to get his own "license to smoke marijuana" in November 2000. Directly after he was licensed, and with his wife and another friend in tow, Teshera reportedly asked Fry about getting some marijuana. He testified that, instead of passing the deal off onto Harvey this time, the doctor handled the transaction herself. According to Teshera, Fry arranged a rendezvous at the nearby fire station, where half-ounce bags of marijuana were then sold to him, his wife, and their accompanying friend. In Fry's car with her, the witness recalled, was a younger woman who was visibly pregnant.

Shortly after this encounter, Teshera decided he wanted to grow his own marijuana, but he rejected Harvey's grow kits as being too expensive and instead bought cultivation supplies from a hydroponics store called "Mystic Gardens." As for the plants themselves, Teshera testified that he bought six rooted clones from Harvey and successfully harvested them ten weeks later. Teshera said he then needed replacement clones in order to start another grow, but had to call Fry's office because Harvey didn't come through for him on the second delivery. This time, he recollected, a meeting was arranged at the local feed store, where Fry and Heather Schafer arrived and sold him marijuana starter plants for ten dollars apiece.

During direct examination, Teshera's story seemed fairly solid. The dates he described matched up with the checks Flynn brought into evidence, and his claims appeared to line up with previous testimony about Harvey's operations. Teshera also kept his statements on a purely factual level, to the point that he risked appearing rigid and mechanical. This was especially true when he answered questions by saying "negative" instead of "no," an oddity that caught the attention of the observers in the gallery. But this lack of passion was to the witness's benefit, and it gave his testimony an aura of realism and precision while being questioned by the prosecutor.

Once the defense attorneys took over, however, Teshera's accuracy was put to the test...and found to be lacking.

Serra confirmed with the witness that Schafer had advised him not to smoke marijuana while driving. Serra also got Teshera to admit that the purchases he described had been done at 10% of the black market price for marijuana. But the heavy lifting was left to Lichter, whose most notable revelation was that Heather Schafer had been at a hospital giving birth on a date when Teshera testified that she had accompanied Fry to sell marijuana to him.

Part of this proof came by documenting the date of birth, and Lichter did so later by providing the baby's passport as well as other evidence of the lengthy, complicated labor Heather had endured at the hospital. Therefore, there was no moment of dramatic humiliation in which Teshera's nose was rubbed in his mistake, but the inaccuracy of his testimony on this point eventually became so undeniable that the lead prosecutor would have to acknowledge it. In the meantime, though, Lichter had plenty of other methods by which to cast suspicion on Teshera's credibility...and he employed them so extensively that even the judge lost stamina and pleaded with the defense attorney to relent.

Lichter noted that Teshera's recommendation had the name of Robin Poseley, the physician's assistant who often performed examinations in place of Fry. In spite of being apprised of this fact, the witness maintained he did not meet with Poseley. Repeatedly, Teshera insisted that he had seen Fry and not Poseley on the day of his examination.

The witness recalled seeing a video prior to having a consultation with Schafer, but he did not remember what the video had been about. Whether he could recollect anything that Schafer had said, however, remained a mystery. "Did you discuss the difference between state and federal law?" Lichter asked about the consultation

Flynn cut in immediately, "Objection!"

"Sustained," Judge Damrell announced. "It's irrelevant."

The defense attorney moved on, confirming with the witness that he had filled out a medical history form at Fry's office. Lichter then took a turn toward the sensational, asking a question that startled observers and propagated a wave of lurid whispers in the gallery. "In that form, did you say that marijuana helped to keep you from *hitting people?*"

Flynn interrupted before the witness was able to answer, and the judge sustained the objection just as quickly, casting a leary eye over at Lichter. But the defense attorney did not pale under this fearsome glance, nor did he let it chill his tendency to make provocative suggestions about the witness.

Laurence Lichter used a variety of tactics against government witnesses. Photo by Vanessa Nelson.

Aside from the insinuation of violent tendencies, there was the matter of Teshera's checkered criminal record…and Lichter had some theories about how this played into his motivation for cooperating with the government.

The defense attorney asked the witness whether he had more convictions on his record than the two he had mentioned while being questioned by the prosecutor. When Teshera denied the implication, Lichter flipped through some papers, determined to detail the witness's criminal past. "There's one for burglary in 1989," he observed, scrutinizing a document.

Lichter then looked up at Teshera for confirmation of this fact, acknowledging the long gap of time. "I know we're going back a bit," he noted.

"I was a minor," Teshera said, taken aback by what he just heard. "I thought that was not on my record." Teshera wasn't exactly shaken, but he seemed slightly precarious at that moment, and he had definitely been caught off guard. It was the first time during his testimony when there was a tiny glitch in his projection of a perfectly strong-and-stoic image.

The diminutive Lichter may have managed to knock the beefy witness off his steadiness, but it would be quite an ethical breach if he had done so by going into Teshera's juvenile convictions. To clear himself of this suspicion, Lichter asked to approach the bench and show the judge that the offense he had unearthed was actually on Teshera's adult record. Judge Damrell, acutely aware of the possibility of ethical wrongdoing, had heavy words of warning for the defense attorney. "Counsel, you better have that one right," the judge cautioned.

The examination of the documents was done at a sidebar conference, during which the courtroom was flooded with white noise to prevent the jury from hearing the discussion at the bench. Observers waited intently for the outcome, but they were left without climax as the parties returned wordlessly to their places. Although there was no official proclamation of the conclusion, Lichter was informally cleared of suspicion – there were no misconduct charges, and he continued to question Teshera on the premise that he had more convictions than he had previously reported.

In fact, as Lichter pointed out, Teshera's 2001 convictions showed *two* counts of "grand theft on a person" as well as the robbery conviction he had acknowledged to the prosecutor. The defense attorney therefore calculated a total of four convictions, but Judge Damrell appeared to consider this claim too much of a stretch. "Counsel, this is not appropriate," he told Lichter coarsely.

Anyway, Lichter noted, three strikes on his record would be enough to subject Teshera to higher punishment if he ran into more trouble with the law. "So when the DEA agents came to see you in 2003," Lichter asked the witness, "weren't you scared you would go back to prison?"

"No, sir, my life had changed by that time," Teshera said smugly. "I was not worried at all."

Lichter tilted his head to the side. "But weren't you on probation then?"

"No," the witness replied. "I had been let out on good behavior."

Lichter explained the probationary periods that follow such releases, then asked, "So couldn't you have been revolved back into prison?"

Teshera answered slowly, "I was not aware of that." The idea seemed to be a surprising one to him, and he appeared as though he was seriously pondering the possibilities and ramifications.

But the defense had gotten its own surprise during the course of Teshera's testimony, and it was time to get things sorted out. The revelation that, in early statements Teshera made to the DEA about his interactions with Fry, he reportedly told the agents that there was no exchange of money when he got marijuana from the doctor. These statements had been documented in the agency's written summary of the interview, but on the witness stand Teshera was directly contradicting the report. While answering the prosecutor's questions, Teshera claimed that he paid for each marijuana transaction stemming from Fry. Lichter gave the appearance of being in a state of disbelief over this development, and launched a series of questions to reinforce the reality of it.

"Mr. Harvey never gave you marijuana for free?" Lichter asked.

"No," Teshera answered.

The defense attorney clarified his inquiry. "You never *told* anyone that he did?"

Teshera's reply was the same, "No."

Lichter kept up his questioning, getting more and more specific. "Didn't you tell the DEA that when you met with Dr. Fry in the parking lot, you were given marijuana for free?"

"No," the witness repeated once again.

Lichter paused for a moment, looking puzzled by the course of the interrogation. "Was the driver of the car the one who gave you the marijuana?"

Teshera was vague. "I'm not sure."

"But you're sure you didn't get it for free?" Lichter asked, pressing.

"Yes," Teshera said confidently. "I'm sure."

The defense attorney concentrated his attention fully on the witness. "Are you sure you didn't tell the DEA that you did?"

Teshera was staunch on this point. "I'm sure."

Approaching the stand, Lichter presented the DEA's report of the interview to Teshera. After giving the witness a moment to look over the document, the defense attorney inquired, "Does that refresh your recollection about receiving marijuana for free?"

"No," Teshera said simply.

"So the DEA statement is incorrect?" Lichter posed.

"Yes," Teshera answered. "I believe it was paid for, yes," he added, referring to the marijuana.

Lichter's gaze at the witness was one of extraordinary skepticism. "Wouldn't your memory of it be better at that time than it is now?"

"No," Teshera replied, his answers sounding monotonous and aloof. "I remember what it cost."

"Is there any reason you would be untruthful to the DEA?" The defense attorney was probing, digging.

Teshera gave his uniform denial, "No."

"Is there any reason you wouldn't be able to tell the difference between what's true and what's false?" Lichter asked.

"No," Teshera answered, his eyes narrowing. "I know what's true and what's false."

Lichter made a short humming sound to himself, then went forward with a new disclosure. "Didn't there come a time when you were losing your job because of your use of marijuana?"

Flynn was on his feet in an instant, making an objection that the judge sustained straight away.

Lichter was not so easily thrown off course. "Didn't Dr. Fry write a letter to your employer?" he asked the witness.

"Objection," Flynn repeated earnestly.

The judge was glowering now. "Sustained."

"Did you pay Dr. Fry for that?" Lichter inquired, his demeanor steady.

"No," Teshera's response was blank in emotion.

Flynn quickly objected, but Judge Damrell just held up his hand. "Let's speed things up, counsel," he urged, aggravated by the course of the cross-examination. "This is taking forever."

Lichter started to reply, but Judge Damrell decided he wasn't done with his lecture. "I had hopes after Ms. Bollinger that this would speed up," the judge said, sighing. "You've had a long time to get ready for this trial. The problem is you take so long between questions."

Lichter blamed the witness. "I didn't know the witness would testify different than in his DEA statement," he said. Then, turning back to the stand, he asked Teshera to describe the transaction that occurred immediately after his visit to Fry's office.

"I believe we met at the fire station," Teshera recounted. "It was just Dr. Fry and Heather." But, when asked to clarify, he added, "I don't remember who handed me the marijuana."

Lichter blazed into accusation. "But now you're not even sure Dr. Fry was in the car, are you?"

"Objection!" Flynn said, arguing that Lichter was misstating the testimony. Judge Damrell was easily convinced.

But the defense attorney had many angles of attack. "Did you say things to please the agents?"

"No," Teshera said, continuing to yield nothing.

"You weren't sure who handed you the marijuana," Lichter summarized, "but then, when the DEA talked to you, you were sure."

Flynn stood up, protesting that Lichter was giving commentary rather than asking questions. The judge agreed, sustaining the objection in a huff. Lichter, however, went right for his zinger.

He asked the witness to think back to the transaction in the parking lot. "What if you were faced with evidence that Dr. Fry and her daughter were having a baby that day?" the defense attorney asked, his volume rising in tandem with the drama of his claim.

Teshera was resolute. Nothing Lichter suggested would sway his answers.

The defense attorney finished there. He had made his point, and, knowing the evidence supported it, he was satisfied. "No further questions," he announced before taking his seat.

Flynn had just one follow-up question. "Is it true that Mollie Fry *was* in the car, but you're not sure it was Mollie Fry who *handed you* the marijuana?"

Teshera promptly concurred, "Yes."

The witness was then excused from the stand, and he left the courtroom with the same swagger he had when he entered. On its own, his testimony had been far too questionable to sway the jurors towards a guilty verdict. Still, Teshera added another pound to the load of testimony against the defendants, and that burden was becoming a heavy one indeed.

Tod Zimmerman

When the prosecution called Tod Zimmerman to the stand, an unassuming man with a forgettable face walked through the courtroom doors. He wore a simple corduroy jacket, sported a salt-and-pepper beard, and underneath his spectacles he appeared vaguely cross-eyed. As he was sworn in, listeners noticed Zimmerman's halting, hoarse voice came out as little more than a whisper at times. It was an effect that made the nondescript man seem shrinking and timid. One might even say that he looked perfectly harmless.

Prosecutor Flynn handled the fragile-looking witness with care, guiding him gently into a narrative that elucidated the details of his single encounter with the defendants years ago.

Zimmerman started off by revealing that he operates a real estate appraisal business, for which he and his wife Doreen inspect residential and commercial properties. In February 2001, their work brought them to the home of Mollie Fry and Dale Schafer in Greenwood, California. In describing the residence, however, Zimmerman made a significant error early on in his testimony.

"It was a large house, with a single-wide trailer on the side and two greenhouses on the property," Zimmerman recalled.

There had been testimony about greenhouse cultivation already, but never before had more than one of these structures been mentioned, even in the prosecutor's opening statement. Flynn hurried on to a different question, perhaps believing that the matter would go under the defense's radar so long as he paid it no mind. If so, it was an unlikely wager. Serra and Lichter had already glanced at each other knowingly from across the defense table, and then leaned in closely to whisper to their respective clients. The issue, clearly, was brewing.

Focused, Flynn concentrated on eliciting a story from Zimmerman that explained what had occurred once he and his wife arrived on the Fry/Schafer property. As the appraiser told it, he glimpsed a couple of children and was greeted by two adult males – one of these men was the owner of the house, Dale Schafer, and the other identified himself as the nanny. Asked to describe the latter, Zimmerman replied, "He was a gentleman that was not well-kept. He was long-haired and he was holding an infant. He seemed agitated that we had come to the property."

Watchers in the gallery whispered, "Mike Harvey," and exchanged concurring nods. The nanny had been identified by the crowd with immediate certainty.

It was at that point, Zimmerman recalled on the stand, that "the nanny entered into a short conversation with the home owner." But Flynn could get no further information about the subject of that talk or about the nanny's concerns. Serra broke in immediately to declare it to be a hearsay response, and Judge Damrell sustained the objection without comment.

"How did Mr. Schafer respond?" Flynn asked.

Zimmerman offered an exact quote. "He said, 'It's cool. Don't worry about it, man.'"

Shrugging off whatever conflict was brewing, the appraisers then proceeded with their work. Zimmerman's first job was taking external measurements of the property. During this task, he would also do visual assessments to check for what he termed "deferred maintenance." In lay terms, he explained, he would be looking for signs of erosion, mold, rot and water damage.

Doreen was charged with making the indoor inspections, and she began her work in the garage. According to Zimmerman, his wife observed conditions atypical for a garage area. It was messy, he said, but the untidiness was not what caught Doreen's interest. "There was a walled-off section, and the walls were exposed," Zimmerman related. "There was silver insulation on them."

Inside, Doreen had gotten her first clue that the situation was out of the ordinary. She had inspected garages before, but in her experience they typically served as quarters for vehicles, storage areas or carpentry workshops. For Mrs. Zimmerman, something in the Fry/Schafer garage was disturbingly amiss, but she nonetheless moved on to check out the rest of the house. According to what her husband said on the stand, there had been no marijuana plants in the garage.

Outside, Zimmerman had found his own room of curiosity – the underground emergency shelter commonly called "the bunker." The concrete structure was built into the hillside, he said, and water was mysteriously flowing out from it. Perplexed, Zimmerman opened the door to investigate. What he saw, he said, was startling.

"I saw three platforms that had marijuana plants growing on them," Zimmerman testified. "There were lights and fans going on inside, and some kind of irrigation system." He had stood in the bunker's threshold for less than a minute, staring, then he shut the door and left the area.

Wanting to work into a reasonable estimate of the plant number, Flynn asked a series of spatial questions. The witness described the bunker as between eight to ten feet wide, and said that there were three wooden planks that ran nearly the length of each wall. Zimmerman believed there had been between 40 to 70 marijuana plants on each of the platforms, and so he deduced that the room contained a total of up to 210 of these plants. They were in buckets containing "a sort of soil," he remembered, and some of the plants had "germinated up to eighteen inches."

"How did you know they were marijuana plants?" Flynn inquired.

"When I was in high school," Zimmerman confessed, "I used to smoke marijuana."

Flynn appeared satisfied by this answer, hoping it would help explain how the witness had, in a mere matter of seconds, identified the type of plants, classified the method of cultivation, and assessed the operation thoroughly enough to offer an estimate of the plant count. The prosecutor also got Zimmerman to justify his actions by emphasizing why he had not scrutinized the discovery longer or more closely. Over Serra's objections, the witness testified about the terror he felt at suddenly realizing his wife was alone in a house with two marijuana growers.

Searching for Doreen, Zimmerman dashed through what he described as an "extremely unkept" home. Serra objected when Flynn asked for details about the condition of the house, but Judge Damrell allowed the description. "There were dirty dishes everywhere, dirty clothes everywhere," Zimmerman said, his voice indicating disgust. "There was food everywhere. It was extremely filthy."

According to Zimmerman, it was equally unclean in the master bedroom where he eventually found his wife. "The bedroom was in the same condition as the rest of the house," he stated. Also in the bedroom, he remembered seeing other objects that confirmed marijuana use and cultivation. At Flynn's urging, Zimmerman listed off some of these items. "Bongs, pipes, vials to store the residue from the pipes, plants in Petri dishes germinating…"

In spite of the alarm and disgust he described, the witness and his wife did not leave the property right away. "We stayed long enough to do the appraisal," Zimmerman admitted. This fact was incongruous with the sense of urgency the witness had described. Staying on to finish the job indicated either that he was a very dedicated worker or that his fears had not been as compelling as he had made them seem.

When the couple finally left, they took a glance back at the property as they rode down the long driveway. "I had a better view of the greenhouses," Zimmerman said about that last look. I could see they had plants growing in them." To his eye, these structures appeared to be full of plants.

Driving away, Zimmerman said, he finally had a chance to talk openly with his wife about what they had seen on the property. "We discussed our findings and the welfare of the children in the house," he related.

Lichter made a hearty objection to this statement, and the judge sustained it readily.

Trying again, Flynn asked the appraiser, "Did you stop on the way back?"

"Yes, in Cool, to use the payphone," Zimmerman confirmed. "We called the sheriff."

With a breezy smile, Flynn relinquished the witness, and Serra stepped up to take over the questioning. The defense attorney, wasting no time, went straight to an inquiry about the two greenhouses Zimmerman had described.

"How far apart were these two greenhouses?" Serra asked.

Zimmerman sounded like he was being asked for information he couldn't possibly provide, "I don't know."

Serra, of course, was not so easily satisfied. "Were they next to each other?"

"No," the annoyance in Zimmerman's tone was becoming more apparent.

"Were they the same size?" the defense attorney pried.

Zimmerman shrugged. "About."

Tony Serra flashed his golden smile at friends and enemies alike. Photo by Vanessa Nelson.

Serra kept prying, "Were they the same color?"

"They both had a white or clear plastic covering," the witness said slowly, carefully.

"And when did you first see the two greenhouses?" Serra asked.

This question seemed easier for Zimmerman. "As I was leaving," he replied.

Serra had been leaning forward as he stood, his hands clasped behind his back. Now he straightened himself fully and looked right at the witness. "If I told you there was only one greenhouse on the property, would that jog your memory?"

173

"No." Zimmerman shook his head slightly, as though brushing off the strain of remembering.

"I see that you're wearing glasses," Serra observed, licking his proverbial chops. "Were you wearing glasses back then?"

The witness swallowed and responded. "Yes."

The defense attorney began to increase his volume. "You don't have double-vision, do you?"

Caught hopelessly in a corner, Zimmerman began getting more formal in his replies. "No, sir."

Serra's next question was the lethal one. He had zeroed in on his target, lined up his aim precisely, and now he pulled the trigger. "Are you as certain about the two greenhouses as you were about all the other details you described?"

Zimmerman sounded perfectly sure. "Yes, sir."

Although Serra could have confidently concluded his questioning with that showstopper, he kept going nonetheless. There was something more up the sleeve of his suit jacket, but it was impossible to discern what it was.

"Did you shut the door to the bunker quickly?" the defense attorney asked.

Zimmerman was now getting evasive. "I shut the door after myself."

Serra tried again. "Did you do it quickly?"

"Not in a panic, no," Zimmerman said, continuing to maneuver.

"In your grand jury testimony, it says, 'and I shut the door quickly,'" Serra read from the papers in his hand. "Do you remember giving that testimony?"

The witness surrendered. "Yes."

Zimmerman's credibility had now taken two serious blows, but he would have to take a third before Serra relented.

"You said that you knew what marijuana plants looked like because you used to smoke pot in high school?" the defense attorney asked.

Zimmerman appeared momentarily more confident. After all, he had already confessed to this indiscretion. "Yes," he answered easily.

Serra raised his bushy eyebrows. "You didn't smoke plants, did you?"

The witness was suddenly more cautious again, and his eyes darted from side to side. For a second, he looked every bit like a chess player scrutinizing the board to anticipate his opponent's next move. "No," he responded.

"You knew what marijuana plants look like because you used to steal marijuana plants in high school!" Serra declared, in full swing with the zealous exuberance of accusation. "Is that true?"

"Yes," Zimmerman admitted, shifting his eyes in discomfort.

"Nothing further," Serra announced, his tone cool and professional again.

The witness was now game for Lichter, who championed another issue: Zimmerman's motivation for reporting the defendants to the authorities.

And the defense attorney got right to the matter. "Didn't you work for the federal government when a property had drugs on it and had been seized by the Drug Enforcement Administration?"

"The federal government didn't pay us directly," Zimmerman explained. "We worked for a subcontractor for the DEA."

Lichter stayed on the witness. "But you knew the purpose was to assist in forfeiture for the DEA?"

"Yes," Zimmerman replied.

Cocking his head, Lichter inquired, "How much money did you make this way?"

Zimmerman was cagey. "I don't know," he answered, almost muttering.

The defense attorney knew what to do with a vague witness, and he went straight into a pinpointing strategy. "More than $100,000?"

Zimmerman denied it flatly. "No."

"Do you hope to get that kind of work in the future?" Lichter asked.

The witness feigned buoyancy. "My company is always looking for work," he said.

After levering his way in, Lichter got to his point. "Did you hope that reporting what you saw at the defendants' home would result in more work from the federal government?"

"No, that wasn't our main concern," Zimmerman claimed. "Our main concern was the welfare of the children."

"Not your main concern," Lichter murmured back in an undertone. His point satisfactorily underlined, he ended his questioning right there.

The ball was now back in the prosecutor's court, and Flynn looked fleetingly uncertain about whether or not to pick it up. For the government, trying to clean up this mess could have done more harm than good, and the young prosecutor made only a single effort at damage control.

"Did you call the DEA or the local cops?" Flynn asked, attempting to disarm Lichter's insinuations.

Zimmerman answered without hesitation, "The local cops."

After that short statement, the testimony was over. The attorneys had no further questions, and Zimmerman was dismissed from the stand. As he exited the courtroom, observers waited expectantly for what would come next.

The government had no remaining witnesses to call. Those who took the stand henceforward would do so for the defense.

Character Witnesses for the Defense

On August 13th, 2007, the defense of Mollie Fry and Dale Schafer kicked off with a series of character witnesses. Supporters of the embattled couple marked the occasion with a demonstration in front of the federal courthouse, displaying signs to motorists and passersby for over an hour before the proceedings began.

Inside the courtroom, however, it soon became clear that the event had put the marshals on guard. What ensued was a typical post-protest crackdown on gallery etiquette.

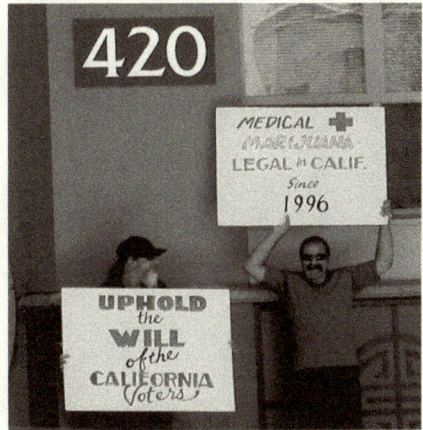

Friends of Dr. Fry and Dale Schafer hold protest signs below an auspicious address marker. Photo by Vanessa Nelson.

This pattern had become noticeable during the trial, with the marshals giving an increased frequency and severity of reprimands to courtroom observers directly following street protests. At these times, the glorified security guards threatened to kick out observers and cite them for behavior as trivial as bobbing their heads. On this day, however, the marshals made the mistake of depriving a water bottle to the wrong guy.

After observer Ryan Landers was ordered to part with his water, the intrepid activist sought the intervention of the defense team and convinced Serra to champion his cause. Promptly taking the matter before Judge Damrell, the defense attorney argued that Landers had a medical condition that required frequent hydration and requested that the water bottle be allowed back into the courtroom.

The judge appeared perplexed by this plea, processing the information by spitting it back out as questions. "He has a medical condition? What medical condition does he have? He has to have water at all times?" Judge Damrell asked, not pausing for answers before he went on to his next question. "What kind of bottle is this?"

Activist Ryan Landers fought to possess a water bottle in the courtroom gallery. Photo by Vanessa Nelson.

Landers fetched the banned bottle for presentation, and upon visual inspection, the judge could find no reason to prohibit it. Seeming perturbed by the undue amount of attention paid to the presence of a nondescript water bottle, Judge Damrell decided hastily, "I'll allow that."

Another consequence of the demonstration was that Pings used it to bolster her daily request for a poll on the jury's media exposure.

"There were a number of people outside the court today, at exactly the time the jurors would be arriving, and they had signs and they were – well, the word 'protest' seems a little strong, but there were *demonstrators*," Pings said with consternation. In her plea to the judge, she also noted her alarm about a headline on the defendants' website that read "Cool Couple Hopes for Jury Nullification."

Judge Damrell listened to the prosecutor's worries, but didn't do much to address them. Later, when the jurors entered the courtroom, he took care to ask them whether they had been exposed to any information or conversations about the case. However, the judge was not particularly anxious about the influence the demonstration may have had on the jurors. He acknowledged that they may have seen some signs while coming to the courtroom, but his concern was whether anything happened beyond the viewing of banner messages. The jury collectively indicated that nothing had occurred, an assurance that satisfied the judge and the prosecutor…for the time being.

Before the day of witnesses could get underway, however, there were some other matters to be discussed outside the presence of the jury. First off, the prosecution was concerned about the responses that would be given when character witnesses were asked questions about the defendants' level of honesty and tendency to obey laws. Although she left her sidekick Flynn to argue this topic in front of the judge, Pings prefaced the matter by alleging that the defense intended to use character witnesses for the purpose of sneaking in references to medical marijuana. The defense attorneys, she claimed, were "trying to do through the backdoor what they cannot do through the front door."

The innuendo in this comment, though seemingly unintentional, inspired a few derisive titters from the audience. The marshals, however, let the laughter slide with just a flash of sour looks as the sole punishment. Following the water bottle incident, they were nursing the loss of some authority.

Serra stepped forward, speaking for the defense. "I guarantee I won't ask anything improper of the character witnesses," he said, palms upturned in a display of honor. "But law abidingness is a character trait."

Flynn clarified the government's requests. "It should be about law abidingness *generally*, not about the medical marijuana law *in particular*," the young prosecutor argued. "With regard to any kind of state law, there is no good faith defense. Your honor has ruled on this. References to a defendant's charitableness, or whether the defendant is a good mother or a good father, is not appropriate…and in drug cases especially, it's just not proper."

Judge Damrell referenced an excerpt from a book of codes. "'…When a trait is an essential element of a charge, it can be raised,'" he read. "That's not the case here."

Serra had a broad interpretation of the statement. "The generic trait of law-abidingness is relevant to *every* case," he asserted.

Flynn, of course, had a different take. He claimed that, in order to have witnesses testify about a defendant's law-abidingness, that defendant must have had his credibility attacked on the stand or in out-of-court statements. The judge took a short recess to consider this claim, ultimately deciding that the prosecutor's assessment did not apply. "The defendants have every right to character witnesses to testify to honesty, veracity, and law abidingness," Judge Damrell declared upon his return.

It may have sounded like a victory for the defense, but first sentences are often deceiving. The judge was not quite yet finished. "Having said that," he continued, "under these particular circumstances, it's not admissible to ask for the basis for their opinion. This invites discussion of specific instances."

"But an opinion without foundation is worthless," Serra declared, only to be met with condescending laughter from the judge.

Sensing the debate was getting too abstract, Pings jumped back in to provide some concrete examples. "Mr. Serra typically asks the witnesses the basis for their opinion on the defendant. Some replies would be 'I've known them all my life' or 'we've been friends for decades.' What I want to prevent are answers like 'I know them from the medical marijuana movement' or 'they helped me with my illness' or other statements the court has ruled inadmissible."

Judge Damrell agreed wholeheartedly. "Yes, those would be getting into specific instances, and I'm precluding that," he explained. "With the issue regarding medical marijuana laws and the conduct relating to this, it's simply not admissible."

And with that castration, the defense moved on to address its individual witnesses.

Chris Conrad

Author and court-qualified expert witness Chris Conrad traveled some 80 miles from the San Francisco Bay Area to testify for the defense, but never made it the final 30 feet up to the witness stand. Regarding Conrad, the prosecutors claimed that the defense did not give proper notice of the proposed testimony.

Flynn argued that the proffer was received too late. "We didn't know about Mr. Conrad until Thursday afternoon, when we rested our case," he told the judge. Furthermore, he argued, the proffer was inadequate. "We got a one sentence email from the defense about what the testimony would be," the prosecutor complained.

Serra explained that he didn't realize they would need Conrad's testimony until a government witness testified about spider mites on the plants seized from the defendants' home. At that point, the defense attorney claimed, Conrad's expert testimony on the effects of spider mite infestation became suddenly necessary. "Their expert precipitated our argument," Serra claimed, and given that the government rested its case ahead of schedule, there was not much time for advance notice.

The judge wasn't buying it. "You gave no proper notice, the prosecution had already rested, and now you're saying spider mites is an issue?" Judge Damrell asked skeptically. "You said from the beginning this wasn't an issue to you. This is not a surprise."

The defense attorney began to explain that he had informed Pings verbally in court about the expert witness, but Judge Damrell would hear none of it. "That's not enough," he roared, cutting Serra off mid-sentence to read aloud the rules for submitting proposed witnesses.

Expert witness Chris Conrad was not permitted to testify at trial. Photo by Vanessa Nelson.

"That's the rule, and it applies to you just like it applies to everyone else in this courtroom," he shouted at Serra.

"Well," the defense attorney said casually, "Conrad will be here."

181

"What?!" the judge demanded, fuming. Given his tone, it seemed he had interpreted the comment as a challenge to his authority.

"He's on his way," Serra clarified, shrugging. "He'll be here later this afternoon."

The judge eased a bit. "Well, it's way too late," he summarized. "You can't bring a witness after the government has rested. The bell has rung. The bus has left the station – the train's out of the station. It's too late."

And, for Conrad, that was that. He was left to enjoy an idle summer afternoon in the state capital.

Joel Bingham

A friend of Schafer's since grammar school, Joel Bingham successfully used his time on the stand to present a squeaky clean image of both himself and his lifelong pal. The small-town postmaster got in several inspiring statements about the defendants, interrupted by only a single objection from the prosecutor.

That objection came as the witness was describing how he and Schafer joined the navy together, only for Bingham to get injured while in service. According to the witness, that was around the time that Schafer helped him out a great deal. "After I was injured, he would take me out and feed me –"

"Objection," Pings broke in, asking the judge to refer to his ruling on this matter. Apparently, this testimony reminded the prosecutor of the statements she had earlier asked the judge to prohibit: specifically, the one she characterized as 'they helped me with my illness.'

Serra was vexed by the interruption. "It's a tactic," he claimed, "to object to every trivial thing, to break the cadence."

The judge was unmoved by the defense attorney's concerns, and sustained the objection without comment.

Amazingly, however, the remainder of Bingham's testimony was given without interruption. When asked about Schafer's law-abidingness, the witness gave a compelling representation. "As long as

I've known him, I don't think he's ever been arrested. I don't think he's ever broken a law. I don't even know if he's gotten a speeding ticket before."

But it was the assessment of his friend's veracity that was the most touching. "Mr. Schafer is probably one of the most honest and trustworthy people I know," Bingham said with palpable emotion. "I believe his integrity is impeccable, and I love him to death."

In response to a short questioning by Lichter, Bingham gave a similarly glowing assessment of Fry's honesty. "Dr. Fry is a very upstanding citizen. She's a very good friend of the family. I do believe she's a very, very good person."

To round it off, the witness also gave Fry strong support with regard to her law-abidingness. "I don't know that she has ever broken the law," he said sincerely.

The prosecution opted not to cross-examine Bingham, so, with a smile and a sense of goodwill; he climbed down from the stand almost as soon as he climbed into it.

Jacob DuCharme

When Jacob DuCharme took the stand, it appeared that the court was going to get another unambiguously feel-good witness. The well-dressed young man carried himself like an Eagle Scout on an important job interview, looking clean-cut and upright from every angle. Serra even did his part to get things started off on the right foot, joking as he struggled to grasp the unusual surname, "Sometimes I mispronounce my own children's names." But no amount of pleasantness could steer the testimony away from the inevitable pitfalls, which began with the prosecution's objections during direct examination.

After DuCharme explained that he and his wife were briefly employed at the defendants' office in early 2000, he was asked about Schafer's reputation in the community. "People held him in the highest regard," DuCharme asserted. "He participated in community events. He's a family man –"

Pings made an objection, which was quickly sustained by the judge. Courtroom observers looked puzzled for a few moments, before remembering what had been said about testimony regarding the parental skills of the defendants. DuCharme was left to amend his sentence, which seemed rather generic in its new state; "Everyone I know has a very high opinion of Mr. Schafer with respect to law-abidingness."

Jacob DuCharme, unlike other former employees of Dr. Fry and Dale Schafer, testified for the defense. Sketch by Dr. Care.

When asked about why he and his wife left Schafer's employment, DuCharme referenced difficulties with Paul Maggy and Traci Coggins, the couple who trained him for his job there. "The problem wasn't Dr. Fry and Mr. Schafer – we love Dale and Mollie. It was Paul Maggy and Traci Coggins – we felt them to be of poor character."

Pings immediately objected. Paul Maggy, after all, had been her lead witness, and her case had a lot riding on his credibility. In response to her concern, Judge Damrell turned to the jury and instructed them to disregard the last comment made by the witness.

In spite of the objections, DuCharme did manage to get some positive statements on the record…and keep them there. First and foremost, he testified that, while at the office, he never saw Fry or Schafer give marijuana to anyone.

About Schafer's law-abidingness, he said solidly, "He was not the maverick individual. He followed the letter of the law, and encouraged others to follow the letter of the law."

Similarly, the witness described Fry as an "absolutely honest, upstanding, vigorous character," and had even more to say about the defendants as a couple. "They both have excellent standing in the community in which they reside, with regard to honesty, veracity and trustworthiness."

This glow of amity was shattered once Pings began her cross-examination. She was intent on destroying the credibility of the man who badmouthed her lead witness's character and reliability, and she went right for the throat.

DuCharme had estimated the duration of his employment with the defendants to be approximately five months, but Pings quickly demonstrated that the actual length was a mere three weeks. DuCharme, admitting the error, attributed his poor memory of the timeline to the fact that the events occurred more than seven years prior.

The prosecutor, however, had another theory for the memory glitch. "When you were working for the defendants, was your ability to perceive what was going on affected by the fact that you were using cocaine?"

The witness, not concealing his surprise at the question, denied the accusation. Pings, predictably, pursued the matter. "Is there a reason why not?" she asked sharply.

"Yes, because I only used cocaine once in my life," DuCharme said with emphasis.

The prosecutor continued, "But weren't you on probation for drug use?"

"No, I was on probation for reckless driving," the witness clarified.

"But isn't it true that when you were on probation, you were given diversion for drug use?" Pings was relentless.

"Yes," DuCharme admitted.

The prosecutor asked the next question with flourish, as though celebrating the cornering of her opponent. "And did you tell Dr. Fry you were on probation for cocaine?"

"I was not on probation for cocaine. I was on probation for wet and reckless driving. I told Dr. Fry about it for full disclosure, that when I was arrested in South Lake Tahoe they found a minute amount of cocaine, that was so minute I wasn't even charged for it."

Pings responded by simply reading off the code for charge of possession of a narcotic controlled substance, as though from a record, but was interrupted by an objection from the defense. "This is not proper impeachment!" Serra declared, and in response, Judge Damrell summoned the attorneys to his bench for a sidebar. At the conclusion of that conference, Pings got DuCharme's paperwork from Fry admitted as evidence. She then marched the document over to the witness stand and declared she had no further questions.

On re-direct, Serra had another idea about what to do with the paper that was just dumped in his witness's lap. "On the bottom of that document, it says, 'Marijuana is still illegal under federal law,'" he began. "In working for the defendant, did you have a belief you were violating the law?"

Pings objected, but the defense attorney quickly countered, saying to the judge, "She opened the door!" Judge Damrell ignored his claim, sustaining the objection instead.

But Serra wasn't done. He turned to the witness again, asking, "Did you ever hear Mr. Schafer explain that statement to anyone?"

An objection came from Pings right away, and the judge was just as quick to sustain it.

The defense attorney kept going. "Did you have an understanding of federal law, or of federal policy, with regard to marijuana?"

Yet again, Pings objected, exasperated. Her objection met its predictable fate and was sustained by the equally exasperated judge.

Serra was persistent. "Did you ever see any crimes?"

Pings objected, right on cue, with Judge Damrell ruling immediately to sustain the objection. They were on a roll now, but the defense attorney cut it off.

"Nothing further," Serra said, taking his seat in order to give re-direct over to Lichter.

Serra didn't stay in his seat long, though. In response to Lichter's first question to the witness, DuCharme explained that he was told in court that he only had to disclose his diversion if he was seeking to become a federal agent or something similar. Hearing this, the attendees at the prosecution's table couldn't help themselves, breaking out in grins and giggles. Serra wasn't going to take that sitting down, and in an instant he was back on his feet, pointing across the courtroom and accusing the prosecutors of "grimacing and laughing." Especially given their close proximity to the jury box, he maintained, this was unacceptable behavior. "The jury sees it!" he declared. "It's very unprofessional!"

The judge, however, had not seen it, but he issued a warning against such reactions in the future.

Elvy Musikka

The final witness of the day was Elvy Musikka, a glaucoma patient who is part of the federal government's Compassionate Investigational New Drug program. Although closed to new entrants since 1991, this program still provides its surviving participants with marijuana that was grown for research purposes at the University of Mississippi. Every month, Musikka is allotted a cylindrical tin of pre-rolled marijuana cigarettes, and to the prosecution's dismay, she arrived at the courtroom to testify with this very same container cradled in her arms.

According to Musikka, the marshals were reluctant to let her pass when they spied the tin. Even when presented with the claim that this was federally legal marijuana, they investigated it suspiciously. Since the marijuana provided by the federal government is often over a decade old, and the manufacture date stamped on the carton had long since passed, the marshals reached the conclusion that the tin was invalid because it had "expired." With much persuasion, however, the witness was finally permitted to escort her marijuana through the courtroom entrance…but she didn't get much further.

Pings was appalled at the thought of Musikka carrying her bounty up to the witness stand, and the judge soon heard all about it. "I understand this next witness is carrying with her a demonstrable object, presumably to show the jury," the prosecutor told Judge Damrell shortly before the jurors returned from their afternoon break. Pings then heightened her tone of urgency to describe what she believed to be contained in the so-called demonstrable object. "I understand she's carrying with her her supply of marijuana that she got from the federal government."

The judge was quick in his decision. "I will not permit her to bring a prop in front of the jury." He ordered the defense to assist Musikka in stashing her tin in the hallway, and then reassured the prosecutor that there would be no discussion of medical marijuana, glaucoma, or the federal program. This established, the jurors were let back into the room to sit in the jury box and await the next witness. Finally, stripped of her tin – and, to some degree, her desired testimony – the nearly-blind Musikka was led up to the stand.

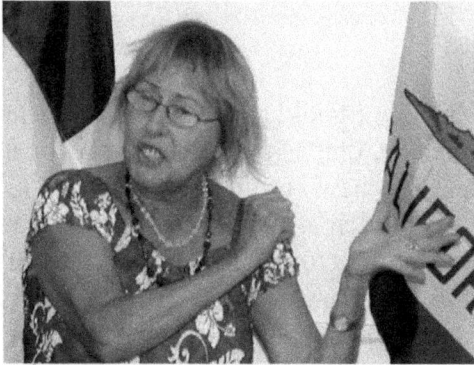

Elvy Musikka receives a monthly supply of marijuana through the federal government, but she was prevented from explaining this program to the jury. Photo by Vanessa Nelson.

But this witness didn't give up so easily. Right as she was taking her seat, she cut off the court clerk who was attempting to administer her oath. "Wait, wait," she said, "what I want to do is ask if I can tell the whole truth –"

The judge interrupted and told the witness just to take the oath, but Musikka continued to speak her piece. "...because I don't want to commit perjury," she concluded.

"You're not going to cross that line," was the comment she received in reply.

Firmly urged once again to take the oath, Musikka relented and swore to tell the truth, the whole truth, and nothing but the truth, so help her God. And, to her credit, the courageous 68 year-old did so to the extent that she was allowed...and a little bit more too.

When Lichter asked her if she was aware of Fry's reputation for trustworthiness, Musikka replied, "She is dearly loved by all of us, and

188

admired, and we feel that she has never done anything wrong in caring for her patients."

Pings was quick to register her opposition to this comment, but, to the amazement of the audience, Judge Damrell decided to overrule the objection. "I'll allow the answer to stand," the judge said, in a rare move favoring the defense.

The witness did not fare so well on other lines of questioning, however. In establishing the background of her friendship with Fry, she twice described attending medical conferences together, but both times an objection from Pings left her with an instruction forbidding the use of the word 'medical.' Musikka was able to do little more to detail her history with Fry, and ended up speaking instead about holidays and weekends spent at the doctor's home.

The witness did, however, get some favorable ideas conveyed to the jury. She repeatedly reinforced Fry's status as a trusted and beloved doctor in her community. Answering about law-abidingness, Musikka said that it was her belief that Fry had never committed a crime. But the witness's most poignant statement came in response to a question about Fry's honesty. "I think she would go to jail before she'd tell a lie," Musikka said with conviction. "I do believe that."

It was a powerful statement to end the day with, especially given that Fry was on trial for crimes that could easily put her behind bars for years. As the last witness, Musikka's words provided the heartiest fodder for the evening's reflection, and she delivered this parting message with feeling and impact. She left the stand with a gracious "thank you," and the court went in recess directly afterwards.

Lichter was even more gracious. As the audience members rose to file out of the courtroom, he gave them a warm verbal salute. "To everyone who came here today – or at least everyone who *wasn't paid* to come here today – thank you. That is the finest character evidence anyone could have given."

Dale Schafer, Part 1

The defense's case had barely gotten underway when Schafer caused a sensation by taking the stand and admitting openly to growing crop after crop of marijuana. Observers looked on with fascination as he teared up while describing his wife's illness, then composed himself enough to detail an articulate account of his successes and failures as a marijuana cultivator. Schafer was not required to take the stand, and so some of the watchers were stunned to see the defendant choose to incriminate himself in this way. During courtroom breaks, they chatted about it unremittingly in the hallway, discussing points of legal strategy with the vigor and intensity usually reserved for sports matches and presidential races.

One of Schafer's motives for testifying quickly became visible, and it appeared to be a sort of chivalry – a falling upon the sword to spare his lady-love. During the course of his day on the witness stand, Schafer insisted some thirty times that Fry had nothing at all to do with his marijuana cultivation. And his assertions to that point were indeed quite believable.

Serra dove into the direct examination of his client, but not without some lighthearted joviality. His first statement was not only comical but also an indication of his familial closeness with his client. "If I inadvertently call you Dale," Serra instructed the defendant, "just reach down and slap me."

Schafer's own dry wit was in harmony with that of his attorney. "I can reach you from here, Mr. Serra," he shot back teasingly.

From there, Serra guided his client through a summary of his early life. Listeners learned that Schafer was born in San Diego but grew up near Sacramento, and that his dad made a living driving a Coca-Cola truck while his mom worked for the Franchise Tax Board. His siblings were two sisters – the older one, a victim of breast cancer, worked as an accountant for McDonald's, and the younger one was permanently disabled and thus unemployed.

The references flew off Schafer's tongue, one after another. Coca-Cola... McDonald's... taxation – what could be more American? But his life-story was already full of foreshadowing, with breast cancer striking down a loved one and lessons in compassion for the disabled. It was a narrative that mixed whimsy and gravity, in seemingly equal amounts.

On the witness stand, Dale Schafer displayed his characteristic affability. Sketch by Dr. Care.

When Schafer first attended college, he "spent more time chasing bikinis than books," and eventually ended up in military service. He went back to school after his time in the navy, getting his bachelor's degree in Social Science from the California State University at Sacramento. It was shortly after that, in the early 1980s, that he first met Fry. He was in law school at the University of Northern California at that time, and she was studying medicine. Once they married, the newlyweds instantly had two school-aged children to raise. They got custody of Heather and Jeremy, Schafer's children from a previous marriage, and it was only a short time later that Fry began having more children. Over the next several years, Geoffrey, Caroline and Tyler (nicknamed "Cody") were born into the family, and they lived comfortably in southern California. Schafer initially worked as an attorney in medical malpractice cases, for which he was lead trial counsel, but eventually decided to set up a private practice lawyer specializing in worker's compensation. By 1996, Fry and Schafer had moved north again, bringing their brood with them to the tiny town of Greenwood. The children liked the new house and the scenic rural setting, and everything appeared ideal for the family. Then, from out of the blue, came Mollie Fry's breast cancer.

Schafer was the first witness to speak in any significant depth about his wife's professional practice or about the evolution of her involvement with medical cannabis. Even though he barred evidence of medical necessity, Judge Damrell allowed Schafer to speak about these subjects in order to explain his reasons for cultivating cannabis. This was a double-edged sword for the defense – Schafer would be allowed to talk about medical cannabis in front of the jury, but only when admitting his own guilt.

Nevertheless, Schafer's testimony marked a dramatic change in the rhetoric of the trial. Up until then, the prosecutor had successfully objected to nearly all the pairings of the words "medical" and "medicine" with mentions of cannabis. Listening to Schafer, however, the jurors got many earfuls of these pairings.

For the defense, Schafer tearfully described his wife's diagnosis with breast cancer and her resulting struggles with chemotherapy and a double mastectomy. "We were told she had a 30% chance to survive," Schafer recounted on the stand, gazing across the courtroom at his wife, who was racked by silent but powerful open-mouthed sobs. "We went through four courses of chemotherapy as soon as the wounds healed from the mastectomy."

After plainly admitting to growing cannabis for Fry, Schafer hit another point of emotional intensity when explaining why he had decided to begin cultivating. "She puked," he said of his wife, tears welling up in his eyes again. "She laid on the floor of the shower and puked, and I would have to clean her off and try to feed her."

Many of the watchers in the gallery had begun crying, and a couple members of the jury appeared to be on the verge of tears as well. The other jurors wore expressions of absorbed concentration and sympathetic concern. In this mood, they heard about how a bald and weak Fry wasted away during her rigorous cancer therapies, unable to hold any food down. "In 1998, her doctor recommended marijuana,"

Schafer recalled. "No other anti-emetics worked, and she was prescribed many anti-emetics. Some were even injectible, I think. None of them worked."

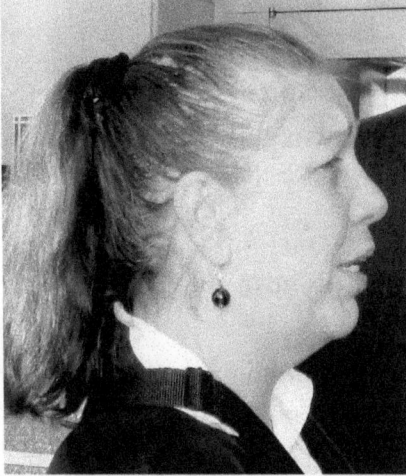

Dr. Fry sobbed openly in court as her husband testified about her battle with breast cancer. Photo by Vanessa Nelson.

As Schafer soon found out, medical marijuana was easier said than done. "At first I tried to buy it," he explained on the witness stand. He then made a comparison that the prosecutor would later try to use against him. "It wasn't like high school – you had to go out on the black market and find it. It was hard."

As Schafer tells it, a friend gave him some marijuana seeds in 1998, inspiring him to try to produce the medicine his wife needed. Even though he had never grown the plant before, he thought it might be easier and more affordable than trying to obtain marijuana on the streets, so he decided to give it a go. There was enough land around the family's home to accommodate a small growing area, plus Schafer already had some experience in agriculture. During his youth, he had spent winters and summers at his grandparent's farm, where he had planted and harvested crops of oats and barley.

"Did you have a green thumb?" Serra asked about his client's days on the barley farm.

Schafer was modest. "I planted it and it grew," he said with a shrug. "That's all."

Marijuana, Schafer realized, differed greatly from oats and barley, so he would need some guidance. He went to Barnes and Noble and got a book on marijuana cultivation authored by Ed Rosenthal. Back at home, he studied the book, and promptly applied his studies. Schafer put his seeds on a plate with a paper towel and germinated them, then put them in cups until what sprouted became big enough to put in the ground. The plants grew to five or six feet tall and flowered, at which time he trimmed and dried them. Schafer admitted to growing just those two marijuana plants in 1998. The bunker where he dried the plants, he said, was already there when his family bought the house.

Serra took Schafer through a list of questions about his wife's role in the cultivation. "Did Dr. Fry help you?"

Schafer seemed glad to answer. "Not in any respect at all," he responded with certainty.

A few questions later, the defendant expanded on this notion. "She never watered a plant, never trimmed a plant, never weeded a garden," Schafer said of his wife. "The most she would do is walk in the garden."

Dale Schafer's cheerful composure broke into tears when it came to the subject of his wife's illness. Photo by Vanessa Nelson.

This explanation, it seemed, was intended to account for photographic evidence that showed Fry in the outdoor marijuana garden. As Schafer would have it, these were not pictures of a proud cultivator posing with her plants or a farmer hard at work in her garden. Rather, they were pictures of a woman recovering from cancer who was getting some fresh air and sunshine by just walking around the yard of her own home. Again and again, Schafer insisted his wife had absolutely no involvement in the cultivation of the plants.

"Why not?" Serra asked his client.

"She was sick," Schafer started to answer with quickness, as though he meant to go through the difficult questions as fast as possible to minimize the pain of the memories. But the speed of his speech

195

crashed into his emotion and he was forced to go more slowly, tearful once again. "She was bald. The chemo had kicked up her arthritis. She was very ill."

"Did you have an agreement with her to grow marijuana?" Serra inquired.

"Yeah," Schafer answered plainly. The response put the watchers in the gallery on the edge of their seats, stunned by the apparent admission. But Schafer immediately continued, clarifying his response in a more familiar way. The cultivation agreement he had with his wife, he told the jury, was this, "I would grow it, and she would stay completely away from it."

Serra went down the line of obligatory questions. "Did you have an agreement with Dr. Fry to distribute marijuana?"

"No," the defendant said, his answer simple but firm.

"Did you have an agreement with Dr. Fry to distribute *clones*?" Serra asked.

"No," Schafer maintained.

It seemed definitive, but it was only the beginning of the questioning about Fry's participation in the cultivation. After discussing the yields of each season, Serra took his client through the same set of questions regarding Fry's involvement with the crop that was just described. And each time, Schafer's answers were nearly identical.

"Did she help you cut the plants?" Serra would ask.

Schafer would answer decisively, "No."

Serra would continue, "Did she help you dry the plants?"

"No," the defendant would reply, shaking his head.

Lastly, Serra would inquire, "Did she help you manicure the plants?"

"No," Schafer would insist. "She has carpal tunnel. She can't do that."

After denying his wife's involvement with each crop, Schafer would give the details about the next year's marijuana grow and explain the developments relevant to each cultivation attempt. He continued this process while testifying about several different grows, spanning 1998 through 2001.

The greenhouse was constructed in early 1999, Schafer said, and he cultivated in it later that year. He also grew some marijuana on his hillside garden patch, for a total he estimated at 20-21 plants for the 1999 grow season. According to Schafer, Mike Harvey was living on the defendants' property and helped out with that year's grow. When Schafer testified about the plant yields for 1999, however, he revealed that only half of the harvest was intended for Fry. Schafer had begun growing marijuana for an AIDS patient by that time, and the other half of the plants were for this man. He had met the AIDS patient, he explained, through a woman who was staying in his home while escaping domestic abuse and being rehabilitated from drug and alcohol addiction.

"Did you consider yourself to be his caregiver?" Serra asked about the AIDS patient Schafer had mentioned.

"Yes," Schafer replied simply.

"Can you explain to the jury what a caregiver is?" Serra urged his client.

"Objection," Pings said, looking anxiously at the judge. "May we approach?"

Judge Damrell agreed to discuss the matter in a sidebar, and Serra went reluctantly up to the judge's bench for the little private conference. When he returned, however, Serra went straight back to questions about caregivers.

"Were you a caregiver for anybody else?" the defense attorney asked.

"Objection," Pings said again, more loudly this time.

The familiar strain was beginning to show again, and Judge Damrell sustained the objection, saying he failed to see the relevance of Serra's question. Pings promptly requested another sidebar to discuss acceptable terminology, but Serra made a rare concession instead. He agreed to simply give up the line of inquiry, grumbling that he didn't want to keep going up to the judge's bench *every time* he asked a question.

Whatever terminology was used, however, Serra was determined to get down to his client's attitudes and his motivations for growing marijuana that was intended for people other than his wife. When asked, Schafer refused to characterize it as distribution when he gave marijuana to the AIDS patient. "I stuffed it into a plastic bag and handed it to him," Schafer said of the half of the harvest that he gave away. "He complained that it wasn't trimmed."

"Did you receive any monetary remuneration for that?" Serra asked.

Schafer was certain in his answer. "No."

"What was your motive for doing that?" Serra inquired.

"Compassion, I guess," Schafer shrugged. "He was sick," he added matter-of-factly.

After giving half of the harvest to the AIDS patient, Schafer trimmed the remaining ten plants for his wife and got about three pounds of bud for his effort. Fry needed this amount to last her until the end of 2000, since the grow cycle for outdoor marijuana plants is usually one crop per year.

But, unfortunately, the yield of the 1999 grow was used up after just a few months. There was a good reason for the accelerated consumption – after the 1999 harvest, Schafer had gotten a doctor's approval to use marijuana. The Fry/Schafer home had become a two-patient household.

Dr. Jerry Powell, who was slated to appear later as a character witness for the defense, advised Schafer to use medical marijuana for a variety of ailments that were rattled off to the jury. First off, Schafer spoke of his hemophilia, stating, "It has caused me a lifetime of bleeds in most of my joints." He also described the ravages of Hepatitis C and the pain of his failed back surgery. Schafer had been taking a long list of prescribed painkillers, but using marijuana helped him cut back on these pharmaceutical drugs. The reduction in prescription painkillers continued up until his arrest in 2005. As part of the conditions for bail at that time, he was denied marijuana use and made to undergo random drug testing as verification of his abstinence.

Although the jury was not told this fact explicitly, Serra hinted around it. "Presently, since this case, what prescriptions do you use now?" he asked.

"The three I mentioned before [extra-strength Vicodin, synthetic morphine and methadone]." The defendant then paused to think of the rest. "Oxycontin," he finally answered, "and Dexedrine to keep me awake."

Schafer estimated that, given his extraordinary pain level, he used more marijuana than Fry did. "I was eating it, so I was probably consuming more than my wife, because eating it takes more material," he explained on the stand. "Eating it was better at pain control and lasts longer. I would eat the crystals with water in the morning and it lasted most of the workday."

At Serra's urging, Schafer detailed this method of ingestion, orienting himself towards the jurors and using hand gestures in his description. He told them he would grind marijuana into a permanent coffee filter and put a vibrator next to it so that it shook all the crystals loose. He would then bottle these crystals up, so that, when needed, he could easily grab a handful of them.

It appears that Schafer engaged in this process frequently after getting his recommendation, and, as a result, he and his wife were out of marijuana in the early part of 2000. Their yearly outdoor harvest would not be ready until autumn, and as an attempt to fill this gap, the defendant claimed that he decided to try growing marijuana indoors.

As Schafer testified, he began this attempt in a grow area constructed in his garage, but later decided to do his indoor cultivation in the bunker room. "I started with six plants in what is called the garage grow room," he testified, "but I call it 'the room of death' because nothing ever grew in there without getting infested with spider mites."

As Schafer told it, this ill-fated grow room had been constructed in early 2000 with the help of a carpenter friend and Mike Harvey, who hung the reflective material on the walls. It was never fully completed, however, thanks in large part to Harvey's ineptitude. "He tried and tried to hang the door," Schafer said of Harvey, "but he could never get it right."

Those six doomed beginner plants, according to the defendant, had come from a man named Don Riniker. They arrived in gallon pots, but Schafer transferred them into buckets and hung 1000-watt metal halide lights over them. Shortly after that, however, those six baby plants became the first victims of the so-called "room of death."

Schafer easily recalled losing the small crop. "They got spider-mites very bad," he reported, only to be asked by his attorney to explain spider-mite infestations. "They're a little bug that loves to eat marijuana plants and lives on the underside of the leaves. I didn't catch the infestation in time. The first sign is little yellow spots on the plants, then there are webs in between the leaves. It looks like a spider's been there."

Although Schafer had made some clones off of these six starter plants, none of them survived. "I killed every one of them," he said, going on to explain to the jury the process of taking cuttings to make starter plants. "You have to care for them," the defendant concluded, "and water them right."

"Did you do that?" Serra asked.

"Obviously not," Schafer replied with an emphasis that seemed somehow humorously self-depreciating. Soft laughter tinkled in the courtroom in response to this drollery.

Though he was ultimately unsuccessful, Schafer said he had fought hard to save the infested plants. As he related, he took the plants out of the room, mopped the floor with bleach and purchased a device that sprayed a pesticide into the room every few minutes. None of these measures worked, and Schafer had to finally give up.

His outdoor cultivation in 2000, however, was much more successful. As Schafer recalled, the harvest began in October, and Mike Harvey was there to assist with the work. Schafer scoffed at Harvey's changing testimony regarding the number of plants – they never reached even a hundred plants, Schafer said, much less the 150 or 250 that Harvey had estimated. As to the exact number that year, the defendant acquiesced to the count made during Sergeant Ashworth's friendly visit. "The police reports say 43," Schafer noted. "I have no reason to disbelieve that."

According to Schafer's testimony, the yield of the 2000 harvest was split in two – half was for him and his wife, and the other half was for Harvey's use. "Mike Harvey wanted to help people and I wanted to help him do this," Schafer said. "He would deliver small amounts of marijuana to sick people."

"Did you distribute any of that marijuana from his 20 plants?" Serra asked his client.

"No," Schafer said with certainty.

"Did you help him in any fashion to distribute marijuana?" Serra queried, being sure to hit on all the technical variations of phrasing.

"We split each plant in half," Schafer explained. "He was given half of the yield to distribute."

When asked if he weighed or packaged the marijuana, or informed Harvey about where to make deliveries, Schafer responded with a familiar series of firm denials.

Serra followed up on the profit angle. "Did you receive money from those distributions?"

"No," the defendant replied, "not personally."

"Did your wife, Dr. Fry, do any of these things?" Serra said, finishing up the string of inquiries.

"Absolutely not," Schafer answered. "She was to stay completely away from it."

When Schafer began to testify about his final grow season, it became clear that history had repeated itself. Just as he had in 1999, Schafer gave away half of the plants after his 2000 harvest. He then ran out of marijuana in early 2001, long before his outdoor crop would be ready for that year. Schafer again tried to supplement by doing a small but ultimately doomed indoor grow in early 2001. This time, the six clones came from a different friend, Rick Garner, but they met the same fate as the clones that came from Don Riniker. Schafer once again tried to grow in the "room of death," and, once again, the clones were infested by spider-mites. If the definition of insanity is to do the same thing repeatedly but expect a different result, Schafer must have been mad as a March hare.

But the clones in the "room of death" were not Schafer's only experience with spider-mites that year. According to his testimony, 22 of the 34 plants seized during the DEA raid in September 2001 were infested plants given to him by a friend to, as Schafer said, "see if I could save them."

"Did they get saved?" Serra asked.

"No," Schafer responded, his voice giving away its first twinge of bitterness. "They were pulled up by law enforcement."

"What state were they in when they were pulled up?" the defense attorney inquired.

Schafer's reply was brief and solid, "They were critically ill."

In addition, Schafer said that three other marijuana plants seized during the bust belonged to a friend, and these plants were kept in pots on the hillside. Therefore, by his own characterization, only nine of the 34 plants seized by the DEA belonged to Schafer – two in the greenhouse, and seven planted in the ground on the hillside.

Serra then addressed a theory that was proposed by the prosecution's witnesses. "Did you, because of your campaign for District Attorney, move a bunch of plants or clones just prior to the serving of the search warrant?" he asked his client.

"If I did, I did a pretty poor job, because there was still marijuana around there," Schafer said, his sarcasm shining.

But Serra pushed for a literal answer, "Did you?"

Schafer obliged, "No."

It was now time for the first of many rounds of arithmetic that would be done during Schafer's day on the witness stand. Serra's math was based on his client's testimony, and it went like this:

$$20 \text{ or } 21 \text{ plants } (1999)$$
$$+ \ 43 \text{ plants } (2000)$$
$$+ \ 34 \text{ plants } (2001)$$
$$= \ 97 \text{ or } 98 \text{ plants}$$

"Adding that up, that doesn't reach a hundred, does it?" the defense attorney asked.

"I don't believe so," Schafer concurred.

Shortly afterwards, as Serra continued asking questions to emphasize this point, Schafer looked over at the jury box and said with solemn sincerity, "It was never over a hundred plants. That was my purpose and goal – stay under a hundred plants."

Whether playing it safe or taking a risk, it wasn't yet clear, but Serra even went so far as to remind Schafer of the two plants he had cultivated in 1998. There was no evidence of this grow, except for the defendant's testimony, so its addition was an interesting move. Even so, it put Serra's official total at 99 or 100, depending upon how many plants had been grown in 1999. The idea was that, even though Schafer wasn't being charged for the 1998 grow, the extra year's yields could still be added in without going over the sum of 100 plants.

Pings, as predicted, did the arithmetic a little differently. First, she cleared up some of the ambiguity by establishing that Sergeant Ashworth's written report on the defendants' 1999 grow showed a count of 21 plants, not 20. Schafer readily agreed to the number in the report, saying he had no reason to doubt it. Unlike the defense, Pings didn't stretch to put the two plants from 1998 in her tally. Rather, she reminded the defendant, and the jury, of what had not been included in Serra's tally – the twelve diseased clones that Schafer had tried to grow indoors in 2000 and 2001.

Therefore, the prosecution's math went like this:

21 outdoor plants (1999)
+ 6 indoor plants from Riniker (2000)
+ 43 outdoor plants (2000)
+ 6 indoor plants from Garner (2001)
+ 34 outdoor plants (2001)
= 110 plants

And this total, she noted, was solid because it was all based on Schafer's own admissions. To take into account the claims of other people, such as Tod Zimmerman and Mike Harvey, the tally would go much higher. But the prosecution didn't need the jurors to make the leap of faith that it would take to believe these witnesses – the defendant himself had testified to every single plant that Pings included in her total.

The issue was complicated by Schafer's claims that many of those plants were not his, and by the question of whether the clones that got killed off by spider-mites ought to figure into the arithmetic. For Pings, however, there was no confusion. Whether the plants "belonged" to Schafer or not, they were on his property and he participated in their cultivation, and she got him to admit to both of these facts during cross-examination. And, as Pings would later tell the jury, it didn't matter whether the clones survived. The plants plagued by spider-mites counted in the total regardless of their life-span, she asserted, so long as they had roots and were alive at some point.

Pings appeared confident in the plant count as she had portrayed it, but just for good measure, the prosecutor spent some additional time on the supposition that there had been *many* more clones than Schafer admitted.

She pointed to Exhibit 138, a photograph of cultivation equipment in the room where Schafer had tried to grow clones of marijuana plants. The picture showed several of the large plastic trays typically used by indoor growers to hold dozens of starter plants. Serra had already asked his client why multiple trays were found in a room that supposedly housed only a handful of plants at a time, but Schafer had merely shrugged off the query. "I don't think they were ever used," the defendant commented on the stand. "I bought a lot of stuff I never used." It was an answer that satisfied the defense attorney, but the prosecutor would be much more difficult to convince.

Pings first got Schafer to repeat the statement that he didn't believe the trays had been used, then she went in for the kill. "But, sir, they have *soil* in them," she said with great emphasis. "They've *been used.*"

Schafer seemed unconcerned by the discrepancy. "I don't know," he said coolly.

It was apparent that Pings was not going to get Schafer to admit that he had grown more plants than he had already confessed. Nonetheless, the prosecutor intended to use all the hinting and suggestion she could summon. If she stayed brief and to the point, she could use the opportunity to remind the jury about evidence that seemed to contradict the defendant.

The garage grow room was a major part of this evidence. By the prosecutor's estimation, Schafer had invested large amounts of time, energy and money in his so-called "room of death," and Pings was highly doubtful that so much construction had been done merely to host a dozen tiny, doomed plants.

She began by listing off the alterations that had been made to Schafer's garage in order to make it into a grow room: someone had built a divider wall to section off the area, installed a door, hooked up an electrical supply, hung reflective lining on the walls, set up a water source, constructed raised shelf surfaces, and provisioned the room with all the necessary equipment such as lighting, timers, and plant nutrients.

Schafer, as one would suspect, downplayed the sophistication of this grow room. The shelves, he said, were merely plywood boards on top of some buckets, and the water pipes were never actually operational. Schafer's descriptions suggested a Mickey Mouse set-up in the garage grow room, but he did admit to investing money in its construction. "I paid for all those things so that I could try to grow marijuana," he explained with simplicity.

The defendant did not, however, admit to investing energy in building the grow room...and, oddly enough, he also denied authorization or knowledge of some of its construction. According to Schafer, the heavy work was done by a carpenter whose wife had offered his construction services as payment for her medical bills to Fry. The hydroponic system, Schafer testified, was set up by a man named Sam, who had begun the work without getting permission. "I stopped him before he completed it," Schafer told Pings, explaining why the water lines had never been hooked up. "When I found out this was going on, I had him stop."

Pings had trouble swallowing the notion that Schafer had been ignorant of the hydroponics set-up until the final step of its completion. "Yet this is taking place in your own house?" she questioned mordantly.

Schafer held to his assertion, also continuing to resist the prosecutor's suggestion that he had grown dozens of clones. Pings reminded Schafer that he had once filed an affidavit in court in Plumas County, stating that he had grown thirty varieties of marijuana. After being made to read the statement and verify his signature, Schafer shrugged off the prosecutor's insinuations as nonchalantly as before. "I don't remember thirty varieties," he said with calm contemplation, "but I have grown different types of marijuana."

Pings then changed gears, shifting into the suggestion that Schafer had maintained a large and constant supply of clones for distribution to his clients. "Did you tell people who came into your office that they could get clones through you?" Pings asked.

"Not through me," Schafer responded, seeming to evade the prosecutor.

Pings pressed, "But you were aware that they called for clones?"

"Yes," Schafer yielded.

In the end, it mattered little whether there had been a dozen, or many dozens, or a few hundred clones in Schafer's grow room. The defendant had admitted to two seasons of six clones each, and if the jurors accepted the philosophy of counting plants that had died prematurely, Schafer's testimony would be enough to put the total over a hundred. That was all the prosecutor would need to secure convictions that carried mandatory minimum prison sentences.

Whatever the actual number had been, the jurors would never know for sure. The prosecution and the defense had different methods of calculating the plant numbers, and nothing could make either side budge. The defense held tight to a total that hovered under a hundred, while the prosecution insisted on 110 plants and hinted repeatedly at the possibility of more. There would be, of course, no compromise between Serra and Pings, and this obstinacy was the expected conclusion of Schafer's testimony on the plant totals.

It was not, however, the end of the defendant's stint on the witness stand...not by a *longshot*. There was much more that both sides wanted to question Schafer about: the testimony of other witnesses, the accusations of marijuana distribution, the validity of his wife's recommendations, and, oddly enough, the names of the songs that were played on the radio station where the doctor advertised her practice. Observers who had been bored by the earlier sessions of repeating arithmetic would be wide awake for the second half of Schafer's testimony, which turned out some unusual surprises.

Dale Schafer, Part 2

During the second half of Schafer's day on the stand, he was able to articulate his side of the stories that were told by other witnesses who sat in that same seat to testify earlier in the trial. Addressing his relationships with the government's informants, Schafer's narrative gave a succinct summary of the testimony presented so far and offered alternative explanations for much of the case evidence. It also opened him up to attack under cross-examination, at which time Pings made accusations of greed and exploitation, casting aspersions on Fry's medical practice as well as the defendants' treatment of their children.

Under direct examination from Serra, Schafer testified about Paul Maggy, the government's lead witness. In the autumn of 1999, Schafer explained, he and Fry had rented rooms at the Embassy Suites in Lake Tahoe in order to hold medical clinics. Through these clinics, the defendants first met Maggy's girlfriend Traci Coggins, who was hired shortly thereafter to help run Fry's office.

"Then Maggy just showed up," Schafer testified, adding that he began trying to come up with ways to make Maggy's presence useful. "We tried to engage him in the office. He was a computer person. My wife and I are not."

The office needed someone with computer skills, Schafer said, because it issued its own identification cards. "We made ID cards for everyone who got a certificate so they could show it to law enforcement," he explained.

In November of 1999, Maggy was hired for this purpose, as well as to perform personal assistant duties for Schafer. The employment only lasted six months, and ended badly. "He had upset a lot of people," Schafer recalled on the stand. "There were death threats coming in for him."

One of Schafer's own negative experiences was related to the duffel bag of marijuana that Maggy had described during his testimony. According to Schafer, this incident occurred in the spring of 2000, when he and his wife had run out of marijuana from their previous harvest. Maggy became a source of marijuana at the time, but he provided only small amounts that the couple consumed quickly. Schafer said he eventually asked if he could purchase an entire pound, and Maggy quoted a price of $3600.

As Schafer told it, Maggy then brought to the office a bag containing twice the agreed-upon amount of marijuana, since his supplier had wanted to make a two-pound deal. Schafer claimed that he wasn't in the office when the bag was brought in, but went to fetch it as soon as he found out about it, because he didn't want any marijuana in the office. He said he took one pound home to keep and intended to give the extra pound back to Maggy, but he became so disenchanted with the deal that he decided he wanted to return all the pot. "He wouldn't take it all back," Schafer testified. "We had already smoked some of the marijuana from the pound we had kept."

This turn of events apparently made relations explosive. The supplier, who Schafer identified as Barry McKinney, supposedly showed up at the office and demanded his money. "There was a message from the receptionist that there was a guy ranting and raving," Schafer said on the witness stand. "I told her to withdraw $3600 and give it to him."

"Did you package it up into little baggies?" Serra asked, referring to Maggy's accusations.

"No," Schafer responded.

"Did you know that Mr. Maggy was soliciting to sell marijuana to people who came to the office?" Serra continued.

"I found that out later," Schafer answered. "I didn't know it then."

As Schafer told it, Maggy was also stealing directly from his employers and acting out of greed. "He and Traci were taking money

210

out of the till," Schafer testified. "We asked them to stop, but they didn't."

Reinforcing this point, Serra had the defendant identify an exhibit that contained four checks from November 2000 written out to Dale Schafer. "There are four checks made out to me," Schafer observed, then turned his attention to the reverse side of those checks. "Four checks endorsed *not* with my signature."

Serra stayed on the subject. "Would you endorse all the checks that were made out to you?"

"No," Schafer told his attorney. "At some point, we got a stamp for deposit to the bank."

"You didn't do your own accounting?" Serra asked.

"No," the defendant admitted, "I'm not real good at that,"

Serra followed up thoroughly and clearly on this issue. "How was the accounting done?"

"The person doing the intake, it was their responsibility to make sure it all added up at the end of the day," Schafer explained. "The staff completed the process."

Serra then got to the main point. "Did you scrutinize what came in and out?"

"I should have, but I didn't," Schafer said with a tinge of woe in his voice.

"Is it fair to say you were not *hands-on* with respect to the checks and the accounting?" the defense attorney asked.

"Yes," Schafer said with emphasis. The attempt to portray him as the naïve victim of greedy, unscrupulous employees appeared to be going well.

"Did you earn a profit with marijuana?" Serra inquired of his client.

"No," the defendant responded.

A little later on, Serra asked Schafer to clarify his financial situation prior to the medical/legal consultation he did with his wife. "Were you doing well in your practice?"

"Yes," the defendant answered. "I had a practice that allowed me to go to events with my family and still practice law."

"Then why give it up?" Serra's articulation of the question was followed immediately by an objection.

"It goes to the motivation for this crime," Pings said, indicating that the jury had already heard that story during the first part of Schafer's testimony.

Judge Damrell began to nod, ready to agree with the prosecutor. Before he could, however, Lichter broke in with sudden vigor. "I object, your honor. It's not a *crime* until there's a *verdict*."

All eyes turned to Lichter. Having stayed silent for much of the day's proceedings, he had been nearly forgotten. But what he said now was so unorthodox and peculiar that it perplexed the judge. "You're objecting to her objection?" Judge Damrell asked Lichter quizzically.

"Yes," Lichter said firmly.

"I second that!" Serra burst out, smiling.

The judge, taken aback by the odd situation, simply instructed Serra to rephrase his question.

Serra complied, turning back to the defendant, "Were you motivated by greed?"

"No," Schafer insisted.

Serra brought up the issue of motivation at various intervals during his direct examination. "Were you *interested* in earning money or a profit with marijuana?" he asked his client.

Schafer flatly denied the notion.

Profit or no profit, there were two marijuana-related businesses with which Schafer was associated. One was HHHR, the acronym whose meaning had been forgotten by most of the witnesses so far. As Schafer reminded the jurors, it stood for Home Health Horticulture Research. "This was something Paul Maggy set up and wanted to run with," Schafer said on the stand. "It was a service to go to people's houses and see how they were situated to grow marijuana...and also to make sure that they had food in their house, that they were doing okay and not destitute, and report back."

As Schafer described it, this was one of the projects Maggy started but didn't bring to fruition, and it never became an official business entity. One of its proposed functions, Schafer said, was to sell hydroponic grow kits. "Paul Maggy brought it up as something that could be done to help people grow marijuana," Schafer testified.

It was an idea that the defendant certainly agreed with in principle. "I wanted people to be self-sufficient, to be on their own and not responsible for other people growing their marijuana for them," Schafer clarified. "Marijuana is more than the price of gold. By growing their own marijuana, they could afford it."

The way Schafer described it, however, these ideals were never born into reality. According to him, Maggy didn't make any progress on the proposal until he was fired. "On the last day, he produced a brochure that talks about kits," the defendant recalled.

It was too little too late, and there was also a catch in the proposal that infuriated Schafer. He claimed that the pitch was to sell the kits for $450, with $50 of that cost to go straight into Maggy's pocket. Fed up with the greed and the lies, as Schafer put it, he fired Maggy that day.

"Did you ever see the kits?" Serra asked.

"Never a full one," Schafer replied. "Just a mock-up with tomato plants."

Serra had one final question about the project. "Did you ever participate in creating the kits?"

"No," Schafer answered.

The defendant went on to describe the second business, Cool Madness, as a way to get a wholesaler's license for purchasing hydroponics materials at cheap prices. The savings, he said, were passed along to their customers, so they could "help people get equipment at a low cost." He took credit for his role in this business, but maintained that it also never generated any money.

Wealth was not even a mention in Schafer's rhetoric. Instead, there was a theme of charity begetting charity: the defendants took people in need into their home, and, while helping these people, also inspired them to help others. These situations began with idealistic good will, but the paths paved with such intentions led the defendants straight to the place where good deeds get punished. Their experience with Mike Harvey was perhaps one of the more illustrative examples of this phenomenon.

"Why did you take him in?" Serra inquired, turning to the subject of Harvey.

"It was the Christian thing to do," Schafer said in a matter-of-fact tone. He then described the situation in greater detail. "We were asked by someone who was a friend, to help. He was drying out from drinking a lot of alcohol. He was physically unhealthy and going through the dt's. We helped him dry out and get healthy again."

Asked about Harvey's duties in the Fry/Schafer household, the defendant detailed a short and seemingly simple list. "For a few hours, he would clean in the house and water the plants, and the rest of the day was his," Schafer explained. "He would do his deliveries one day a week – that's all."

Schafer, as before, admitted that he was aware that Harvey was distributing marijuana. The firing of Maggy had halted development of projects aimed at helping indoor cultivators, and, as Schafer put it, he was continually getting calls from people in need. "People were constantly asking if there was any way they could get help growing their marijuana, and some of them were extremely ill," Schafer stated, explaining his reason for approving Harvey's marijuana delivery service.

As Schafer had authorized, the deliveries were supposed to be in quantities of an eighth of an ounce, and they were supposed to be free. The only charge, Schafer said, would be a $10 delivery fee, to be paid only by those who could afford it.

"But Mr. Harvey charged more?" Serra inquired of his client.

"Yes," Schafer replied.

"How did you find that out?" the defense attorney asked.

Schafer flashed a look of dismay. "When the UPS packages were seized," he said, describing the incident that marked the beginning of the criminal investigation against him and his wife.

Serra queried further on this topic, "Did you tell him to send marijuana through UPS?"

"No," Schafer insisted.

Serra turned to the recorded evidence from Harvey's deliveries, getting Schafer to confirm the theory that the "sample numbers" on the upper left of the receipts referred to numbered plants from his garden. This was a crucial point for the defense – since the "sample numbers" didn't go above 35, Serra suggested, it stood to reason that there had only been that many plants grown that year. Such numerical evidence stood in opposition to the vague claims of government witnesses like Mike Harvey and Tod Zimmerman who alleged that the defendants grew hundreds of marijuana plants at a time.

This line of questioning also gave Serra a chance to slip into the jurors' minds an explanation about why Schafer had methodically recorded which plants were which: he was keeping track of his different strains, a practice crucial for growers of medical marijuana. "Were you familiar with cannabinoids that had some relation to the person's needs who was using them?"

Serra, hands clasped behind his back, faced his client as he asked the question. He didn't see Pings maintaining a low hover over the seat of her chair, waiting for the right moment to pounce with an objection. But Schafer chatted about THC and CBD, sativa and indica, all without interruption. He didn't explicitly utter the forbidden words "medical marijuana," and, besides, the prosecutor had only to wait until cross-examination to get her points across.

But before finishing his direct examination, Serra wanted to elicit Schafer's side of the story when it came to the claims made by Sean "Nacho" Cramblett. If Schafer was indeed truthful in his testimony, then Cramblett was yet another unscrupulous user who took advantage of the defendants while times were good, and then bit the hand that fed him when the going got tough. This destructive pattern appeared to be all too common for Fry and Schafer.

As the defendant related, Cramblett was a friend of Maggy's who had come onto the scene in late 1999, when Schafer was in need of the services of a glass-blower. This need, Schafer said, came from the idea that his wife should use a water-pipe to consume marijuana because this method is healthier for the lungs. The concept made good sense, but Schafer still had to explain the reason the water-pipe had to be custom-made. "We wanted to make a pipe with a red cross and 'Dr. Fry' on it," Schafer testified. "It's a hard process. It's like making hard candy with writing inside of it."

Cramblett was eager for the job, even agreeing to barter his wares. "He came to a clinic and said he was a glass-blower, but he didn't have money for a recommendation and wanted to swap," Schafer explained. "The $150 fee was waived, and I got three or four good little water pipes."

As it turned out, Schafer was so impressed with the results that he and his wife made a loan of $8500 to Cramblett a few months later. Schafer characterized this loan as the funds that Cramblett would use to start up his own glass shop, an endeavor for which he had written up a detailed business plan. According to Schafer, the loan was documented by a promissory note for repayment on a specific timetable, paperwork that was signed by all parties as well as a few witnesses. Schafer insisted that the loaned money was not, as Cramblett had suggested on the stand, payment offered to induce the young glass-blower into growing marijuana for the defendants.

Schafer vehemently denied ever giving, or receiving, any clones from Cramblett. Another thing the defendant never received was repayment – he testified that he was given only one check, for $750, towards the amount of the loan. Cramblett had been arrested shortly after the loan was issued, and was being prosecuted for marijuana cultivation in Lake Tahoe. Fry and Schafer traveled to one of the scheduled court appearances, but the result of their attendance was described as "a ruckus."

Cramblett had hired attorney Randy Moore, a move that didn't seem necessary in Fry and Schafer's view. "We thought he should be able to defend himself," Schafer reasoned. But this difference of opinion was not the only disagreement Fry and Schafer had with Cramblett over his legal strategy. As the case progressed, it was apparent that part of

216

Cramblett's defense was that Fry and Schafer were the actual owners of the plants for which he was being prosecuted.

Serra asked his client if he had legally declared ownership of the evidence in question. "Did you represent that the plants were yours?"

"No," Schafer told his attorney unequivocally.

"Did Dr. Fry represent that the plants were hers?" Serra asked.

Schafer's answer was the same as before. "No."

Getting these distinctions sorted out was crucial business for the defense, and Schafer's attempt to shield his wife from incrimination continued through to the end. Serra, concluding his direct examination, made sure to emphasize this point by re-phrasing a few of his questions. "But when you say you grew plants, you mean *you,* not Dr. Fry?"

"Yes," Schafer answered quickly, "that's what I mean."

When asked about the length of his marriage, Schafer was more cautious. "We've been married for – let me make sure I get this right..." Schafer paused at that moment, appearing to be calculating carefully but with a wry grin, "...it will be twenty-two years this year."

This was the kind of understated humor that Schafer employed several times during the course of his testimony. As usual, it communicated beautifully to the jurors and even won a few knowing smiles and tiny chuckles from amongst them. The role that Schafer affected was one his audience knew well: the husband who must maintain perfect recall of the milestones of a marriage lest he face accusations that he does not value the relationship enough to remember. It worked for Schafer precisely because he had already conveyed so much love and devotion to his wife. If he hadn't demonstrated adoration, he might have evoked the image of the hen-pecked male. Instead, he came across as sweetly obliging, and, most importantly, someone with whom the jurors could relate.

By talking about the length of his marriage, Schafer shifted into a point about intertwined identities. He suggested that the long duration of his relationship with his wife, and the closeness that they shared at home and at work, sometimes resulted in the mental effect of merging

217

themselves into a single entity. This phenomenon, he claimed, was what was responsible for Fry using the term "we" as she chatted on the undercover tape about growing marijuana plants and helping others to cultivate. "It's the 'royal we,'" Schafer insisted on the stand.

Laurence Lichter's direct examination of Schafer was remarkably brief, using him to defend Fry by confirming a single point about a single date.

The date in question was November 30th, 2000. That was the day government witness Jeffrey Teshera claimed Fry examined him and then arranged a meeting in a parking lot for a hand-to-hand sale of marijuana. Teshera couldn't recall whether the sale was done by Fry herself or through the defendants' daughter Heather Schafer. As Lichter showed through his questioning, it was highly unlikely that either woman made such a sale on that particular day. The defense attorney got Dale Schafer to explain the reason.

"On November 30th, we spent the majority of the day visiting at the hospital, Mollie and me," Schafer said, explaining this day immediately followed the complicated birth of Heather's first child.

"She didn't see patients that day," the defendant said of his wife. "Rob Poseley saw patients that day." Looking over an exhibit of Jeffrey Teshera's recommendation, Schafer confirmed his statement. "I can tell Rob Poseley did this exam because his signature is prominent. Dr. Fry is just a counter-sign."

Heather, the defendant confirmed, went to the hospital on November 28th and she finally gave birth by cesarean section on November 29th. To prove this birthdate, the child's passport was admitted into case evidence.

"So on the 30th she wasn't selling a baggy of marijuana, was she?" Lichter asked slyly.

Schafer denied the possibility of such an occurrence, noting that Heather was not discharged from the hospital until December 2nd.

Lichter wrapped up his quick questioning. "You were never in a parking lot with your wife or anyone selling a lid of medical – or any other kind of – marijuana, were you?"

218

Schafer's answer was plain and solid. "No."

The prosecutor prickled at this portrayal of Schafer as a family man who stayed devotedly by his daughter's side as she struggled through the difficult birth of her first child. In fact, Pings was so perturbed that, during a jury break, she argued for presenting as evidence the unaltered photos of the Fry/Schafer offspring handling and trimming marijuana. It was a proposal that shocked the judge, who said the photographs could not be admitted "in the interest of fairness," but Pings persisted with her argument nonetheless.

"Well then, in the interest of fairness, all references to him as a loving father should be stricken," the prosecutor said of Schafer. "He's raising two kids he got sole custody of and he's at his daughter's side when she gives birth...but it's not fair to tell that to the jury without them knowing he has young children in there, trimming bud like a little sweatshop."

Judge Damrell, not persuaded by the prosecutor's impassioned rhetoric, was staunch in forbidding the jury to see the picture of children manicuring marijuana. "That is so inflammatory, Ms. Pings," the judge declared. "Exhibit 167 is so inflammatory, so prejudicial..."

Pings looked for other avenues to remedy her grievances. "Can there be curtailment of their representation of Mr. Schafer as a family man?" she asked eagerly.

"If the defense wants to push that door open," Judge Damrell said with heavy contemplation. "The door is ajar. The defendant is being presented as a family man, and we're getting close here. The jury is getting a misimpression, and they're being told something that's not true. They think Mr. Harvey is the only one trimming those plants," he said, sighing as he gazed down at the picture.

"I'm telling both parties – this is a close case right now, on this issue," the judge continued. "To tell the government someone can be allowed to not tell the truth on the stand...I can't do that. But to allow the photos of the kids...I can't do *that*." The judge was conflicted, and the solution he urged was one of a standoff between the defense and the prosecution. If it went as he pleased, neither side would move – the defense would not go further in portraying Schafer as a family man, and the government would cease its fight to admit the photos of the children trimming marijuana buds.

The defendants posed outside the courthouse with their sons Cody and Geoffrey. Photo by Vanessa Nelson.

It was an unlikely cease-fire, and Judge Damrell was visibly frustrated by it…until, as it appeared, he let off some of his steam in the form of admonitions to the gallery. "This is a court of law," he lectured in his most stern voice, addressing the day's various minor outbursts. "This is not a stadium where you cheer your team on. I have advised the court officers to remove anyone who speaks out loud or makes a gesture, from here on out." He paused for emphasis, then asked the observers collectively. "Do you understand?"

Those sitting in the gallery, having just been threatened with expulsion for any speech or gesture, looked back at the judge dumb and motionless. Most were reluctant even to nod, as some observers had been hassled by court officers for "head bobbing" during the first few days of the trial. The gallery was completely mute, and the silence seemed to infuriate Judge Damrell.

"Can you hear me?" The judge shouted out to the audience, exaggeratedly emphasizing each word. The sound evoked a comparison to a drill sergeant attempting to mold an army of soldiers,

but the courtroom audience responded with less enthusiasm than most new recruits. Still, the few timid acknowledgements he received were enough for Judge Damrell, who permitted the proceedings to move forward again.

The comedic value of this interlude, however, was outdone by the many bizarre moments of Schafer's cross-examination. The last part of his testimony quickly became a battleground, with the prosecutor making her attack on the legitimacy of Fry's medical practice.

In her campaign, Pings focused on the ages of Fry's patients and the conditions for which some of them were issued recommendations. The prosecutor acted appalled that the doctor wrote recommendations to treat asthma. The implication, which was never contested, was that smoked cannabis would be especially harmful for asthmatics, and thus, Fry made her recommendations irresponsibly. Unless the jurors happened to know that marijuana can actually dilate bronchial passages, they were quite likely to swallow this idea.

Pings continued the attack by questioning Schafer about Cramblett and his medical condition. Pings described this patient as a "kid," even though he had been 22 years old at the time of his recommendation, and mockingly asked the defendant if he was aware that his wife had issued a recommendation for a "sore elbow."

Schafer, however, was on point. "I was aware that he had osteochondritis, yes," he said confidently. It appeared to shut the prosecutor up…momentarily.

Thwarted on that example, Pings shuffled her notes, then went on to suggest that Fry targeted children through her practice. Schafer testified that he believed his wife wrote recommendations for a few minors, but stressed that this was done with parental consent. The prosecutor responded with a rapid fire of statistics that were allegedly gleaned from an analysis of several thousand patient records seized during the 2001 raid of Fry's office and storage facility.

Pings first asked Schafer if he was aware that, as of September 28th, 2001, his wife had written 130 recommendations for people under the age of 20. After the judge overruled the defense's objection, the prosecutor presented another statistic, asking if 175 of the recommendations had been written for individuals under 25 years of age. The defense repeated its objection on grounds of relevance, and once again the judge overruled it. Next, Pings switched tactics to imply that a significant number of Fry's patients were criminally suspect, asking Schafer if he knew that 339 of the recommendations were issued to those who had pending criminal cases or who were on probation. Yet again, the judge allowed the questioning to proceed in spite of objections uttered in unison by the defense attorneys.

Absent a frame of reference, it might have slipped past the jury that each of the figures quoted was a very small percentage of the total, which exceeded 5,000 patient files. With this understanding, it was easy to see that issuing recommendations to persons under 20 years old was actually an exception to the norm in Fry's practice. Without this knowledge, however, there was only the sensationalist mirage created by the prosecution.

Pings wasn't done, however. She had more ammunition against the doctor, and she was prepared to reach as far as she was permitted. Attempting to further show that Fry targeted youth and drug criminals, the prosecutor began listing some of the songs that were played by the radio stations on which the doctor had advertised her practice.

It was a bizarre stretch of logic, but it was given an air of legitimacy by Pings's serious and outraged tone of voice. With an atmosphere of supreme drama, the prosecutor asked Schafer if his wife had advertised on a station that frequently played a song called "Because I Got High." When Schafer said he didn't know, Pings hit him again, asking if another of those songs had been titled "Tweaked" by the band Crystal Method. The prosecutor pronounced the song titles and the band names with such a mood of shocking exposure that they superficially sounded like revelations, even where the logic fell short. Schafer again shrugged off the questions with casual disregard, his demeanor downplaying their significance.

Although the most far-fetched of Pings's suggestions had involved Fry's clinical practice, she had plenty of venom for Schafer himself.

Some of the prosecutor's attempts to cast doubt on Schafer's character were either half-hearted or bungled. Early on in her questioning, she referred back to the defendant's comment that finding marijuana to buy for his wife had been difficult. "You said that it was 'not like high school,'" Pings reminded Schafer, glancing down at her notes. "Did you use marijuana in high school?"

Serra's objection on grounds of relevance was sustained, and Pings dropped that question. She followed, however, with a series of false leads. "Isn't it true that you traveled to Canada to obtain seeds from a man named Marc Emery?" she asked in an accusatory tone.

"No," Schafer said, looking at the prosecutor with bewilderment. "I did not."

Pings, apparently without viable evidence on that point, left the trail cold. It seemed she was taking a shot in the dark by bringing up the famous Canadian seed-seller who was awaiting his own prosecution by the United States government. Leaving that path, Pings started a new line of questioning that quickly confused matters even more.

As it appeared, the prosecutor had some kind of dirt to expose regarding the woman that the defendants took into their home in order to help her escape an abusive husband. However, the point Pings was trying to make got repeatedly sidetracked when she mistakenly identified this woman as the defendants' accountant. "I think you got the wrong woman," Schafer eventually told the jumbled prosecutor.

But Pings was just warming up to the sport of insinuation, and by the end of her cross-examination, she had done her best to sink her teeth into the effort.

"You've cast a certain amount of blame on Mr. Harvey for what you're charged with," Pings said, posing it as more of a comment than a question.

"I think I'm taking responsibility for what he did," Schafer returned calmly. "I authorized him to do it." And the defendant remained serene, even as the prosecutor proceeded to needle him about taxation and accuse him of exploitative profiteering.

Pings's methodology was at first cold, mathematical. She reminded the defendant that the September 2001 search had yielded the records of approximately five thousand recommendations issued by his wife. Since the charge for this service had ranged from $150 to $200 each, Pings estimated that Fry had made over a million dollars by issuing recommendations between 1999 and 2001.

"If you say so," Schafer acquiesced, going along with the prosecutor's math. "I accept that."

When Serra had the chance to ask further questions of his client, he went straight to these financial claims and kept his focus there. "I want to do a little arithmetic," he told Schafer, who nodded in approval. Serra then turned to the jury and smiled charmingly, "That was never my specialty."

The defense attorney's point was that the gross income from Fry's recommendations was more likely to be under $750,000 throughout the course of three years. The standard fee was $150 for much of that period, according to his client, and Fry often waived fees for ill patients with financial difficulties. All of that income was spread over a three-year period, making an average of $250,000 per year, which was hardly an unreasonable amount for the combined income of a professional couple.

Still, this figure did not reflect the costs of running the business, and according to the defendant, there was a great deal of overhead. As Schafer testified, the rent for the offices was $5,000 per month, and several thousand more went to paying the salaries of the physician's assistant and various other employees of the business. By the calculations that were worked out between Serra and his client on the stand, it was figured that the defendants had an annual take-home income of only about $60,000 each.

Pings was still persistent once she got the witness back. "You didn't report this on your tax returns, did you?" the prosecutor asked, trying to build up to a zinger.

"I did," Schafer asserted in a direct denial of the accusation. Although he couldn't recall the precise amount he claimed in these filings, it seemed reasonable that, so many years later, the defendant couldn't remember these exact figures offhand.

Pings was hungry to prove that the defendants were profit-minded, bringing into evidence a price sheet from Cool Madness. Going down the line of products, the prosecutor identified items for which the business marked up the price by as much as 55%.

224

"This was just a proposal," Schafer tried to explain. "It didn't go into effect."

This claim scarcely seemed to matter, as the prosecutor continued to list item after item and rattle on about excessive mark-ups. The much-discussed grow kits, she showed, also had a price that was inflated to be approximately double the cost of the materials.

In addition, Pings set forth the theory that Fry made a killing from giving testimony in court. "Isn't it true that, after that $200 fee, you charged them $4000 to come to court to authenticate that piece of paper?" she asked about Fry's patients.

"No," Schafer said simply. The prosecutor then showed him a document that quoted a $4000 figure for a full day of court testimony and $2000 for a half-day. "No one was ever charged that," Schafer responded, shaking his head slightly.

As he put it, the notary seal on the recommendation conveyed enough legitimacy for most purposes, but there had been twenty or so cases when his wife was subpoenaed to testify about a recommendation's validity in court. With these cases, however, he recalled that Fry was rarely reimbursed for her services, and she didn't push for payment from those who had difficulty with funds. Schafer estimated that his wife was compensated for less than five percent of the cases in which she testified, and that he wasn't sure she ever received the amount of payment the document quoted.

The cross-examination then came to a rather abrupt ending when Pings asked Schafer about specific testimony for which Fry had allegedly charged $125 per hour. "Isn't it true that Dr. Fry testified in Yolo County?"

Schafer responded with vague recollections of the case, only to be met with a bizarre inquiry from Pings, "And isn't it true that she testified for the use of marijuana for the treatment of hemorrhoids?"

"I don't recall that she testified that," Schafer answered.

The prosecutor left off her questioning there, ending the day's proceedings on a seemingly strange note. However, the subject matter she raised had earned her a scattering of silly grins from the jury, and it was likely that she hoped for this sense of frivolity to be the lasting impression of the defendant's testimony. If the jurors were to go home for the night with an idea about medical marijuana in their heads, Pings would probably prefer it to be a giggle about hemorrhoids rather than a fit of sobbing over breast cancer.

After hours on the witness stand, Dale Schafer spoke confidently to the press about the ordeal. Photo by Vanessa Nelson.

Whatever the parting thoughts on his testimony might be, Schafer stepped down from the witness stand with an air of success. He had protected his wife, described his personal experiences with medical marijuana in full detail, conveyed his dedication to his family, and even prevented the prosecutor from portraying his home as a sweatshop. And in spite of the strain of the long day on the stand, Schafer looked positively radiant. Contrasted with the government's parade of informants and undercover agents, the defendant was golden in his warm, calm glow.

Rob Poseley

As the defense's case began to come to a close, the looming question was whether Fry herself would take the witness stand. Rumors had been circulating that she would be testifying, and oftentimes these rumors came straight from the doctor herself. However, Fry was also the primary source for rumors that she would *not* be taking the stand. In short, her decision was not yet cemented, leaning one way and then another as her defense continued to take shape. Fry watched, speculated, intuited, and prayed, over and over again, but her decision remained mired in mystery.

As the days went by, the window of opportunity was slowly closing, and on the eve of her last possible chance, she was still officially unsure. During her daily guest appearance on Christine Craft's radio program, however, it seemed that Fry was expressing a nearly-steady inclination to testify. Joking that she would be able to prepare for the ordeal by getting a good night's sleep on the adjustable firmness of her "sleep-number bed," and reminding herself that she had God at her side, the doctor seemed more confident than ever.

Given this attitude, many in attendance in the courtroom were expecting to see Fry take the witness stand the next morning. But it soon became known that the doctor had ultimately decided against testifying, and called instead was her former physician's assistant Robin "Rob" Poseley. It was a strangely appropriate turn of events. After all, acting in place of Fry had been Poseley's job for years, and he took to the task as naturally on the witness stand as he had in the doctor's office.

But Poseley's appearance had been preceded by its own set of rumors. He was currently employed as a fire-fighter and paramedic in El Dorado County, and there had been some whispered discussion about him coming to the witness stand wearing a fireman's uniform. No doubt such garb would have added some pizzazz to the proceedings, but it would have been more than just visual novelty. Fire-fighters, as it turns out, are presently near the very top of the list of professions trusted and respected by Americans. Bringing the witness to the stand in full uniform might have looked like a ploy by the defense to increase his credibility with the jury, and would have certainly provoked attack by the prosecution. Instead, Poseley entered the courtroom wearing inconspicuous business-casual apparel.

Rob Poseley took a break from his firefighting job to testify for the defense. Sketch by Dr. Care.

In spite of dressing down for the appearance, Poseley projected every bit of his typical straight-laced image. He stood with perfect posture in his robust frame and gave a relaxed smile from under a well-groomed moustache. When the court later heard that Poseley had been mistaken for a cop during his first attempt to interview with Fry, no one seemed very much surprised by the revelation. The witness seemed smoothly amiable, upright and self-assured.

As it turned out, his composure would serve him well.

Over the course of the next hour or so, Poseley was tossed around almost like a hot potato. With all the direct examination, cross-examination, re-direct, re-cross, and many fierce outbreaks of objections, there was a great deal of back-and-forth between the attorneys. Those observing from the gallery often looked as though they were watching a tennis match, but certainly this was nothing unusual. It had been a contentious trial, and the spectators were accustomed to nearly every witness inspiring a battle between the two sides.

Of course, things typically took a while to accelerate into conflict, and it was no exception with Poseley's testimony. He began, as expected, by detailing his background and his training, and then describing how he came to be employed by Fry. Lichter handled the questions, guiding Poseley through a chronology that took him from college in Minnesota to medical school at UC Davis and hands-on training at Sutter Cardiac Hospital. When he completed his course of study, Poseley had become a Physician's Assistant.

"Can you prescribe medicine as a P.A.?" Lichter inquired.

"No, but you can make a transmittal, and this can result in a patient getting a medicine," Poseley explained.

Lichter was still curious. "Can you give medicine right in the clinic?"

"A physician can do that," Poseley replied, "but not a physician's assistant."

Lichter continued, "What about morphine?"

"That would require a triplicate prescription and require a physician's signature." Poseley's answer was prompt and confident. The witness seemed to know his stuff.

Poseley went on to describe applying for work with Fry when she was seeking a P.A. for her practice. The job interview had ended with a prayer for divine guidance, and this left Poseley with a positive feeling about the job. Prior to being hired, he discussed his required duties with both Fry and Schafer.

"Why would Dr. Fry need to hire a P.A. for such a small clinic?" Lichter asked.

"Dr. Fry was very sick," Poseley responded. "She was physically ill. She needed help."

He had been optimistic about taking the job, but Poseley also had some very specific concerns about the conditions of his employment.

"I am not a cannabis user," he revealed. "I don't have a need for it, and I don't enjoy how it makes me feel. So part of our agreement was that there wouldn't be cannabis in the clinic." And, he testified, during the years he worked at the office, he never saw Fry or Dale Schafer distribute cannabis.

Poseley readily gave his opinion that a legitimate medicial clinic would not be a place where marijuana was kept, used or distributed. Nor, furthermore, would it be a place where marijuana was recommended for recreational, rather than medical, use. "For the people who were going to get recommendations, it was going to be the real thing," he added.

Pings issued the day's first objection. "Self-serving hearsay," she said to the judge.

Judge Damrell nodded heavily, "Sustained." He then told the jury to disregard the witness's last comment.

At Lichter's request, Poseley described the typical procedure followed by patients who visited Fry's clinic. After filling out forms, the patients would watch an instructional video and have a consultation with Schafer. Then they would be examined by Poseley, who would make what he called "an evaluation using all senses." This examination would start with taking a patient's vitals and then move on to include visual, auditory, olfactory and tactile components, as necessary.

"Would you and Dr. Fry would go over cases together?" Lichter asked.

"The physician can go over the chart and review notes," Poseley told the attorney. "We didn't go over every case together, but she would go through all the chart notes." Then he added, "We made very sure that the people who came to our clinic were legitimate."

Pings interrupted here, objecting to the use of the word "we."

"Only say what *you* saw," Judge Damrell ordered the witness.

"I saw that every patient who came in was required to have records," Poseley asserted. "I had people who came in and said, 'I just want to get high.' Those people never got a recommendation."

Lichter asked the witness whether Fry herself had such high standards in relation to her practice, but Pings blocked the answer. Though the prosecutor objected to questions about the legitimacy of Fry's motivations for running her practice, Poseley was allowed to testify about his former employers' honesty and trustworthiness.

"I believe she is a person of integrity and can be believed," Poseley said about Fry.

Regarding Schafer, he was equally complimentary. "He is a man of integrity and honesty," Poseley declared. "When he said he would do something, it would get done."

Poseley knew of Mike Harvey, describing him as an alcoholic who had been living at the defendants' home. When asked about Harvey's alleged marijuana deliveries, Poseley claimed to know very little. "I understand this gentleman was distributing cannabis through the mail," he said. "I don't know why."

Poseley's employment with Fry also acquainted him with Paul Maggy, who was working as Schafer's personal assistant as well as helping out with computer work for the office. Poseley's testimony about Maggy, however, was not at all flattering. "I have a very poor opinion of Mr. Maggy and his ability to tell the truth and be honest," he testified.

"Did he have a business on the side?" Lichter asked about Maggy.

Poseley said simply, "It was my understanding that he did."

Pings quickly spoke out against this line of questioning, and the judge sustained the objection.

Lichter tried another topic. "Did patients ever bring marijuana to the clinics?"

"When that happened, I instructed the office staff to have that person take it outside," Poseley answered. "If Dr. Fry or Mr. Schafer were there, I would ask them to handle it."

As Lichter questioned him, Poseley denied that he ever saw marijuana being sold at the clinic. In addition, he had no knowledge of any arrangements being made at the clinic for such sales. Poseley also testified that the office staff held meetings, during which Maggy was present, but said that the distribution of marijuana was not discussed at these meetings. "Not once," the witness maintained.

When Lichter asked about the grow kits, Poseley mentioned that there was a mock-up grow kit in the office for display, but it contained a tomato plant. He claimed he never saw a grow kit with a marijuana plant in it, and that he was not at all involved with the distribution of these kits.

The defense attorney then came to the matter of Jeffrey Teshera's heavily disputed claim about being sold marijuana directly after getting a recommendation from Fry. Poseley appeared to bolster the defense's argument that Fry had not examined patients on the day in question, as Teshera had claimed. Looking over Teshera's recommendation, Poseley said with certainty, "If I signed it, I did the exam." He then added, "I wouldn't sign it otherwise."

On her first go at cross-examination, Pings set out to undermine the basis for Poseley's opinions about Maggy. Since Poseley had begun working at the office in April of 2000 and Maggy had left the next month, Pings pointed out that Poseley had only a matter of weeks to get to know Maggy and observe his behavior. Poseley granted the accuracy of the prosecutor's dates, leaving the jury to wonder whether the witness was a remarkably quick judge of character or if he had leapt to conclusions about Maggy.

Next, Pings pointed out that the hiring process for Poseley had been a little more tense than he had described to Lichter. After going to Cool to inquire about the want ad for a physician's assistant, Poseley had initially been turned away, according to the prosecutor.

"Isn't it true that you went to Mr. Schafer's office and he denied everything, thinking you were a law enforcement officer?" Pings asked the witness.

"That's inaccurate," Poseley replied. "That's a misstatement."

This denial encouraged Pings to present a 2004 report made by DEA Special Agent Brian Keefe, who had interviewed Poseley about his involvement with the defendants. "It says you told the agent that a friend from Chico had seen the ad for a physician's assistant," Pings read. "You went to Cool, but you were unable to find the doctor's office, so you went to the attorney's office. Traci Coggins and Heather Schafer were there, but they wouldn't help you because they were worried you were law enforcement."

Poseley acknowledged making these statements, but clarified that these initial suspicions were easily overcome. After that, he was quickly hired and began working closely with Fry. Poseley estimated he had been to the defendants' home about ten times, during which he saw some sickly marijuana plants in pots and some healthier ones growing in the ground. During these visits, he testified, there was no place on the property where he had been restricted from going or looking. Under questioning from Pings, however, he admitted that he never saw the bunker.

When the cross-examination came to the topic of the grow kits, Poseley once again declared that all he ever saw was a display kit containing a tomato plant. To the prosecutor, that was just more repetition – she wanted to get deeper into inquiries about the manufacture and distribution of the grow kits.

"I understand your claim is that it was a tomato plant," Pings told the witness. She then referred back to Keefe's report of the interview with Poseley. "But you said that Dr. Fry and Dale Schafer sold the kits as part of HHHR?"

"Yes," Poseley replied.

According to the prosecutor's reading of the report, Poseley had listed many people who were involved in assembling the kits. Pings read these names out: Traci Coggins, Paul Maggy, Heather Schafer, Heather's boyfriend Randy Gabourie, Mike Harvey…

"That's inaccurate," Poseley insisted. "I said Traci and Paul were involved. The rest of those people I just identified by picture."

Pings tried to clarify the claim. "So your testimony is that Heather Schafer, Randy Gabourie, and Mike Harvey were *not* involved in assembling the kits?"

"Correct," Poseley answered.

"And the kit on display at the office was the same type of kit that Paul Maggy was distributing?" Pings asked.

The witness readily confirmed this fact.

Pings next turned to whether or not Fry smoked marijuana in her office. On that point, Poseley was ambiguous but nonetheless offered some leading descriptions.

"There were times when there was an odor similar to cannabis – it probably was cannabis – coming from Dr. Fry's office," he explained.

The prosecutor followed up. "Did you see any other people smoking marijuana there?"

"No," Poseley said, his tone definite.

Following this denial, however, he admitted that both Schafer and Fry had offices with closing doors, and that when these doors were closed, he could not hear or see what was going on inside. Pings made an effort to emphasize this point, likely in the hope that the jury would speculate that anything might be going on unobserved behind those closed doors.

Leaving these possibilities up to the jurors' imaginations, the prosecutor turned next to questions that focused on Fry's practice – specifically, how it was run and how it was promoted. When asked, Poseley testified that, although he had not actually heard the radio ads or read the newspaper ads about the office, he had been aware that Fry was advertising.

"Would it be fair to say that the practice was only for writing marijuana recommendations?" Pings inquired.

"*Mostly*," Poseley said, emphasizing the word as though it were a correction. He acknowledged that the examination of patients for the approval of marijuana was the primary function of Fry's practice, but he held back from saying that this was the *only* type of medical service given in the office.

Pings brought up a disclaimer on Fry's forms that said she was not the "treating physician" of the patients to whom she issued recommendations. She then asked Poseley if he knew this to be true.

"I don't know what that term means," Poseley said plainly.

"This goes back to – the purpose of the clinic was just to recommend marijuana," Pings told the witness.

"The purpose of the clinic," Poseley explained, "was to provide relief and care to people who were sick."

"Did the clinic offer diagnostic services?" Pings asked.

"No," Poseley replied.

The prosecutor kept going, "Did it offer physical therapy?"

Again, the witness answered, "No."

Pings pushed, "Did it prescribe any other pain medicine?"

"No," Poseley disclosed.

Pings gave her inquisitive face. "So people had to come in with medical records because your office didn't do x-rays or other tests?"

The witness was clear on that point. "Correct," he said.

"Did you ever give a recommendation even without records, but just for a 30-day recommendation?" Pings asked pointedly.

"If the physical exam was commensurate with the complaint, we would do that," Poseley answered.

But Pings had a more controversial question up her sleeve. "Did Heather Schafer ever persuade you to give a recommendation you didn't want to give?"

"Objection!" Lichter called out suddenly.

Judge Damrell barely glanced up from the papers on his bench. "Overruled," he declared coolly.

Pings took the witness back to whether he had been talked into giving recommendations against his judgment. "Yes," was Poseley's simple response.

For those in the know, it was clear that Pings was circling around the issue of the infiltration of Fry's practice by undercover DEA agents. Particularly damning for the defendants was evidence that one agent posing as a patient was able to obtain a full-fledged, one-year recommendation without providing any medical records. If shown to be true, such an occurrence would sharply contradict the defense's assertions about the office policy as well as the legitimacy of Fry's practice.

But Pings took her time while working up to confrontation on this point – first, she wanted to talk about the questionnaires that Fry's patients were made to fill out.

"On the questionnaire, did it ask people if they had a spiritual presence in their life?" she inquired.

"Yes," Poseley conceded.

Pings continued, "Did it ask people how they took marijuana – with a pipe, a joint, or a water pipe?"

"Yes," Poseley replied, then went into further explanation. "We made a push to have them take it orally."

"As in a Rice Krispie treat?" Pings asked, making a snarky reference to testimony about the cannabis-infused Rice Krispie treats prepared during a seminar run by the defendants' daughter Heather Schafer.

"Yes," Poseley said soberly.

Pings then referenced a series of questionnaire items that asked Fry's patients about how marijuana helped them with various aspects of life, and to what degree. As Poseley confirmed, the survey-takers were asked if marijuana made them more or less able to solve problems, more or less able to appreciate life, and more or less able to enjoy being with their families.

"Did you see these questions on intake forms anywhere else you worked?" Pings asked.

"No," Poseley acknowledged. When he was asked if he helped out with creating the questions for the form, however, his answer was mixed. "Yes and no," he replied nonchalantly. "Some questions were for research Dr. Fry was doing for her own purposes. Some were ones I put on."

By finally bringing up the recommendation issued to the undercover agent, Pings did her best to crack the witness's composure. "I did the exam," Poseley said when confronted with the documentation. "It shows non-approval. Many people didn't get approval, or got provisional approval."

The chart may have indicated non-approval, but Pings remarked that a full-term recommendation was issued to the undercover agent nonetheless. It was a conflict in stories that required some significant explanation, and what followed was the climax of tension between the prosecutor and the witness.

"Mr. Poseley, you're trained to detect med-seeking behavior, aren't you?" Pings started in.

"Yes," Poseley agreed.

"And this person walked in and got this recommendation, right?" the prosecutor continued.

"Yes," Poseley said again.

"And you didn't catch that this was *not* a 30-day approval?" Pings poked at the witness.

"The way we did it was that the front office would affix the note on the recommendation that limited the recommendation," Poseley explained.

The prosecutor kept prodding. "So you signed it without a 30-day limit?"

"I thought I answered that," Poseley said, his brow furrowing. "I signed it with the intent –"

Judge Damrell wouldn't let the witness go any further. "Just answer the question," he told Poseley. "You're not being asked for your intent."

Poseley sighed, complying. "That does not have a 30-day note," he said, talking about the undercover agent's recommendation, "and it has my signature."

But Pings didn't want an accumulation of related facts. She wanted her question answered directly. "Did you sign this recommendation without a 30-day note?" she insisted.

The witness started again to talk about procedure and intent, but the prosecutor stuck like glue to her question. "Yes," Poseley finally insisted.

Pings relented, and the witness went back into Lichter's hands.

The defense attorney wanted to clear up a 9-day discrepancy between the examination and the date of Fry's signature on the agent's recommendation. Lichter began asking the witness, "When Dr. Fry was very ill, did she at times write out –"

"Objection!" the prosecutor said, clarifying that the question was leading.

The judge agreed with Pings, and Lichter quickly restated. It was clear that the prosecutor didn't want the jury to hear any extra mentions of Fry's poor health, and the question wasn't blocked when Lichter omitted this topic from the question. "Did Dr. Fry fill out forms prior when she knew she wouldn't be in the office?"

Poseley acknowledged this to be true. He also explained that the date next to the doctor's signature indicated the day she had signed the form, and this sometimes differed from the date the recommendation was notarized and thus officially issued.

Lichter directed Poseley's attention to the documents from his medical examination of the undercover agent. After giving the witness time to fully review the papers, the defense attorney asked, "This document shows you didn't give your normal recommendation to this person, doesn't it?"

Over the prosecutor's objections, Poseley testified that his chart indicated the agent's recommendation had not been full-fledged. He read aloud the notations that showed the approval was only provisional: "Pending," "No [Medical] Records," and "30 Days."

The phony patient, Poseley said, had described a severe back injury resulting from a motorcycle accident in 1989, and claimed that he was in extreme pain. "He reported an 8 or 9 on a scale of 10," Poseley stated about the counterfeit patient. "He said he couldn't sleep." The 30-day approval would allow him to get immediate relief while he located and obtained the medical records necessary for a full, year-long recommendation.

238

Looking down at the documents, Poseley couldn't resist a particular observation. "Of note to me is the statement, 'I sign under penalty of perjury that all the above information is true and correct,' signed by a Mr. Joe Riley."

Poseley's comment mattered little in the substantive sense, since undercover agents are legally permitted to commit perjury, but perhaps he hoped he could get across to the jury a subtle point about the hypocrisy of such a situation.

Meanwhile, the defense attorney stayed focused on the intake forms the undercover agent had filled out. Lichter asked question after question about the survey details, fleshing out a portrait of the agent's elaborate undercover identity. Poseley reported the imposter patient had indicated marijuana helped him with pain control, anxiety control and insomnia prevention, but had no effect on the functioning of his gastrointestinal tract. He said he had grown up as the third-born of five children, and had served in the U.S. Marines until getting an honorable discharge, after which he worked part-time as a drafting apprentice. As he wrote on the forms, the supposed patient experienced depression and anger, had no spiritual presence in his life, and he lived alone.

For the prosecutor, Lichter had gone far enough with his point. "Objection, your honor," Pings broke in. "The witness is reading."

The judge had also reached a limit. When Lichter tried to argue against the objection, Judge Damrell let his exasperation show. "Oh, come on, counsel!" he said to the defense attorney. "How much more of this?"

Regrouping, Lichter got down to his main point, asking the witness, "How did the recommendation get issued after you limited his verification?"

"This could only have been a clerical error at the front desk," Poseley said, still seeming a bit mystified that this could occur. He could not recall who worked at the front desk that day, but Poseley's explanation appeared to satisfy Lichter and he concluded his questioning for the moment.

When she stepped up for her re-cross, the prosecutor came in like gangbusters. "Is it fair to say that you can't write a prescription for marijuana because it's illegal under the Controlled Substances Act?" Pings demanded of the witness.

Poseley began his answer by mentioning the Health & Safety Code, but the judge cut him off and ordered him to simply answer the question.

Lichter stepped up, objecting. "He's giving a legal opinion," he argued about the witness's testimony.

"Overruled," said the judge, again ordering Poseley to answer the question.

"Yes," he replied, acknowledging the prosecutor's explanation for why marijuana couldn't be prescribed.

This sounded conclusive, but once the witness was back in Lichter's hands, the struggle was resurrected. As soon as he had the chance, Lichter put Pings's question before Poseley again.

"Are you asking for my legal opinion?" the witness asked.

"Objection," Pings cut in, sounding annoyed.

Lichter was undeterred, "I'm asking for –"

"Objection," the prosecutor repeated, her repetition starting to sound automatic.

The defense attorney continued to ignore her. "I'm asking for –"

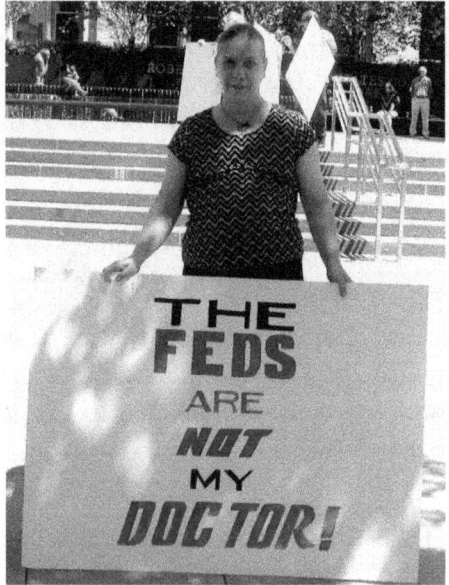

At a public protest, Dr. Fry challenged federal laws that restricted her practice of medicine. Photo by Vanessa Nelson.

"*Objection!*" Pings insisted. She had finally been provoked into shouting, but quickly she calmed herself and requested a sidebar. The attorneys gathered around the judge's bench and, although their words were intentionally drowned out by white noise, they spoke with lively facial expressions and gestures.

Lichter returned to his witness at the conclusion of the sidebar. Clasping his hands together, the defense attorney asked, "You testified that a physician cannot write a prescription for marijuana?"

"Yes,' Poseley granted.

Lichter continued, "Under federal law –"

The defense attorney was cut off by yet another objection, and Judge Damrell warned Lichter that he was leading the witness. Nevertheless, the very next question put to Poseley was about whether the situation was different under state law.

Poseley answered with ease. "Yes, in the dozen or so states that –"

"Objection!" Pings called out, interrupting the witness.

"Sustained," Judge Damrell said, his eyes narrowed at the defense attorney.

"Did you know that doctors can write recommendations for marijuana under federal law?" Lichter asked.

"I'm unclear about that…" Poseley replied, hesitating.

Lichter went to his next question while the witness appeared to be still pondering the last point. "But when you were writing recommendations, were you doing anything you believed to be illegal?" the defense attorney asked.

"Objection!" Pings cut in again.

This conflict soon resulted in a sidebar, but the informal conference ran so long that it cut into the jury's regular mid-morning break. After the jurors filed out of the courtroom for a ten-minute respite, the judge and the attorneys frantically tried to wrap up the heated debate at the bench. There was pointing, frowning, and wide gesturing…and then, as it appeared, an eerie calm.

When the jurors re-entered, a tentative truce had been declared for purposes of efficiency. Judge Damrell announced that the defense intended to conclude their case before the afternoon, so that closing arguments might begin by the end of the day. After a morning of seemingly endless disputes, the jurors were suddenly being promised light at the end of the tunnel.

Nevertheless, Lichter had a few concluding points to make with his witness, hoping to get the newly-cheerful jury to consider that the undercover agent may have manipulated the evidence.

"You said the provisional notice was supposed to be affixed to the recommendation?" the defense attorney asked.

"Yes," Poseley verified.

Lichter began to speculate. "Is it possible the agent could have removed it?"

Poseley readily acknowledged the possibility. "Yes."

"Is it possible that it fell off?" Lichter asked.

"Yes," the witness agreed.

Lichter had one final question. "And it's a fact that your chart notes reflect your intentions?"

"Yes," Poseley answered, seeming to appreciate this small attempt at vindication.

"No further questions," Lichter announced with a sense of satisfaction. Poseley was then promptly excused from the witness stand, leaving the watchers in the gallery wondering what would come next.

Rebuttal Witness Brian Keefe

Right in the middle of the defense witnesses, Special Agent Keefe was brought to the stand yet again. He had been called by the government as a rebuttal witness, ostensibly to refute suggestions made during the defense's case.

The most significant of these suggestions was the one made by Rob Poseley. On the stand, he had speculated about how an undercover DEA agent could have obtained a full-fledged marijuana recommendation from Fry's office when chart notes from the examination indicate only a temporary 30-day approval. Poseley testified that perhaps the front desk had misinterpreted his directives and issued the wrong type of recommendation. Or, he proposed, the DEA agent could have altered the document by removing a marker that indicated it was only a temporary recommendation. It was this matter that prosecutor Flynn sought to clear up, first and foremost.

Flynn established that Keefe had been on duty during this operation and present after undercover agent Joseph Brock emerged from Fry's office. The prosecutor then confirmed that Keefe had seen the recommendation Brock had been issued. "Was anything appended to that document that was later removed?" Flynn asked the witness.

"No," Keefe said, simply and firmly.

The prosecutor then turned to evidence about the seminar that had been infiltrated by undercover agent John Nolan. Keefe was asked to identify many of the papers that Nolan had taken from the seminar, categorizing them as registration forms and informational documents.

"There are also many pamphlets regarding growing and cloning," Keefe commented, describing the seized literature.

Serra objected strenuously. "This is opinion and conclusion of what their objective was," the defense attorney claimed. The effort was in vain – the documents were admitted into evidence and Keefe's statement remained on record.

Bolstered, Flynn listed a series of items – cloning products, hydroponics equipment, and beverages priced at $1 per bottle – and asked Keefe if these items had been available at the seminar. Serra was more successful with his next objection, however, and the judge agreed that such a question was out of the witness's scope. In fact, he went a step further and instructed the jury to disregard the statements.

The prosecutor continued his examination, using what appeared to be more solid evidence. He presented a pricing sheet for Cool Madness, Schafer's hydroponics supply business. Over Serra's objections, Keefe interpreted the document as showing a 70% markup on every single product offered. Of markup, the agent said, 55% was invested into the business and the remaining 15% was a sales commission for the employee.

When Schafer was on the witness stand, he testified that he had not authorized or accepted the price list. He claimed it had been prepared and submitted by Paul Maggy, at the time he was fired. Flynn challenged this story with a single question to Keefe, "Isn't it true that Mr. Maggy was gone since May?"

"Yes," the agent responded, "to my knowledge."

Flynn's suggestion was that, if Schafer had rejected the price sheets, it was reasonable to believe they would have been thrown out during the four months that elapsed between Maggy's departure and the defendants' bust. One could see the point the prosecutor was attempting to make, and it might have been more convincing had the defendants been portrayed as tidy and well-organized about house-keeping. Instead, the government had presented witnesses who made a point of testifying about how dirty and messy the Fry/Schafer home had been. In such a setting, it would be easy to imagine a dozen copies of a discarded price sheet getting lost in the flotsam of an extraordinarily cluttered household…perhaps even for many years.

244

During his cross-examination, Serra went more broadly into the subject of the Cool Madness price lists. According to Keefe's answers, the sheets had been seized during the September 2001 search of the defendants' home, although he did not recall where in the house they were found or how they had been placed at their time of discovery. Keefe admitted that no similar documents had been found in the searches of Schafer's office or Fry's clinic, nor were they referenced in the advertisements Fry ran for her practice.

"So, you don't know whether my client rejected these?" Serra inquired, referencing the price sheets.

"No," Keefe answered.

Serra continued, "And in these lists, there's no mention of the clones, the *plants*, or marijuana, the *product*?"

Keefe hesitated. "I would have to see it again to refresh my memory," he said of the price sheet exhibit.

"We *just* looked at it!" the defense attorney protested. Indeed, the collective mind of the courtroom had already been numbed by Flynn's laborious look at item after item on the price list in order to demonstrate a universal 70% markup.

Keefe gave up his request to see the exhibit. "Not that I recall," he conceded.

"So there was nothing illegal there, not even *federally*?" Serra emphasized the final word with the full force and drama of his vocal talents.

"Not to my knowledge," Keefe yielded.

"You can buy them in a hardware store," the defense attorney muttered. It was more of a comment than a question, however, as he didn't pause for a response from the witness.

When Serra directed the witness to look at the law enforcement photos of the price sheets, Keefe acknowledged that he had not taken the pictures. "So you don't know if they were found like this or laid out for this photo?" Serra asked.

"No," the agent replied.

"Isn't it the procedure that, if a photo can't be taken there, where the item is found, you take it somewhere else?" Serra pushed.

"We try to take it where it was found," Keefe answered. When prompted again for a more direct reply, he said, "I can't think of when I've ever done this."

The defense attorney refused to accept the evasive responses, pressing his question on the witness until he eventually confessed that this was indeed a law enforcement practice. It was a hard-won battle, just as the cross-examination about the UPS packages proved to be.

For this line of inquiry, Serra took Keefe back to the time when the DEA had been alerted about the seven packages from Cool that contained marijuana. The agent disclosed that Schafer had phoned the DEA about retrieving the packages. The call had been a quick one, Keefe claimed on the stand, in which the defendant had merely asked for the property back. However, the agent did not recall whether or not he had taken notes on the conversation.

"Did he say he had a legal right to marijuana and that they were not attempting to evade law enforcement?" Serra asked about Schafer's call.

Keefe granted a quick agreement. "Yes."

"So you knew he was an attorney?" Serra queried.

"I don't know," Keefe replied.

"Your report says he claims to be the attorney of the recipients," Serra pointed out.

The witness shrugged, his gaze going downwards and to the side. "Okay…"

Serra persisted, "So you learned during the conversation that he was an attorney?"

"I don't know," Keefe reiterated, sticking firmly to his declaration of ignorance.

"Would it refresh your recollection to read the report?" Serra asked the witness, handing him a document that was grudgingly accepted. Keefe looked at the paper silently for a few moments, as the defense

246

attorney looked up at him expectantly for a response. "Is your memory refreshed that you knew he was an attorney?" Serra finally urged.

"Yes," Keefe admitted. He appeared weary at this point, and when he was excused from the stand shortly afterwards, the agent looked truly exhausted.

Fatigue, it seemed, was entirely proper – this case had been a long road for Keefe. In addition to all the behind-the-scenes duties, he had to testify twice before the jury, handle the government's evidence and escort its witnesses, and be at Pings's beck-and-call for the entire duration of the trial. But, in light of his prior experiences with the case, the trial itself was the least of the trauma he had suffered. His ordeal is chronicled in the case discovery, which goes into great detail to document one particular incident that was especially distressing for Keefe.

The report is DEA-6, which contains signed statements entitled "Surveillance of SA [Special Agent] Joe Brock by Unknown members of the Medical Marijuana Movement on 10-22-2001," and, "Surveillance of SAs Joe Brock and Brian Keefe on 10-22-2001."

According to DEA-6, the incident began during an October 2001 court hearing in the defendants' case. It ended when Keefe and a fellow agent ran for cover under a freeway overpass and hid out in Old Sacramento, waiting frantically for their supervisor to respond to their pleas for rescue. Under most circumstances, an exciting story would exist in between such a dramatic beginning and ending. However, in this case, it wasn't so. From the start of the hearing to the conclusion of the desperate rescue mission, very little time had elapsed...and even less activity.

First off, Keefe and his colleague Joseph Brock had been startled to find that the defendants' supporters were holding a protest outside the courthouse during the hearing. On alert to possible threats, the agents quickly became suspicious when they learned that one of the defendants' supporters was returning to a car that had been parked in the same lot as the agents' vehicles. The pair drew no comfort from the fact that the lot is the one closest to the courthouse and with the most available parking. Instead, Keefe and Brock became convinced that they were being stalked by "a white male, with long brown hair, wearing a brown suit" who was destined for "a small dark-colored import vehicle, possibly a Nissan" in the lot. But Brock confronted the man before he got to the suspected Nissan.

DEA-6 reads: "SA Brock observed the white male walking rapidly towards SA Brock. SA Brock noted that when the white male saw SA Brock, he immediately slowed his pace, and continued walking towards SA Brock. When SA Brock was approximately 10 feet from the white male, SA Brock asked the white male if SA Brock could help the white male with anything. The white male told SA Brock, 'No, lots of people park their cars over here.' The white male asked SA Brock if there was a problem. SA Brock told the white male that there was no problem as long as the white male was not following SA Brock. The white male stated that he was not following SA Brock."

U.S. Marshals have been apprehensive about protests by the defendants' supporters. Photo by Vanessa Nelson.

During a subsequent hide-out in the nearby train station, a rattled Brock attempted to call for help. His supervisor's cell phone was off, so Brock paged him…and waited. But after emerging from the station and walking back towards the courthouse, he and Keefe were dismayed to find that the aforementioned possible Nissan and a Volkswagen were circling the area where the demonstration was taking place. This heightened the agents' paranoia. It was not considered that the cars could be making the rounds to observe the protest. To the agents, the vehicles were circling in order to stake them out, and they turned back in their tracks. Soon afterwards, however, they came to believe they were being surrounded.

As written in DEA-6: "During SA Brock and SA Keefe's movement to the other location, SAs Brock and Keefe observed Dale SCHAFER, a defendant in the above referenced case. SAs Brock and Keefe observed that SCHAFER's vehicle was parked in very close proximity to SA Keefe's OGV (Official Government Vehicle). Also during SAs Brock and Keefe's movement to other location, SAs Brock and Keefe observed several individuals who were present in the courtroom at the aforementioned hearing, positioned in close proximity to SA Keefe's OGV. SAs Brock and Keefe were unsure if Dale SCHAFER or the aforementioned individuals were involved in the surveillance of SAs Brock and Keefe. SAs Brock and Keefe agreed that the appropriate course of action to take would be to leave their OGVs in the present location and arrange for the safe and secretive pick-up of SAs Brock and Keefe by a third agent, in an effort to elude any possible surveillance."

The two agents ducked out under the I-5 freeway overpass and into the safety of Old Sacramento, with its cobblestone streets and horse-drawn carriages and raised wooden sidewalks. Even though the scenery evoked an image of Old West-style lawlessness, it was only a tourist attraction, and the agents waited amidst the protection of cotton candy and overpriced t-shirts. But the sense of shelter evaporated when Brock received a return phone call from his supervisor, who admonished the agents for running from their vehicles in fear. The supervisor, Kyle Scott, refused to order a pick-up for the agents and instructed them instead to return to their OGVs. When Brock asserted that he and Keefe were under the threat of surveillance, Scott simply said that the agents should attempt to elude surveillance by departing the area in their vehicles and returning to the Sacramento District Office.

When Scott hung up, Keefe and Brock were left with the horrifying prospect of returning to the parking lot. Rather than facing this fear, however, Brock was able to arrange a pick-up by his colleague John Nolan. Readers will remember Nolan as the undercover DEA agent who claimed to get a contact high from Rice Krispie treats during a seminar about cooking with marijuana extracts. He was too overwhelmed by the influence to drive home from that class, but he swooped in like a hero in his OGV and rescued the two stranded agents. This fairytale ending is recorded in DEA-6 as: "Several minutes later, SAs Brock and Keefe were successfully and secretively pick-up (sic) by SA Nolan. SAs Brock and Keefe returned later that same day to pick-up their OGVs." In the end, the agents had been brave enough to go back to the scene of their trauma that very same day.

But the agents weren't the only ones in the case who were paranoid about surveillance. In fact, right after Keefe's second stint on the witness stand, a juror anonymously reported fears that his face had been portrayed in too much detail in courtroom scenes drawn by a sketch artist. No pictures had been released to the media, but the juror had his concerns nonetheless, and these worries magnified once they reached Judge Damrell's ears. It was time for action – the sketchbook was seized and handed to the judge by a marshal.

Flipping through the book, Judge Damrell identified and confiscated those drawings he felt to be an infringement on the jury's facial privacy. "These would harm them in their deliberative process," the judge explained. The sketchbook was then returned to the artist, plucked of all its transgressions.

But Judge Damrell was in a less powerful position when it came to protecting his own image, as evidenced by a lunchtime incident. The severity in his voice, as he related the occurrence to the court afterwards, tried to convey the enormity of its significance.

"This afternoon I was having lunch at a Thai restaurant," the judge began. "The defendants and a number of their supporters were present, and that's all very natural."

The unnatural part was ushered in by the appearance of a camera. "There was a photograph taken where I was in the foreground," Judge Damrell revealed in a tone of indignation.

"I see the gentleman sitting here in the courtroom now," the judge said, eyeing the cameraman disapprovingly. "I was having lunch with my former law clerk."

"If anything is done with the photo," Judge Damrell warned crossly, "it shall be excised."

Serra stood up, assuring the judge with promises yet to be arranged. "It shall not appear on the internet," he pledged.

Outside the courtroom, conversation hummed about why the judge had reacted to the incident so harshly. The prevailing theory was that Judge Damrell's former clerk, who was described by witnesses as young and blonde, was a lunch partner he preferred to keep secret. Whatever the reason for the outrage, the episode was yet another reminder of the unblinking eye that watches vigilantly over the paranoid.

Doctors In The House

The defense's case ended with a muzzled whimper on its last day of testimony, as four doctors were called to the stand and forced into saying very little. There was nonetheless a feeling of fluid amity in the proceedings, especially with the extinction of cross-examination by the government. However, the prosecutors still made their presence felt through objections that frequently inhibited the testimony.

Dr. Robin Daus

The first witness was Dr. Robin Daus, a tall, middle-aged woman with glasses and shoulder-length dark hair. Her eyes shined clear through the cover of her spectacles, and she conveyed an even sense of sincerity.

In response to Serra's questions, Daus revealed that she became acquainted with the defendants two decades ago and has remained close to them ever since. "Mollie and I went to med school together," she told Serra. "At that time, Mollie and Dale met each other and got married."

In the beginning of the twenty-year friendship, the witness had seen Fry and Dale Schafer so frequently that their lives became intertwined. "They're one of the reasons I moved to San Diego," Daus divulged. "I have not seen them as much since they moved up here. I probably talk to them once or twice a year, and see them every few years."

During that time, she assured Serra, she had been in a position to observe the character traits of her friends. And in spite of their geographical separation, Daus believed that she could still speak about the defendants' character in the present tense. "I don't believe character traits change," she explained, before going on to elaborate.

"I think Dale is one of the most honest people I've ever known," Daus said of Schafer. "In general, Dale's not a renegade. He has certain beliefs he feels very strongly about, and he is willing to fight for them."

This statement had a positive ring to it, but was full of ambiguity nonetheless. Serra pushed for an unequivocal assurance that Schafer was a law-abiding man. "I think Dale tries to uphold the law," the witness obliged, coming close to the desired level of certainty.

When questioned by Lichter, Daus spoke similarly of Fry's law-abidingness. With regard to other character traits, the witness made a perfectly definite pledge about Fry. "She has been extremely trustworthy and honest," Daus said with unmistakable confidence.

"Were you familiar with her reputation in the community while in San Diego?" Lichter asked.

"As far as I know, she didn't break any laws while she was there," Daus replied earnestly. "I didn't hear anything negative about her with regard to trustworthiness or honesty."

The testimony was left at that, and Daus cleared the witness stand for the next doctor.

Dr. Philip Denney

When Lichter called Dr. Phil Denney as a witness, he was summoning a man who was familiar to many in the gallery. The medical doctor had set up a private practice in El Dorado County nearly thirty years earlier, and many of the defendants' supporters knew him as their physician, their friend and their neighbor. He was a benevolent-looking figure as well, with a fluffy white beard and soft but twinkling eyes. And when he was shown in, Denney spoke with both a gentle voice and a tone of personal conviction.

"How did you meet the defendants?" Lichter asked the witness.

Denney began, "I met Mr. Schafer when he presented as a patient –"

Prosecutor Pings, no doubt irked by hearing the word 'patient,' interrupted with a question. "Is this a character witness or a personal witness?" she demanded.

Lichter confirmed that this was a character witness, and, after a nod from the judge, Denney continued. "After that, I saw them in the store, at the post office...places like that," he said of the defendants.

As a neighbor and friend of the defendants, Dr. Phil Denney provided solid character testimony. Sketch by Dr. Care.

When assessing Fry's law-abidingness, the witness stated, "She's very much a law-abiding citizen, as far as I know." Asked about whether Fry was truthful, Denney gave an enthusiastic and certain assurance of the defendant's honesty.

The defense attorney didn't get much more out of the witness, however. When Lichter inquired about a professional association between Denney and Fry, Pings stood up and argued that this was not an appropriate question for a character witness. She made the same objection when Lichter began to ask Denney about Paul Maggy. The judge sustained each of these objections, and soon Lichter was out of questions.

Serra, however, managed to go places where his colleague had been barred, eventually eliciting from Denney a damning statement about Maggy. But first the witness described to Serra the frequency of his contact with the defendants. "We both live in a rural area served by a single road," Denney revealed. "We're both on the road committee. We see each other a couple times a month."

The defense attorney then asked a series of questions about Schafer's character traits, giving the witness latitude for some glowing assertions. "I find him to be a very honest and trustworthy human being," he said of Schafer.

"He has an outstanding reputation in our community. It's excellent," Denney continued. "He has made every effort to be a law-abiding citizen, as far as I know. He has a sterling reputation for being law-abiding in his community."

"Are you familiar with the reputation of Mr. Paul Maggy?" Serra asked, squeaking past the prosecutor's warning signals.

"No," Denney said simply.

But it was quite a different matter when the defense attorney asked for the witness's personal opinion of Maggy's truthfulness.

"He has proven, in my experience, to be a liar and a thief," Denney said decisively.

It was a compelling statement with which to conclude, so Serra wrapped up his questioning right then and there. The prosecutors remained seated, scribbling notes half-heartedly, and Denney was excused from the stand.

Dr. Jerry Powell

Next to testify was Dr. Jerry Powell, a medical professor specializing in hematology and oncology. Powell gave Serra a lengthy and impressive résumé of schools and medical institutions, but indicated that he presently worked at the University of California at Davis. There, he said, he taught students and interns, conducted research, and took care of patients in the cancer center. Powell also, as it turned out, was the director of the hemophilia treatment center, and this is what brought him into contact with the defendants.

"Dale Schafer is one of those patients that I care for," Powell told Serra. "Since the early 1990s, we've had a continuous doctor/patient relationship."

Asked about frequency of contact with Schafer, the witness answered, "At minimum, once a month. That's how often I have to see him to write his pain prescriptions."

Pings objected to the response, likely worried that it would cast a sympathetic light on the defendant. Judge Damrell, sustaining the objection, turned to the witness and instructed him to simply answer the questions without embellishment. Powell nodded and agreed.

256

"How long is each meeting?" the defense attorney inquired.

"A few minutes to write a pain prescription," Powell replied, "or an hour if it's an acute medical episode."

"Are you close enough to him to be able to assess character traits?" Serra asked about Schafer.

"Yes," the doctor responded. "I –"

Pings issued another objection, prompting the judge to instruct Powell to give a simple yes or no answer. Later, however, the doctor was permitted to elaborate without interruption. "As a physician, I have to bond very closely with my patients," he said. "I know intimate details."

Serra asked about his opinion of Schafer's honesty, and the witness was effusive. "Oh, it's a very high opinion," Powell gushed. "He has always been on time –"

"Objection," Pings broke in. "Non-responsive."

Judge Damrell agreed. "Sustained," he said plainly.

The defense attorney then inquired about Schafer's reputation for law-abidingness, commenting to the witness, "I hope you can tell the jury without another interruption."

"It's very high," Powell answered, sticking strictly to the question this time. "He's very law abiding."

And, with that, the penultimate doctor was excused from the witness stand.

Dr. David Ostrach

Dr. David Ostrach arrived in a motorized wheelchair, flanked by a white wolf. He made his way to the front of the courtroom without issue, but when he got to the witness stand, there was a problem. The electric lift that was supposed to raise him to the level of the stand's microphone was staunchly uncooperative. The clerk tried time and time again to get it to work properly, requiring Ostrach to ride in and out of the lift each time. Eventually, surrendering to failure, the clerk just decided that the witness would have to remain on ground level and speak into a handheld microphone. This was a trying experience, but it would be far less exasperating than dealing with the numerous interruptions in his testimony.

Another doctor hailing from UC Davis, Ostrach identified as a pathologist, but also disclosed that he has focused on environmental issues and training service dogs ever since his illness worsened. The professional autobiography was kept short, after which the examination got into full swing. But when Lichter asked about Fry's reputation for truthfulness and law-abidingness, Ostrach earned his first objection.

Dr. David Ostrach's testimony was hampered by the suppression of any and all references to the medical use of marijuana. Sketch by Dr. Care.

The witness began, "Approximately seven and a half years ago –"

Pings cut him off. "Objection!" she announced. "Non-responsive."

Sustaining the objection, Judge Damrell informed Ostrach that the reputation question was solely relating to the factors of truthfulness and law-abidingness. "Truthfulness and law-abidingness are the only questions," he repeated to the witness.

Ostrach made another go at it. "I was aware of her reputation. That's why I was referred to her as the expert in –"

"Objection!" Pings interrupted. "It goes to specific instances."

"Sustained," the judge said, turning back to the witness to give his instruction on the question yet again.

More obediently this time, Ostrach answered, "Dr. Fry is absolutely law-abiding, both by reputation and by personal experience."

Expanding on the idea of experience, the witness uttered another objectionable statement. "Dr. Fry is one of my many doctors –"

258

Pings quickly abandoned explanations in favor of exclamations. "Your honor!" she cried out, gesturing her exasperation. Thus summoned, Judge Damrell instructed the witness to talk about his personal experiences with Fry without speaking of his relationship to her professionally.

"We are colleagues," Ostrach attempted, "and I have gotten medical advice from –"

Pings broke in again, repeating her plea, "Your honor!"

"Don't answer about medical advice," Judge Damrell ordered the doctor.

Guiding the witness back to the topic, Lichter reissued his question in a way that stressed the inquiry into Fry's law-abidingness. "She has always told me to follow the letter of the law," Ostrach replied. "No bending of the law. I don't believe she's capable of it. She's one of the most highly-respected physicians in her field –"

"Objection," Pings said, breaking up the doctor's narrative. Trying to expedite the examination process, the judge had Ostrach simply move on to the question about Fry's reputation for honesty and integrity.

Again, however, the witness failed to untangle the professional references from his personal statements. He appeared to view personal reputations and professional reputations as intertwined concepts. "In my personal opinion," he remarked, "she's absolutely one of the most kind, honest, compassionate –"

Pings bolted at another medical marijuana buzzword, stepping in to object. Judge Damrell tried to mend the breach by ordering the word "compassionate" striken.

Lichter began to ask his next question, but it did not go without disruption. "When you visited with Dr. Fry, was there a muscular –"

Pings shouted this time, "Objection!"

Judge Damrell turned to the jurors, instructing them to disregard the question.

"I wasn't aware I'd asked it," Lichter commented.

The judge glared at the defense attorney, incensed. "Do you have any further questions?" he demanded.

"I do," Lichter answered pertly, "but not character questions."

Judge Damrell was livid. "Don't roll your eyes at me!" he fumed. "This is not argument. This is not a debating society. I've ruled!"

The battle culminated during a lengthy sidebar, during which white noise prevented observers from hearing the sounds that issued from angry faces. Lichter emerged appearing unscathed, however, and proceeded with a couple additional questions for the witness.

"Did you use marijuana before visiting Dr. Fry?" the defense attorney inquired.

Ostrach never got to answer. The question was instead killed by another successful objection from Pings.

"Did you see Dr. Fry about whether medical – no, not medical – whether a recommendation for marijuana was appropriate?" Lichter asked slyly.

"Yes," Ostrach answered. "I was referred to see if it was appropriate." Following this, he was excused from the witness stand…even though, of course, he hadn't been on the witness stand.

"I apologize for this courtroom," Judge Damrell said as the doctor began to wheel away. It was unclear whether he was referring to the equipment malfunction or the conduct, but it was likely an all-encompassing statement.

"No worries," Dr. Ostrach replied cheerfully.

"I *do* worry about it," the judge shot back, shaking his head.

The Prosecution's Closing

"They Grew, They Distributed, They're Guilty"

When Pings addressed the jury for her closing arguments, she did so with something beyond self-assurance. Her tone, her words, and her facial expressions carried with them a sentiment that was akin to annoyance. This attitude clearly conveyed the message that the whole case was so brain-numbingly simple that its further consideration wasted the time and energy of a whole courtroom of participants. To a jury that had been looking increasingly restless, a pledge that this case was open-and-shut was like music to their ears.

The prosecutor put it quite simply, telling the jury, "You've already heard from the most important person you'll need to hear from to make your decision, Dr. Marion Fry, talking to what she thought was a customer."

Pings then played a tape that had become all too familiar to the jury – the recording introduced during the testimony of Special Agent Keefe, which detailed a conversation between Fry and an undercover agent posing as a patient. The courtroom lights were dimmed so that listeners could read along with a screen showing a transcript, since the tape was garbled with audio hiss in some spots and occasionally unintelligible. The strange part about the arrangement was that the recording itself was an official case exhibit, but the transcript was never admitted into evidence. This was an odd situation, especially given the poor quality of the audio and the dutiful attention the jurors paid to the screen each time the tape was played. They appeared to be relying upon the transcript for comprehension in some places, giving this document a weight that was disproportionate to its actual evidentiary status.

In spite of this, however, Pings maintained her stance that there was nothing further to consider. There was not a hint of ambiguity in her argument, and for this she was rewarded with looks of relief from her audience as she recapped what Fry had said to the undercover agent. "She told him that if he needed clones, she would give them to him," the prosecutor summarized. "She told him she was growing marijuana at her house. She told him she had a clone room, a mother room, an outside growing area, and a 'big old greenhouse.' She said she had someone there to cultivate the plants, but he failed miserably and she ended up losing an entire crop of 45 plants. She said she kept trying to help him take care of the plants." Pings scanned the jurors' faces in a moment of pause before telling them precisely what they wanted to hear. "You heard from Mr. Schafer that he grew and distributed marijuana, essentially admitting that he too is guilty. You heard from both defendants from their own mouths that they are guilty of these charges. That's all you need to make your verdict."

Pings assured the jurors that they need not worry about the circumstances or history of the defendants' involvement with marijuana. She emphasized that it was their duty to focus on the charges themselves, which covered a strictly-defined period from August 1999 through September 2001. "What happened between Dale Schafer and his wife in 1998 is not to be considered," the prosecutor said discreetly, carefully avoiding mention of things like cancer or compassion. "Under the law you are to apply, the possession, distribution and manufacture of marijuana are illegal for any reason."

The prosecutor acted as though she could have easily concluded at that point, but with an air of generosity went on to list more seemingly straightforward, effortless damnations. Going through the requirements that were to be proven in each part of the conspiracy charge, she resurrected in short mentions the cast of characters that had taken the witness stand.

First off, Pings claimed, both defendants were part of an agreement to sell dried marijuana and marijuana plants. In fact, as she described

262

it, Fry and Schafer did *everything* together. "Their offices were together, both contributed the source of customers to this conspiracy, jointly owned the house where marijuana was cultivated," the prosecutor said, attempting to merge the defendants into one unified entity. If she could group Fry and Schafer this way, she could get two guilty verdicts by skillfully playing out a single hand. "What they did, they did together," Pings emphasized.

The prosecutor reminded the jurors of Sean Cramblett and his account of obtaining marijuana from the defendants. As she recounted, Cramblett had offered Fry glass pipes in exchange for dried marijuana, but it was Schafer who showed up later and made the trade. "That was one transaction where marijuana was distributed, and they were both part of it." Pings then took the time to inform the jury that the legal definition of distribution includes sales as well as trades or gifts. "They both handed over baggies and had others that did it for them," the prosecutor said of the two defendants.

Next in the prosecutor's review was Jeffrey Teshera, who testified that he had received multiple in-home marijuana deliveries from Mike Harvey as well as several UPS deliveries. The products in question, he clarified, were dried marijuana as well as starter marijuana plants. In evidence was a receipt from Harvey's book to Teshera's wife, with a memo for "Rx plants and general hydro." In fact, all of these deliveries were paid for with checks written out to Dale Schafer, one of which was shown to have been endorsed by Fry before deposit. Pings used this example to emphasize the financial connection between the two defendants, but she wasn't quite finished mining quotes from this witness.

On the stand, Teshera said that Fry had set up a meeting spot and personally sold him marijuana hand-to-hand at that location. Unfortunately for the prosecution, however, the defense attorneys had made a significant showing that the witness gave an erroneous date for this encounter – rather than leaving her office to meet Teshera, Fry had been in a hospital all day long to coach her step-daughter through a complicated childbirth. Pings, quite predictably, did her best to downplay the flawed testimony. "You'll hear from Mr. Lichter that Mr. Teshera got the date wrong," the prosecutor acknowledged. "But it's not the *when* of this transaction that is important – it's *where* this deal happened that's important." Pings then described the location of the meeting, portraying it as a sleazy, clandestine drug deal in a vacant parking lot.

After discussing a few cumulative witnesses, Pings turned to the evidence involving Mike Harvey. "He testified that he made intensive deliveries, and it was corroborated by the testimony of other people," Pings summarized Harvey's testimony. "He said the defendant gave him marijuana to distribute, and Mr. Schafer essentially admitted this." The prosecutor reminded the jury that the links between this witness and the defendants were woven with many tight threads. Harvey drove the defendants' jeep to make these deliveries, and that his receipt book was found in the defendants' office during the September 2001 raid. And just to make sure to emphasize the idea that Fry was also in on the deal, Pings recalled that the raid had turned up a triple-beam scale in Fry's bedroom, where Harvey had claimed she weighed out the delivery packages. Even though this revelation did nothing to conclusively demonstrate Harvey's honesty on this accusation, Pings certainly acted like it did. "You know he's telling the truth," the prosecutor said to the jury about Harvey, using a voice of great earnestness.

Having summed up the examples of the conspiracy to *distribute* marijuana, Pings moved on to discuss another part of the charge: the conspiracy also involved an agreement to *cultivate* marijuana. And to make this showing, Pings came back to her prized piece of evidence and once again quoted from the undercover tape. She called Fry's speech a "sales pitch," but she also wanted these words to have an undue amount of weight and veracity. Oddly enough, the jury was asked to assume that such advertising language is by nature extraordinarily honest and representative of objective reality. It seems to go against common sense, but said in Pings' no-nonsense tone; it came off as perfectly reasonable. "You can't get more evidence than a sales pitch to her customer," Pings declared.

Fry did use fatal language on the undercover tape, but it was not the language of salesmanship – it was the language of connections, of relationships. She repeatedly said "we" when talking about her

264

husband's business of selling grow kits, and also about the marijuana plants that were being cultivated at the couple's home. "Her own words tell you what she did," Pings said of Fry, speaking to the jury. "You knew there were outdoor plants – Sergeant Ashworth said there were 21 plants outdoors in 1999 and 43 plants outdoors in 2000, and then the DEA found 34 plants when they executed the search warrant."

Pings spoke about indoor cultivation as well, although in her typical fashion, she acted as though this consideration was actually unnecessary. "You saw the plants, and the photos of the search and heard from the defendants' own mouths – you knew they grew plants," Pings said to the jurors, implying that the evidence was obvious. But the crucial finding would be whether the number exceeded a hundred plants, and for this charge the figures were a little wobbly. Proving it would require Pings to get the jury to believe in extensive indoor cultivation that was never seen or discovered by law enforcement.

During closing statements, prosecutor Anne Pings acted as though she and the jurors shared a shrewd understanding of the case. Sketch by Dr. Care.

"Dale Schafer said he only had a few plants [indoors], but you know there were rooted clones in there before the DEA arrived," Pings phrased her speculation as undisputed fact. "Fry said, 'Just call up – we always have a system to make clones.' And when the DEA arrives, there was still a roomful of nutrients and equipment for growing indoor plants."

In this way, the prosecutor was asking the jury to assume there had been more plants than were actually found. After all, a belief in unobserved plants was necessary for tipping the plant count over a hundred. Pings also employed this strategy while discussing the other charge the couple faced: a substantive count for the actual cultivation of marijuana. On this charge, the prosecutor wanted the jury to believe the plant count was higher than the number that was observed and recorded by law enforcement. After all, the police count from the three relevant grow seasons hovered just under a hundred. Ashworth had recorded 21 plants at the defendants' home in 1999 and 43 plants during his 2000 visit. Adding in the 34 plants that were seized in the 2001 raid, and the count comes in at just 98. To get the total over a hundred, Pings relied heavily on testimony from various witnesses to help conjure up a belief in an undetermined number of indoor plants.

Starting off, the prosecutor aimed high and asked the jury to have confidence that there had been many of these plants. Harvey, she remembered, had said that hundreds of clones were being grown at the defendants' residence. But Harvey's ever-shifting testimony was a slippery place for Pings to stand, and she remained there for only a moment. Witness Tod Zimmerman, who had appraised the Fry/Schafer house in February 2001, got a much more lengthy mention from the prosecutor.

Zimmerman had testified that he saw marijuana clones laid out on tables in an indoor grow area, estimating there were three rows containing up to seventy plants per row. That room alone would have held well over a hundred, in the prosecutor's account, and possibly even more than two hundred plants. And, in her view, Zimmerman's story was exceptionally credible because she could conceive of no ulterior motive for his testimony. "His testimony is key because he doesn't know these defendants at all," Pings asserted about Zimmerman. "He sees many people and many houses, but he was so concerned about seeing these plants that he got worried about his wife being inside the house with Dale Schafer and Mike Harvey."

Pings didn't shy away from addressing some of the flaws in Zimmerman's account. Sure, he may have gotten a few tiny things wrong during his testimony, like recalling the number of greenhouses on the property, but the prosecutor stressed that these events happened a long time ago and that it was natural for some details to be hazy in his memory. That's precisely why the prosecutor encouraged the jurors to pay attention to Zimmerman's actions rather than the minor errors in his account, and to make logical conclusions about the meaning of his behavior at the time. "He saw so many plants that he ran to call the sheriff about it," Pings said of the witness. "His actions that day speak louder than his words here in the courtroom seven years later."

The prosecutor then attempted to cast doubt on Schafer's earlier testimony that he had only grown six clones at a time, and that he had done so with great misfortune. If that had been the case, Pings concluded, then Zimmerman would never have been so alarmed. "There's no way he rushed out of that house to call the sheriff if all he saw were six spider-mite-ridden clones," Pings speculated about the real estate appraiser. Besides, she said, logic dictates that Schafer would have made better use of the grow room after going to such lengths to set it up. "Surely he paid a carpenter to put in a wall, and to put in electricity, and to install lighting, for something more than a few clones."

After several sardonic comments, the prosecutor again spoke of Cramblett. This time, she referenced his testimony that the defendants gave him forty marijuana clones and a loan to buy equipment for the cultivation of these plants. Pings put a point on the fact that Cramblett was only 22 when he got involved in business deals with the defendants, saying the word "twenty-two years old" with such heavy emphasis that it made it sound like this was itself a criminal charge of some kind. With increasingly vivid language, the prosecutor jogged the jurors' memories about Cramblett and his story on the stand. "Remember the brunch where they went upstairs and all smoked pot, and Dale Schafer asked him, 'Hey, you want some morphine?'" Pings recounted for the jury, trying somewhat comically to deepen her voice to deliver Schafer's line. "After this bizarre interlude, they went on tour outside and he saw plants in the bunker. Mr. Schafer handed him trays of forty clones, and he said this forty was just a small dent in the number of plants that were there."

The prosecutor also made sure that the jurors understood that Cramblett had good reason for having a sharp memory and keen recall about those particular clones. "He remembers those plants well," Pings said of her witness. "Those are the plants he got arrested for. And Dr. Fry came to court and said, 'Those are my plants!'"

Speaking of Fry's words, the prosecutor was all too happy to direct the jurors' attention back to the undercover tape one last time. On the recording, Pings pointed out, Fry makes the comment that she lost all 45 of her plants while someone else was taking care of her crop. "Flip that on its head, and that means that there were 45 plants alive at one time," Pings ventured. She continued to urge the jury to follow her reasoning that there must have been many marijuana plants on the property shortly before the raid. This allegation was supported not only by logic, but also by Fry's description of having 45 plants and Heather Schafer's comment about cleaning out the house in preparation for her father's campaign for District Attorney. The cleaning comment, according to Pings, was what had motivated the police to get the search warrant as soon as possible. But, as the prosecutor told the story, it was already too late – the family had been cleaning out the house, just as Heather said, and by the time the officers got the warrant and executed it, there were only 34 plants left to be seized on September 28th, 2001.

As she wrapped up her speech, Pings was left to do her ultimate calculation, and she regained her air of generosity for this task. Regarding the witness accounts about hundreds of marijuana clones, the prosecutor offered to leave them out of the final count. Law enforcement reports had totaled 98 plants, but all it took to break the hundred mark was Schafer's testimony about cultivating two different sets of six clones. This brought the count to 110, but if the jury needed more convincing, Pings reminded them that they could include the 45 plants that Fry mentioned on the undercover tape. "There's no requirement that the plants lived forever, that it was a healthy plant or a strong plant," the prosecutor clarified. "It doesn't matter if it ever had spider mites, just if it had roots and was alive."

Giving parting advice to the jury, Pings spoke like a sports coach. "Keep your eye on the ball," she urged with determination. "Remember the testimony of the witnesses who got marijuana hand-to-hand. Remember Mr. Schafer's testimony that he grew plants and gave them away. And remember the words of Dr. Fry on the undercover tape."

For poetic fulfillment, the prosecutor finished with the very same words she had uttered at the beginning of her closing statement. "They grew, they distributed, they're guilty," she repeated about the defendants, completing a rhetorical circle with words of simplicity and confidence.

Tony Serra's Closing: *The Crucible of Justice*

When it comes to closing arguments, Serra has an undeniable sparkle. By his own observation, however, "sparkles are a surface manifestation," and this holds true to the defense attorney himself. The internal phenomena behind his shine are fluency in emotive lyricism and a gift for perfectly-punctuated oratory. Simply put, his speeches are a spectacle and an experience.

"I've been doing this a long time," Serra said as he started off, " but I always have butterflies every time I step to the podium for closing."

With a gracious excess of words, he thanked the jurors for their patience and attentiveness. "This is the crucible of justice, and you participate in it admirably." He bowed his head slightly in appreciation.

"You are the figurative peer group of our clients." Serra gestured towards Fry and Schafer at the defense table. "You should *feel* that. You should give the justice that you would want for you and your loved ones."

Serra's form was beginning to take shape, the rhythm and speed of his speech finding balance with the pace of his imagery. "Dr. Fry and Dale Schafer are not aliens," he told the jury. "They are in the bosom of their community. They are good people. Give them justice."

He wanted the jurors to recall the scales of justice hanging in the entry to the courthouse. "The scales of justice tilt. They bend. They bend towards *mercy*. They bend towards *compassion*." Serra stated that morality is a part of every case, announcing with conviction, "Law that is divested of morality cannot perpetuate itself."

271

Part of that morality was reflected in the testimony of the character witnesses, and Serra put great emphasis on this concept. "It was extraordinary to see the girth and magnitude of the character witnesses," he observed, noting the demographic range of these people. "All different levels of society came forward to attest to Dr. Fry and Dale Schafer's good character. Other defendants don't come with such pedigree, such community—"

"I'm sorry, your honor, but I'm going to have to object," Pings broke in, taking issue with the reference to other cases. Judge Damrell, while clearly not pleased with objections during closing, curtly advised Serra to talk only about this current case.

Serra got back to his point, continuing to sketch a portrait of his client – a man who was raised and schooled locally, who joined the armed forces, became a lawyer, and married a woman with whom he raised five beautiful children. The family was, as Serra described it, happy and prosperous, and the lifestyle exemplary. The couple built their professions, became a valuable part of their church and their community, and deeply devoted themselves to their children. "Is that not the American way? Is that not the American dream?" Serra then gestured towards Schafer, who had a look of humility as he sat near his wife. "Is he not symbolically our son, our brother, our father?"

Jurors were reminded of the catastrophe that befell this family when Fry was diagnosed with breast cancer, and how Schafer testified tearfully on the stand about his wife's struggle against death. "You saw him emote. You think that was somehow counterfeit?"

At the defense table, Fry was gripped by full, open-mouth sobbing, but she did it all in perfect silence, reminding the audience of Serra's description, "She's all courage…she's been hurt but she's so brave." The defense attorney was passionate in his appeal, and all ranges of his address fell neatly into their distinct grooves. He had hit his stride.

After failing to find relief with a number of conventional therapies, he recounted, Fry found that she was helped by marijuana. Serra then tried that term out, reciting it over and over with careful articulation. "Marijuana. Marijuana. Marijuana. Marijuana. It's not a dirty word."

The defense attorney explained that words acquire positive and negative connotations through social constructs. He listed other words

272

– narcotics, methamphetamine, terrorism, molestation – and acknowledged that they get automatic cerebral and emotional reactions. "If this case did anything at all, ladies and gentlemen of the jury, understand that marijuana, for her, Mollie Fry, and for him, Dale Schafer, is medicine." Serra jumped immediately forward into the assertion that this was not a defense, and that his descriptions were merely providing context. "It was an epiphany, an enlightenment, a bolt of lightning…it was an angel of mercy for her, as it has been for many—"

Pings raised her second objection at this point, indicating that she desired a sidebar to discuss the matter, but the judge merely reminded Serra to keep his comments specific to the case at hand. "Proceed" said the judge.

The defense attorney nodded, returning directly to his narrative about the impact this medicine has had on the defendants. It saved Fry from pain and despair, rescued her from death, brought her redemption… and the family's priorities were reordered accordingly. As a result, Schafer voluntarily chose to devote his practice to a specialty that earned him less money, a move that contradicted the government's claim that the defendants were motivated by profit. "What they were doing, from their perspective, was *good*. What they were doing, from their perspective, was *right*. And what is good and right can never be illegal."

Serra quickly tacked on the clarification that he was describing the defendants' mindset, but this amendment was not enough to satisfy Pings, who simultaneously shouted out her objection. "It's not a defense," Serra admitted, but he directed his focus back to the defendants' reputations for honesty and trustworthiness.

Vouching for his client, of course, were the extraordinary character witnesses that Serra mentioned earlier in his speech. He briefly traced their history back through English common law tradition and into Middle Eastern practices of justice that extracted 'an eye for an eye.' In this system, as Serra described it, "Justice was swift, and punishment was certain."

The defense attorney also highlighted the brutality of those trials. "They would take the accused to the stoning wall, and the jurors, more or less, would stone him or her to death." However, if a respected member of the community placed himself in front of the accused at the wall, the participants were faced with two options: either kill both parties, or exonerate. That, as Serra drew the comparison, was the function of the character witnesses in this case. "They come forward and say, 'Spare them. These people warrant your judgment, your compassion, your fervent consideration of the evidence."

Schafer's honor was not only confirmed by these witnesses, the defense attorney suggested, but his character was also demonstrated in the testimony he gave on the stand. "He said he grew marijuana," Serra recalled from Schafer's testimony. "He doesn't expect to walk out of here without a conviction."

It was surprising to hear that the defendant, in essence, expected a guilty verdict. But there was method to this madness – Serra then told the jurors that they could trust Schafer's testimony because he had taken responsibility and spoke honestly about his deeds. This showed his integrity, his honor, his veracity. As such, the defense attorney concluded, his client's word has far more weight than the word of a witness like Paul Maggy. Just in case any of the jurors were wondering precisely *how much* more weight, Serra went so far as to suggest a rate of conversion: his client's word was over twenty-five times more valuable than the word of the government's lead witness. The jurors were urged to consider Schafer's testimony with an eye to its greater worth, giving special attention to his declarations that his wife had nothing to do with growing marijuana. "His word alone, because he has integrity, raises reasonable doubt."

As for the witnesses who testified against the defendants, Serra advised the jurors not to rely on their testimony. They were lacking in credibility, the defense attorney proclaimed, and he followed up with detailed descriptions of the character flaws of these witnesses.

With regard to Maggy, Serra had many points of concern. "Dr. Denney testified that Paul Maggy is a liar and a thief, in his opinion," the defense attorney reminded the jurors, going on to detail Maggy's extensive criminal history. "You can't ever take the word of a liar and a thief over the word of an honest human being, a wholesome human being."

274

Beyond deception and theft, however, there was another factor that made Maggy's testimony suspect. Just like so many other witnesses on the government's case, he was seeking leniency in sentencing. Serra reiterated that giving testimony in this case was a requirement of the plea deal Maggy took to avoid a 5-year mandatory jail sentence in his own cultivation case.

"You get a few vignettes that symbolically open the door to your understanding," Serra said to the jurors, going on to describe the fear Maggy was experiencing during his interviews with federal agents. "They put him in cuffs and interrogate him. 'We know there were more plants than that! How many plants were there?!' He gets the idea. He sees a crack in the door of the jail. He will say anything to save his own skin. He is flawed. He is a coward. You can't believe a word he says."

The defense lawyer compared this situation to the highly problematic practice of extracting confessions through torture, and then went on to call it a form of bribery. "The government says, 'Give us what we want, and we will give you years of freedom,' and what is more valuable than money? Liberty." As with other forms of bribery, Serra implied, the result is corruption. "This system produces, ultimately, a system of justice that has no validity, that has no integrity. How can the building blocks of truth be built through witnesses who are paid?" he asked rhetorically. "They'll say anything."

The defense attorney's poetic symbolism was vivid. "These are the halls of justice," he continued. "And into our halls comes that viper, that flawed human being, that Judas, and wants you to take his word and condemn this beautiful couple!"

Mike Harvey, Serra contended, was not any better than this. "The Judas syndrome comes easily to the weak," he said.

The defense attorney informed the jurors that one of the factors they can use to weigh the credibility of a witness is the manner in which that witness testified. "Do I really need to say much?" Serra asked about Harvey's testimony. "He stuttered. He contradicted himself. He had a look of blankness like the proverbial deer in the headlights. He made admissions of almost hateful bias against Dr. Fry."

Referring back to a contentious time during cross-examination when he called Harvey a rat, the defense attorney was without regret. "I called him an ugly name," Serra recalled. "I don't take it back."

Tony Serra was most enthralling when given the chance to deliver a monologue. Photo by Vanessa Nelson.

The better analogy, however, was saying that these traitorous witnesses preyed upon the defendants like spider mites preyed upon Schafer's hapless clones. "The spider mites come around – they want the money, they want the ease, they want to suck off the gravy." Serra shook his head at the shame if it all, concluding to the jurors. "I beseech you to never convict on the word of a Mike Harvey."

As for Sean Cramblett, the defense attorney saw him in a similar light. Like the other witnesses Serra described, Cramblett testified in exchange for leniency in his own criminal case. But there was another factor that complicated things with this witness – the obvious financial motive. "He ripped my client off," Serra alleged, referring to the $8500 loan Schafer made to Cramblett. "That was no agreement to grow marijuana. That was for his glass-blowing business." The loan, of course, was never repaid. And, as Serra suggested, if Cramblett's testimony could get the defendants in jail and out of the way, it might never have to be repaid.

The prosecutor's objections lulled during the middle of Serra's closing statements, but Pings was suddenly on her feet again once the defense attorney began discussing the testimony of real estate appraiser Tod Zimmerman. Serra reminded the jury of the witness's insistence on an inaccurate recollection of two greenhouses on the defendants' property, but more important was the revelation that Zimmerman admitted to the theft of marijuana plants during his youth.

"Marijuana is medicine," Serra began, but an objection from Pings stopped him in his tracks. The defense attorney turned to the judge. "This is in the instruction," he explained.

"*I* will instruct," Judge Damrell insisted.

Serra, however, went right back into contentious territory. "He stole marijuana from sick people," he started to recount about Zimmerman.

Pings objected yet again, petulance peeking through. Judge Damrell's irritation was becoming similarly transparent. "Stay away from the law I will be instructing on," he warned the defense counsel.

"Okay," Serra yielded. Turning back to the jury, he said of Zimmerman, "I will just say that he stole plants, and leave it to you to conclude who from." Suffice to say, in the defense's characterization, the real estate appraiser was a thief who belonged in the same category as the aforementioned witnesses. Since their testimony was unreliable, Serra asked the jurors to take it out of their consideration. "Once you do that, there's not much left," the defense attorney noted. "She mentioned them every other word in her closing," he said of Pings's references to the suspect witnesses.

Serra then turned to what he called the centerpiece of the government's case – the recording in which Fry encourages the undercover agent to grow his own marijuana for medicine. The defense attorney acknowledged there were times when Fry used the term 'we' when talking about providing marijuana clones, but he denied that the defendant ever actually intended to refer to herself. "If she said 'we,' she meant my client, and my client told you the truth," Serra said to the jurors. After all, he continued, "There is a 'we.' We're human beings and it's a beautiful thing." To illustrate, he directed the jury's gaze out into the gallery and asked them why the seats were all filled. "They're filled for *these people*," he answered, indicating the defendants.

Serra next reinforced the notion that Fry's interest was in being a doctor, which meant helping patients and gathering statistics while doing so. The argument was that the testimony about her intake forms demonstrated a focus on research, and one of the reasons for its importance was due to the relative newness of her field. "We were in the infancy of something," Serra emphasized. "We were in a whole new medical world."

The defense attorney paused long enough to let the idea penetrate the brains of the jurors, but promptly hopped to the next stepping-stone. "It's not a defense," he said in a conciliatory tone. He claimed he was just giving context, and continued to do so with some other analogies about promoting new theories and fields of research. "In the old, old days, if you expostulated that the earth circled the sun, you were prosecuted. It was heresy. At another time in history, you were ridiculed if you didn't believe the earth was flat. Another time in more recent history, if you taught Darwinian Evolutionism in some corners of this country, you were prosecuted."

As far as applying these concepts to the current trial, Serra began to address the jury about their duty. "If the ulterior motive is to stop the medical marijuana movement, then—"

Pings was quick to object, claiming that the defense was speaking about jury nullification. Serra maintained that he was addressing government witnesses and their biases, but Judge Damrell was unwilling to take this statement at face value. "You're talking about the government?" he asked skeptically.

Serra answered, continuing the argument that any bias that was rooted in political motivations would erase the credibility of the government witnesses. To explain the bias, he expanded his scope. "We're not here, really, on just one case—"

"Objection, your honor!" Pings's vigor had increased to true outrage, which was mirrored by the judge's reaction.

The angry opposition only seemed to fuel Serra. The defense attorney launched into a series of questions he wanted the jury to ask itself about the prosecution's intentions. First of all, he mused, why did the raid occur in the midst of Schafer's campaign for district attorney? And why, Serra wanted the jury to wonder, was Pings so involved with this case? The prosecutor not only orchestrated the grand jury proceedings, offering immunity and eliciting testimony, but also participated so heavily in the investigation itself that she was even present for the raid of the defendants' home. "Has she overstepped the bounds of a lawyer who's supposed to be in the courtroom?" the defense attorney asked, his voice getting louder and louder as the intensity of his accusations increased.

While Serra was in the middle of a heated point about the prosecutor losing her objectivity and all directives coming from Washington D.C., Pings yelled out her final objection. She had Judge Damrell's full backing, and he was heavy right back at Serra. "You're way out of line here!" the judge said sharply, instructing the jury to disregard yet another of the defense attorney's comments. "You're out of the ballpark of biased witnesses here. You're supposed to be going over evidence in this case."

Serra went on to a description of what must be proven to find guilt in a conspiracy charge, telling the jurors yet again that there is ample reasonable doubt in this case. In parting instruction to them, he urged fearlessness. "There is no negative connotation when you find someone not guilty. It doesn't mean the system has misfired. It doesn't mean there's injustice," he assured the jurors.

"'Not guilty' are the two most beautiful words in our system," Serra concluded, beaming. "It means you have, as the conscience of the community, addressed the issue and resolved it. It's beautiful, it's strong, and it's appropriate for this case."

Laurence Lichter's Closing:
An Angel On Her Shoulder

Since his colleague's closing arguments had stretched to the end of the previous day, Lichter got to make his final statements to the jury as soon as they arrived out of the fresh sunlight the next morning. Unlike the prosecution, the defense had no foundation of facts to stand upon – no damning undercover tapes to play for the jurors, no two-digit arithmetic to run them through again and again. Like Serra before him, Lichter had only persuasion to work with – the art of words to weave concepts of morality, empathy, and a fundamental understanding of justice. It was a difficult task, but Lichter did it with astonishing ardor.

"The first thing I notice when I come into the courtroom is that my client, Dr. Fry, is not alone," he said, positioning himself in front of the jury box. "I know *you* see her with her husband, her family, those that care for her and show up from time to time. But *I* see her with an angel on her shoulder. That angel is the presumption that she is innocent, and it hasn't moved."

Lichter clasped his hands together. "That angel will not move, and not because [Dr. Fry] loves God and goes to church every Sunday…not because she has presented evidence that she is truthful, has integrity, has virtue…not because she strives to understand and comprehend the law…not because she has dedicated her life to healing illness and injury…not because she is what has become a rarity—a country doctor…not because she has been a pioneer in her medical specialty, or because she has sacrificed time with her family for her profession."

The point was hard to miss. Perhaps Lichter's "angel" wasn't there for any of those reasons, but all the better for him that it wasn't. That gave the defense attorney the opportunity to emphasize the merits of his client indirectly, as though her virtues were such solid facts that they could almost be taken for granted.

"The angel is there because Judge Damrell has told you she is there. The angel is there through the judge's instructions," Lichter continued with keen enthusaiasm. "I don't have to tell you she's there. It's the law that she's there. In this case, the presumption of innocence will never be removed from her shoulders because the evidence doesn't justify it."

The defense attorney then launched into a sympathetic portrayal of what the jurors had learned from the evidence presented by the prosecution. It had been shown, Lichter noted, that Fry's heart and home were open to people in need. She had taken in a woman escaping a violent husband, children in crisis, and recovering alcoholics like Mike Harvey. Lichter argued that, with such an open house, there was no need for surveillance by law enforcement. Nonetheless, case agents had flown over in airplanes, and they had done so with such

During his closing, Laurence Lichter described the presumption of innocence as an angel sitting on Dr. Fry's shoulder. Photo by Vanessa Nelson.

frequency that they couldn't remember how many times in total.

Lichter asked the jurors to see the absurdity of spying on a house whose owners would gladly open their doors and invite the cops in for coffee.

And, the defense attorney noted, that's precisely what had happened with Sergeant Ashworth. When Fry became aware that her home was being staked out, she had called up the sheriff's department herself and invited them over for a tour of the property. Ashworth, Lichter reminded the jury, "broke bread with Mollie and Dale" and "led Dale and Mollie to believe they were friends." The defense attorney paused for a moment, as though to recognize the atrocity of such an act. He then asserted that pretending to be a friend is something different than undercover work. "When you think about this case, think about the morality of that," he urged the jurors.

In addition, Lichter stressed, the jurors should consider whether it was right that "federal and state policemen camouflaged themselves as the sick" when they came to Fry's clinic. The defense attorney contended that, even if such investigative techniques were considered acceptable, they were nonetheless ineffective.

"There is only one instance we have where one visit was incriminating to Dr. Fry, but it points to *innocence*, not to *guilt*," Lichter declared. "The reason these imitation sick people were sent to Dr. Fry was to get marijuana, and we know that not one of them got *one stick* of marijuana from Dr. Fry or Dale Schafer, despite the stories, phony medical records, etcetera. And only one in ten of them did get a recommendation, based on false medical history, by fooling the doctor, who had a big heart, who had taken an oath to never reject the sick and the infirm."

As Lichter put it, the reason the agents didn't get any marijuana was because Fry was operating by the adage of "if you give a man a fish, he eats for a day, but if you teach a man to fish, he eats for a lifetime." That saying so embodied the doctor's philosophy, Lichter claimed, that she became irrepressibly enthusiastic when it was brought up by the undercover agent who posed as her patient. According to the defense attorney, this was the background story of the taped conversation the prosecution had become fond of playing for the jury.

"It starts out with Dr. Fry saying 'grow your own,'" Lichter said of the undercover tape. "We don't hear the context, what happens before or after, just this portion in evidence. We hear he gets [marijuana] from friends, but what he really wants is to control his own destiny, 'grow your own,' and Dr. Fry gets excited because this is what she believes. The agent says, 'I'm trying to get started – where do I start?' She doesn't say, 'go read a book,' or, 'go buy it on the street corner.' No. She says 'we,' then corrects herself and says that her husband has a service to help these particular people learn to grow marijuana."

Lichter then reinforced the idea that Fry encouraged her patients to grow their own marijuana because she was concerned they might bankrupt themselves or get into legal trouble by obtaining it some other way. "She wanted her patients to suffer less, not suffer more," the defense attorney explained. "She wanted to help them be legal under federal law, as she understands it."

"Objection, your honor," Pings said, on her feet in a flash. "This is not in evidence."

Judge Damrell glanced down from his bench wearily. "Stick to the evidence, counsel," he told the defense attorney.

"I'm just saying what she said on the tape and what she meant by it," Lichter responded, a mild hint of defiance in his tone. "Ms. Pings talks about Greenfire, but there's no evidence in the case about Greenfire –"

"Objection," the prosecutor cut in again, only to be ignored.

Lichter continued on as though Pings hadn't said a word, "…but if you've read the newspaper—"

"Objection!" the prosecutor shouted, though her voice had the character of a nervous laugh.

Once again the referee, Judge Damrell instructed Lichter to comment only on the evidence of the case.

"I'm commenting on common knowledge," Lichter countered, smiling his familiar half-smile.

"Stick to the evidence," the judge said succinctly.

Appearing to comply with the order, the defense attorney returned to his speech describing his client as kind and compassionate. Fry was concerned about patients who were poor, he claimed, and she wanted to help them find ways to get medicine at a reasonable cost. "There's a difference between two people caring about the same thing and an agreement between two people to participate in an enterprise to break the law," Lichter set forth. "It's no defense that the defendant tried to comply with the law, but there's certainly evidence of it."

Pings was on her feet again. "Objection!" she proclaimed loudly. "There's no evidence of that."

Judge Damrell's eyes were heavy on the defense attorney. "Counsel, stick to the evidence."

And indeed Lichter stuck to the evidence...at least for a while.

First, he went back to the much-played undercover recording of his client. "On the tape, Dr. Fry says there is some marijuana at home for her...but that she didn't water the plants," Lichter pointed out. "She noticed they were unhealthy and tried to talk to [the gardener] about it." Lichter claimed that those were the most incriminating statements the agents had gotten from Fry on the subject of whether she grew or distributed marijuana herself.

There had been other witnesses who testified about these activities, the defense attorney admitted. In his view, however, the testimony of these witnesses was suspect because they lacked credibility. "People didn't talk about Maggy the way they did about Mollie," Lichter noted about the character witnesses. "The real conspirators are Mr. Harvey and Mr. Maggy. Maybe they thought it was legal, maybe not, but their motive was to make money."

The sidelong reference to state law passed the scrutiny of the prosecutor, and Lichter continued uninterrupted. He next cast suspicion on Jeffrey Teshera, who had testified about someone from Fry's office selling him marijuana, but who had been unsure whether it was Mollie Fry herself or Heather Schafer. At any rate, Teshera's testimony about the date of the sale had been blown out of the water by the defense attorneys, who provided evidence that both Fry and Heather Schafer had been at the hospital all day long on that particular date. Logic would have it that Teshera was either confused or deliberately untruthful – either way, his testimony wasn't credible.

Instead of merely dismissing Teshera as an unreliable witness, however, Lichter played the devil's advocate. Even if the witness had merely confused the date, Lichter argued, "We don't know where [Dr. Fry] would have gotten the marijuana to sell him. Mr. Poseley said he never saw any marijuana in the office. You heard that from an honest person."

Lichter reminded the jurors that Fry had proselytized for her patients to grow their own marijuana, and was thus an unlikely dealer. The defense attorney then made his riskiest argument so far, saying, "And even if it was true, and [Teshera] did buy 1/8 ounce from Dr. Fry or Heather Schafer – he wasn't sure which one – then maybe Mollie committed some crime, but it wasn't a conspiracy." Using a series of anecdotes about receiving pharmaceutical drugs from his own doctor, Lichter suggested that his client theoretically selling marijuana to Teshera would be akin to a doctor giving a patient a sample of a prescription drug. "That doesn't fit into the goals of the conspiracy," Lichter said, concluding his point.

After all, the defense attorney stated, a charge of conspiracy involves an agreement between two or more persons. There was no reliable evidence of an agreement between the doctor and her patients, he argued, but there was evidence of a pact between Fry and her husband. "There was an agreement – for Mollie *not* to be involved in Dale's attempt to be...a farmer."

But due to the closeness between husband and wife, Lichter explained, Fry often slipped in her speech and used the term "we" when she really meant to refer only to Dale. The defense attorney speculated that the reason for his client's verbal slips dated back centuries. "There was a time in English common law when a woman's identity was merged with that of her husband, and this tendency still exists psychologically for a lot of women," Lichter lectured. "Her husband had given up much of his lucrative business for her. Husband and wife are so intertwined in a common property state, but it involves more than this for conspiracy. What existed between Dr. Fry and Dale Schafer was not conspiracy – it was love."

Lichter's words began to burn at this point, seemingly heated by both passion and outrage. "What's twisted in this case is that his love for her has been twisted into an accusation of criminal conspiracy –
286

how can that be?" the defense attorney demanded from the mute jury. "He got involved for her sake, and, later, for the sake of her patients. How can that ever be twisted to be used against him?"

The defense attorney then reinforced his point with an unexpected analogy. "At the same time federal agents were meeting with local law enforcement and sneaking around the defendants' home, other people were planning to knock buildings down," he told the jurors, adding that they might want to consider if their tax money was used wisely in this instance. "9/11 – *that* was a conspiracy, not what happened between Mollie and Dale."

Waxing philosophical for a moment, Lichter reflected about the saying that liberty is always unfinished business. For this reason, he asserted, his client's activist leanings were a positive, and even patriotic, thing. Activism, he argued, changes the world for the better. "That's how this country works, if a law isn't working," Lichter declared. "If this country didn't do this, we'd still have slavery. Years after the last black man got the right to vote did the first woman get the right—"

Pings could feel the subject of jury nullification nearing, and she broke in with a vigorous objection.

Judge Damrell was not quite as certain as the prosecutor, but intended to be thoroughly cautious nonetheless. "I don't know where this is going," he said to Lichter. "*I* instruct the jury to follow the law as *I* instruct it."

"I don't think anyone doubts juries are better with women on it," Lichter countered, continuing on with his statements. "But, as I was saying, liberty is unfinished business. This case requires wisdom and a little bit of courage."

Looking up at the jurors, Lichter addressed them directly. "Ultimately, you're the ones who sit as judges," he said in a tone of high emotion. "You decide whether Mollie Fry is a criminal, or a frail human being who falls short of criminal activity. "

The defense attorney then capitalized on the importance of the jury's decision. It was one of the few things in this technologically advanced world, he claimed, that couldn't be computerized. "There's a reason, in modern society, that we still have trials with juries," Lichter said with reverence. "A computer has not compassion, sympathy for human suffering...cannot hold back tears or let them flow, cannot understand love, cannot tuck children into bed at night with a kiss. A computer can't experience what humans do – suffering, or the shared rhythms of another's heartbeat. A person is flesh and can understand what is important to another flesh."

In an odd bit if science fiction reverie, Lichter began to contemplate the future of medicine – largely, that the National Institute of Health and the big pharmaceutical companies would develop tiny robots that could be implanted in our bodies to constantly repair them from within. "It will be run through our cooperative system that rewards people with money," Lichter speculated. "But that won't happen for Dr. Fry. She was interested in the smallest ways to help people with their health. We need doctors like Dr. Fry who say to other doctors, 'The emperor wears no clothes. There are better ways and better medicines. There are cheaper ways to medicate—'"

"Objection, your honor," Pings cut in, her brow furrowed from the effort of following Lichter through his futuristic fantasies and into another attempt to sermonize on the medicinal virtues of marijuana.

"Counsel, you were over the line again," Judge Damrell said, his voice deepening into tones of warning. "The jury is to disregard those comments."

Thus blocked, Lichter turned back to discussing the credibility of the prosecution's witnesses. "As you watched them up on the witness stand, couldn't you *smell* which witnesses were telling the truth?"

What happened next was swift and chaotic. The defense attorney began drawing, admittedly, from the symbolism used in this author's published reports of Maggy's testimony. Describing the witness's background in mortuary science and proclivity for hanging upside down, Lichter reconstructed a classic horror-tale creature. "He is the very image of a vampire!" the defense attorney declared emphatically.

The jury box and the gallery broke out in what appeared to be a round of involuntary laughter, which, though the giggles were quickly stifled, put the courtroom marshals on alert. They fixed on a scapegoat for the prohibited mirth, and they quickly crowded into the aisleway

288

around the row in which she was seated, demanding that she leave the courtroom immediately. "What...me?" the target asked incredulously, but her words of disbelief were taken only as resistance and she was threatened with forcible removal from her seat. In shock, she stumbled out to the aisle with her cane, tripping dreadfully over another woman with a walker who sat in the aisle seat.

A few compassionate observers followed the accused giggler out into the hallway, where she had been left to shed tears of dismay at her harsh and inexplicable banishment. Those who remained in the courtroom heard Lichter move on to discredit real estate appraiser Tod Zimmerman's testimony, using much less colorful imagery.

The defense attorney backed up his contention with a few points. First of all, he said, Zimmerman had vowed up to the very end of his testimony that there had been two greenhouses on the defendants' property, when, in reality, there was only ever one greenhouse. Plus, Lichter added, this witness had a motive to lie about the defendants because he had a financial interest in their house being taken away by the government. "He actually benefits financially from forfeiture," Lichter said with a flourish of revelation. "He was quick to call the police, and I don't think it was out of any kind of regard for the children, do you?" he asked the jury rhetorically.

"I'll make your work easy – compare the quality of the prosecution's witnesses versus the quality of the defense's witnesses," he said, still speaking directly and intently to the jurors. "Think about what a criminal is, and don't be afraid to find 'not guilty.'"

It sounded like it was going to be the end of his closing argument, but it wasn't. Lichter still had more to say. In fact, he had a lot more to say...but was prevented from saying most of what he intended.

He got in some final rhetoric about the angel on Fry's shoulder. "Since we have the presumption of innocence and proof beyond reasonable doubt, we have a bias in this room, but not one I'm ashamed of – it's a bias toward *freedom*," he announced. "There is an angel on her shoulder – the presumption of innocence that remains there until and unless all of you decide to knock her off."

Lichter also got in a few high-minded quotes, such as the classic, "If we are to keep our democracy, there is one commandment – we shall not ration justice." But when he began to talk about quotes he had read on the courthouse steps, it appeared that he had somehow wandered into taboo territory.

"Each day that I enter this beautiful building, I find that I am not like Tony Serra," Lichter mused. "I am not looking up at the sculpture. I am more like the little tramp in the Charlie Chaplin movie, shuffling along looking at the sayings that are engraved on the ground." The defense attorney hesitated for a moment, perhaps giving the jurors a chance to consider their own recollections of these etched quotes, then continued. "One of the building's engravings reads: 'Fairness is what justice really is.' Another, 'There are not enough jails, not enough police—'"

Pings couldn't take any more. "Objection, your honor!"

Judge Damrell's voice was heavy, fatigued. "The stones on the building are not the law the jury will consider," he commented grimly.

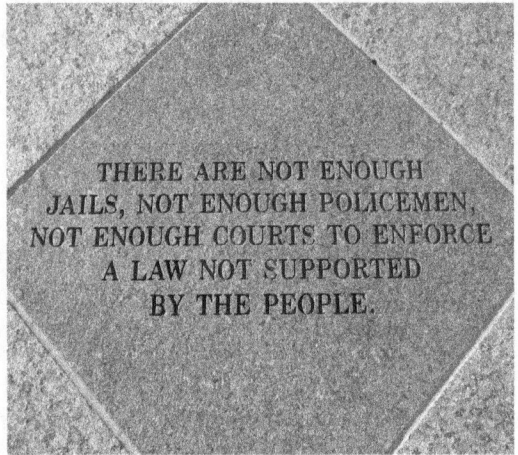

THERE ARE NOT ENOUGH JAILS, NOT ENOUGH POLICEMEN, NOT ENOUGH COURTS TO ENFORCE A LAW NOT SUPPORTED BY THE PEOPLE.

"I will be happy to proffer the rest to the court," the prosecutor announced, eager to avoid a reading of the quotations.

Laurence Lichter's closing statements were cut off when he referenced the engravings at the courthouse entrance.
Photo by Vanessa Nelson.

Lichter wasn't giving up. "It isn't appropriate for closing argument?"

"Yes," the judge conceded, "but you're going overboard."

Lichter threw in one more quote, looking as though he was sweeping it under the rug. "'In a civilized world, law floats in a sea of ethics,'" he blurted out, before leaving the stones to rest.

For a few sentences thereafter, Lichter spoke in generalized ideals, and the prosecutor and judge watched him with calm expectance. "Man does not defer to woman, or woman to man – in front of a jury, you are all equals," he said in reverence. "Please focus on wisdom, not on power. I know everybody wants to go home. What's important is that the justices of the Supreme Court are very seldom unanimous. It was 6 to 3, I believe, in a recent relevant decision."

Although the defense attorney didn't dare to flesh it out, his vague comment referred to the 2005 U.S. Supreme Court ruling in Raich v. Gonzales. This decision gave the government standing to enforce the federal prohibition of marijuana regardless of state law allowing for medicinal use. It was a tremendous disappointment to medical marijuana activists, and also the beginning of a surge of cases pushed forward in the federal courts. The Raich ruling even precipitated the prosecution of Fry and Dale Schafer themselves, as they were indicted and arrested just days after the decision. Given Judge Damrell's tightening impatience, trying to explain the Raich case in his closing argument might well have landed Lichter with a charge of contempt.

But the defense attorney was bold enough to attempt to describe another case he was forbidden to mention. He began to transport his listeners back to William Penn's heresy trial in England, when the jury refused to issue a guilty verdict because they did not believe the defendant should be imprisoned merely for giving a political lecture. The evidence against Penn had been overwhelming, and the trial was expected to be merely a matter of going through the motions. However, everything got thrown off track when the jury decided to acquit because they did not believe in the law under which the defendant had been charged.

This concept, called jury nullification, led to the jurors in Penn's trial being imprisoned without food or drink. When the famous patriot came to the American colonies, however, his contribution to the developing legal system was to make sure that no one would be punished for jury nullification in the United States. And although that ideal holds true, it is a whispered truth that's seldom, if ever, permitted to be explained to the jury in a courtroom. The feared consequence of such an explanation is that it might be used to influence the jurors – influence them, as it turns out, to make a decision that is based on something more fundamental than the evidence presented in one specific case.

Since it allows citizens to make choices about the laws that govern them and their peers, jury nullification could easily be seen as an integral part of the democratic process. But it also threatens the rigid power structure of the prosecution and the judge, and so jury nullification has become a concealed concept. If it's part of the family of democratic processes, it's not a well-known member. It's more like democracy's crazy aunt who's kept up in the attic and out of sight. Every now and then, people hear it bumping around, but it's never officially brought out and shown. The only glimpse of it the jury got in Lichter's closing argument was a measly half-sentence. "William Penn," the defense attorney began, "he was arrested for heresy and the jurors were punished for—"

Pings took no chances, jumping to her feet as soon as she heard the patriot's name. "I object to this," she said firmly to the judge.

Lichter gave a glance back at Pings, and quickly extended a finger. It was, however, his index finger, and it signified a request for what he said next. "Just one more sentence," he told the prosecutor, as though reassuring her.

"Counsel, it's outrageous!" Judge Damrell bellowed down. "I think you know it's not a proper argument."

Having pushed his boundaries to their breaking point, Lichter turned back to the jury and finished up his speech. "My faith is in you," he concluded. "You know the answers. You've smelled the truth. You see the angel on her shoulder." He gave another of his endearingly quirky half-smiles, then turned and went back to his seat.

Judge Damrell had done his best to keep his cool in front of the jurors, but after they filed out of the room, he let the sparks fly. "Counsel, I find it very ironic that you did a very good job of stating the merits of the government's case," he said sourly to Lichter. "The jury nullification comment…this is not one of those cases. This is a case to be decided on the evidence. This is totally unnecessary."

Serra spoke up then, quizzical in the face of the judge's anger. "I said my client was guilty of growing less than a hundred plants – how is that jury nullification?"

Judge Damrell shook his head. When he spoke, he put the full emphasis of forceful enunciation into the two words he spoke. "It's unfortunate," he said to the defense attorneys. And with that he rose and walked out of the courtroom for a break.

Prosecution's Rebuttal: *Be You Never So High*

When it came to closing statements, the prosecution got the last word. Since the burden of proof was on the government, its side was given the chance to make a speech rebutting what the defense attorneys had said in their final remarks to the jury. And, of course, Pings seized the opportunity readily.

"We are not here about the defendant Mr. Schafer's love for his wife," the prosecutor began. "We are here about marijuana, a drug being sold hand-to-hand…a drug that's clandestine, illegal."

Pings continued, her tone containing an implied appeal to common sense. "This case is about $450 kits with clones," she asserted. "This case is about checks to U.S. bank accounts in Mr. Schafer's name so that everyone could later pretend it was for legal fees. It's about posting photos of their harvest on the internet. It's about advertising on hard rock radio stations."

The prosecutor was then interrupted by a jolt of banging sounds, as the judge, without comment, began to loudly adjust his microphone. She paused in mid-thought, waiting calmly to resume. And when the auditory domain was hers once again, the prosecutor attacked Fry's statements to the undercover agent about the legality of marijuana-growing cooperatives.

"She says 'oh, you can have these small little grows,' and even if that was true, *even if that was true*, she doesn't talk about small groups," Pings said of Fry. "She thinks she is different and the law doesn't apply to her."

The prosecutor mocked the claims that Fry was a humanitarian, saying that she perverted the adage: 'you give a man a fish, he eats for a day; you teach a man to fish, he eats for a lifetime.' Dr. Fry's version was profit-oriented, Pings professed, and it came through loud and clear on the undercover tapes. "She's offering to sell him a fishing pole for $450!"

Re-emphasizing the notion of greed was still on the prosecutor's agenda, but it was also imperative for her to defend the conduct of her witnesses. "The defense called them 'suffering imitators,'" Pings said, referencing the officers who infiltrated the seminars run by Heather Schafer. "Did Agent Nolan look sick or unhealthy? Assume what you will about being able-bodied, about his physical fitness. He used a piece of paper that he whited-out and Xeroxed. There is nothing wrong with what he did."

Pings made her declaration using her most reasonable voice, stressing each word. "Law enforcement is allowed to use undercover tactics."

The prosecutor addressed another of the defense's points – that the undercover agent who drew Fry into the recorded conversation about cultivation had, ultimately, not walked away with marijuana. However damaging the words on the tape might be, the agent had gained only speech from the endeavor. The prosecutor challenged this notion by suggesting the agent had instead been a victim of a bait-and-switch technique.

Rather than simply selling a baggie of marijuana, Pings argued, Fry had been focused on arranging the sale of a house-call consultation service in addition to dramatically overpriced grow equipment. "It's like going to Circuit City for a TV, and you get hustled for a new deal," the prosecutor said, fashioning an analogy to which the jury was likely to relate.

When it came to the defense's speculations about the motives of the real estate appraiser, Pings threw up her arms. It was a hopeless conspiracy theory, as she saw it. "There's no evidence he had something to gain by calling the sheriff to report these clones growing," Pings said of Zimmerman. She then smiled at the jurors and scoffed, "If you understand the theory, you're way ahead of me."

The prosecutor even made an effort to strengthen the weakest links in her case, saying the defense attorneys had abused witnesses like Sean Cramblett, Mike Harvey and Paul Maggy. "Mr. Serra came in here and raised his voice and called people names," Pings recounted. "Mr. Lichter came in and, not so loudly, called people names. Today you heard: liars, vampires, vipers, rats."

This was all unfair language, in the prosecutor's view, to describe people who had helped law enforcement to identify and stop criminal behavior. She explained to the jury, with gravity in her voice, "The government makes deals with people to get information about what happens inside the operation or the organization."

Pings agued that witnesses like Cramblett, Harvey and Maggy had done exactly that – they were able to tell federal agents about what was hidden from sheriff's deputies when they came to inspect the defendants' property. Without these "rat" witnesses, Pings pointed out, investigators may not have had a clue about the true extent of the defendants' cultivation.

The prosecutor wondered aloud about what it really meant to refer to these witnesses as rats. "If you're called a rat, it means you're not loyal," she reflected. "If you were loyal, you would have gone in and lied to the grand jury."

Maggy may have gotten some time off his sentence in exchange for his testimony, but Pings stated that he didn't get off scot-free – he served over a year in jail and then reformed his behavior. "Mr Maggy moved out of the marijuana lifestyle and on to a new family," the prosecutor noted. "He's called a liar – where are the lies?"

As for Harvey, Pings couldn't swallow the idea that he had been in charge of the marijuana distribution operation. She urged the jury to similarly reject this theory. "If Mr. Harvey was running this organization, he didn't do a very good job," the prosecutor sneered. The money had all gone to the defendants, she argued, through checks made out to Dale Schafer and occasionally endorsed by Fry.

"They came in here and called him a thief," Pings said of the defense's allegations against Harvey. "There's no evidence of that about Mr. Harvey."

The prosecutor then made a sly jab at the defendants' personal judgment. "Maybe you wouldn't hire him to babysit *your* kids, but that doesn't mean he's untruthful," she commented about Harvey.

Pings also recalled that the defense had reinforced the idea that Zimmerman and Jeffrey Teshera were robbers, calling the accusations hypocritical. "It's a little ironic, when they're the ones selling marijuana to criminals," she said of the defendants. "These are *their* people. We didn't choose them."

Besides, Pings argued, Zimmerman had been up front about his record. "He admitted to you about his high school pranks," she maintained. "But this isn't about high school."

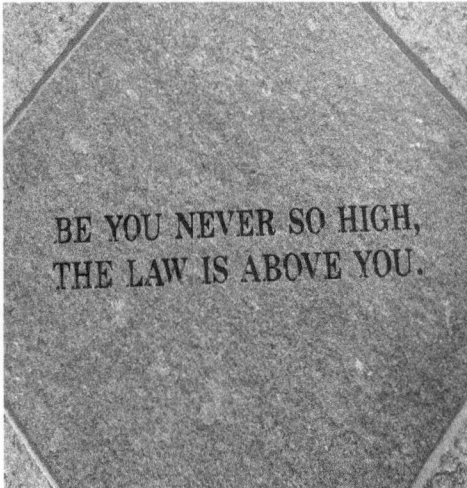

During her rebuttal, prosecutor Anne Pings successfully quoted the courthouse engravings. Photo by Vanessa Nelson.

It was, Pings said in a tone of great dismay, about marijuana being recommended to minors and to people with criminal cases. It was also, she reminded the jurors, about greed and a hydroponics business that put a 70% markup on every single product. "[The defendants] came out way ahead of where they started when he had a worker's compensation practice," the prosecutor claimed.

"Mr. Lichter talked about the quotes on the courthouse steps," Pings continued, appropriating her opponent's tactics. "My favorite quote is: 'Be you never so high the law is above you.'"

She immediately leveraged this line into an attack on the defendants. "These people think they are above the law. They are so self-important, so arrogant, that they think they must be victims of some government plot straight from Washington D.C.!"

Pings tried to show that the developments in the case had been commonplace. "Young people get arrested for marijuana all the time," she began.

"Objection!" Serra cut in. "This is outside the case."

Judge Damrell, however, disagreed. He allowed the prosecutor to continue her argument.

"Young people get arrested for marijuana all the time," Pings repeated.

Lichter then interrupted with his own clever objection. "Not in *federal* court," he pointed out, subtly attempting to raise the issue of jurisdiction.

With a deeper frown this time, the judge again instructed the prosecutor to go on.

"People in rural areas get arrested for growing marijuana all the time," Pings continued. "They sent marijuana, the drug, through an interstate mail service! They were practically begging for arrest. They never stop! The calls were coming in from Mr. Zimmerman, from the UPS. Was Agent Keefe supposed to just sit there with his hands over his eyes?"

Pings upheld the argument that the case was not an attempt to thwart Schafer's run for District Attorney. "The investigation was not because of his campaign for D.A. That train had left the station nine months earlier when Agent Keefe got the call from UPS." The prosecutor acknowledged the impact of Heather Schafer's statement that the family was cleaning out the house due to the campaign. "It's why they did the warrant then," Pings said of the agents. "It's not why they did the case."

And the case itself, the prosecutor reiterated, was essentially a simple one. "It's about growing marijuana. It's about distributing marijuana. Both defendants have told you, from their own mouths, that's what they did." Pings then ended with the phrase that had become the mantra of her closing statements. "They told you they grew, they distributed, they're guilty."

As one would expect, Pings had used her considerable powers of inclusiveness. That is to say, she had skillfully conveyed the notion that she and the jurors alone comprised the in-crowd. They shared the bond of being the only people in the courtroom smart and sensible enough to be hip to truth and to resist being blinded by illusion. In doing so, the prosecutor was able to connect with the jurors with a closeness that gave her a distinct advantage. The defense had asked the jury for compassion, but Pings appealed to something much more powerful. She reached to the jurors at the places they were most vulnerable – through human vanity and through the pleasure of being received into a clique. She did not issue a challenge for the jurors, as the defense attorneys had done. Rather, Pings flattered them. Every sentence of her closing was delivered in a way that tightened the feeling of intimacy and inclusion, and she was remarkably convincing.

The courtroom had been packed extraordinarily full for the closing statements, but most of the audience consisted of the defendants' friends and family members. This imbalance, in fact, had been maintained for the majority of the trial. Aside from a sprinkling of fellow prosecutors, who flowed in and out as their schedules allowed, Anne Pings had few allies seated behind her. But during her closing remarks, she had one particularly special supporter in the audience.

An elderly woman sat in the aisle seat of the second row behind the prosecution's table, and during the break between closing statements, Pings had come out to the gallery to greet her warmly. The old woman's daughter, as it turned out, was one of the prosecutor's close friends and classmates. She had come to see Pings perform her final appeal to the jury, and she sat with a mixture of composure and enthusiasm as she drank in the spectacle. Nevertheless, the old woman sat alone – her daughter had been unable to come. She had been stricken with breast cancer, but the same disease that had transformed the defendant's world had claimed the life of the prosecutor's friend.

This fact was just a footnote to the day's proceedings, in that it did not impact them directly. Nonetheless, when the old woman disclosed the story to the curious listeners in the gallery, she instilled a poignant sense of tragedy that endured throughout the afternoon of jury deliberation and remained for the announcement of verdict.

The Verdict, With A Quickness

Although the morning's speeches had been quick-paced and exciting, the final afternoon of the trial lost that momentum. The reading of the jury instructions provided quite a lull, and these recitations crawled past the noon hour without hurry. Many of those in the gallery appeared eager for their mid-day meal by the time Judge Damrell got to the end of the document.

There were no big surprises here. For the most part, the jury instructions were standard and expected. After detailing the charges and their necessary elements, the judge covered the issue of admissible and inadmissible evidence. Regarding testimony or exhibits that mentioned the medical uses of marijuana, the judge explained, "It was admitted for the limited purpose of providing context for which evidence is inextricably intertwined." Continuing, the jury instructions got less ambiguous. "You cannot consider the claim that the defendants were manufacturing marijuana for medical purposes. Federal law prohibits the possession, manufacturing, and distribution of marijuana for any purpose."

After the reading finally concluded, the jurors proper were separated from the alternates and escorted to the room where they would begin deliberations following lunch. Judge and counsel remained behind for a moment to address some housekeeping matters.

Largely, the discussion concerned the locations and arrangements for various exhibits the jury might request to view during deliberations. Of key concern was which pieces of evidence would be put in the jury room for independent examination and which pieces of evidence would not. Pings then began to speak about some particular evidence:

301

marijuana and grow equipment seized during the raid on the defendants' property. "Your honor, we have nutrients, we have scales, controlled substance—"

"That's not going in," Judge Damrell stated firmly and abruptly.

Pings chuckled. "That's not what I'm asking," she said, going on to inform the judge that these materials would be held just off site, in an adjacent building.

"The scales can go in," the judge decided, relaxing a little. "Just not the marijuana."

Court then recessed for lunch, and remained recessed for deliberations. The process of deciding the verdicts was expected to be a lengthy one, given the complexities of the charges and the required findings. In their overview format, the counts seemed simple and fairly straightforward – both defendants were charged with the exact same crimes, two counts that related to the manufacture and distribution of marijuana. But the charges were much more complicated than this description.

The first was Count 1, a conspiracy charge for the manufacture and distribution of marijuana during the time between August 1999 and September 2001. This charge did not require that an actual crime be accomplished, but only that there was an agreement between two or more persons to commit a crime. To be found guilty, a defendant had to have become part of the conspiracy while knowing its goals and taking steps towards accomplishing them. In his instructions, the judge clarified that aiding and abetting made someone part of the conspiracy.

There were three subsections of the conspiracy charge, and guilt on each part could be determined independently from the others. These were the alleged goals of the conspiracy, and they included: distribution of processed marijuana, the manufacture of marijuana plants, and the distribution of marijuana plants. A guilty verdict on the count as a whole would require a finding of guilt on at least one of these elements.

If the jurors found guilt on either or both of the last two goals of the conspiracy, which involved marijuana *plants*, they would then make a finding on whether or not the number of plants in question exceeded a hundred. This decision would be made separately regarding the manufacturing and distribution elements.

As for Count 2, it was much less complex. It was a charge for the actual manufacture of marijuana, which had to be done knowingly by the defendant to have a finding of guilt. In the event of such a verdict, jurors once again had to determine if the number of plants actually cultivated was over a hundred.

Accounting for all of the determinations to be made, jurors had a maximum of sixteen decisions to agree upon. They had to reach verdicts regarding both of the counts and the three goals of the conspiracy charge, and, if there were conclusions of guilt, they faced three more decisions about plant counts. The jury had to go through this process with consideration of each defendant, and then fill out the verdict and finding forms once the group reached unanimous agreement. And all of this could only occur after first making another crucial decision – choosing a foreperson.

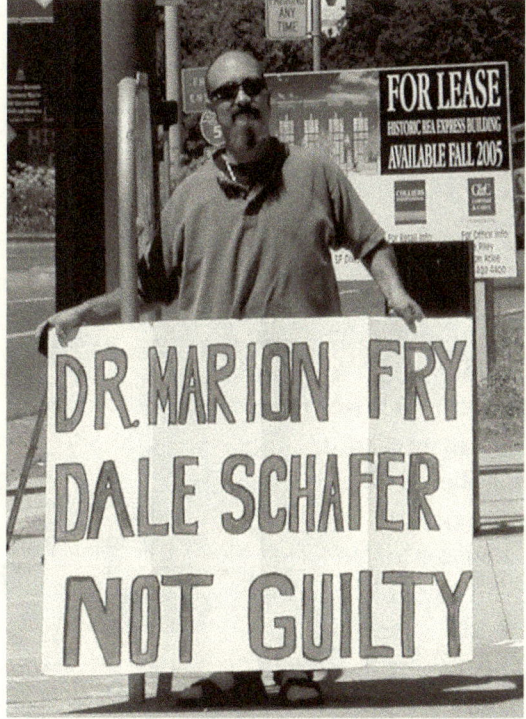

At an intersection in front of the courthouse, a supporter of the defendants displayed an optimistic prediction of the verdict. Photo by Vanessa Nelson.

With so many details for the jury to discuss and agree upon, they were expected to deliberate for a considerable length of time. It was therefore a surprise when, little more than an hour later, the jurors sent a note to the judge indicating that they had a question about determining plant numbers. They wanted to know if all of the plants had to be alive at the same time to be included in the count. Instead of answering with an explanation, however, Judge Damrell referred them to the appropriate section in the instructions. He then sent them back to the jury room to read these instructions and continue deliberating.

The news was a bad sign for the defense. After all, the jury was only to consider the issue of plant numbers if a guilty verdict had already been reached. Of course, it seemed improbable that the jurors had all settled in and come to agreement so quickly – to do so would require accord so precise it would nearly have to be choreographed. It could be that the jurors were pondering details in an exploratory way, and had stumbled accidentally into a theoretical discussion of the protocol for counting plants. To do so, however, would require optimism so expansive that it pushed the bounds of realism.

Fry knew the omen well, and she cried heavily in the hallway outside the courtroom as the deliberations wrapped up. "It's all my fault, it's all my fault," she blubbered with tearful desperation into the shoulder of a friend, who held her and gently asked the reason for her guilt. "Because I got cancer," Fry admitted

Dr. Fry and her daughter Caroline shared moments of bonding and concern during the jury deliberation. Photo by Vanessa Nelson.

with soft tones of self-blame, choking on her sobbed words. "That's what started all of this."

"Oh yeah, Mollie, that's right – why did you have to go and get cancer? I told you not to do that," the friend said, playfully demonstrating to Fry that she was being far too hard on herself. The sweet little joke inspired a pained attempt at a smile from the doctor, who began trying to pull herself together to brace for the verdict.

In fact, the defendants braced themselves together, as a family. Parent and child, brother and sister, husband and wife, all hugged and
304

held hands tearfully as they waited. There was not enough comfort in the world to *erase* the agony of those few hours of limbo, but the love of family was certainly enough to *minimize* it. There was an end to the wondering, however, and it arrived with an astonishing quickness.

Just over an hour after returning to the deliberation room, the jurors issued their announcement – they had reached their verdicts. Parties were gathered up and attorneys summoned to the courtroom, and by approximately 4:30pm the jurors entered to deliver their fateful news. The process of deliberation, all told, had taken just a couple hours.

The courtroom was packed with observers, who rose and watched with keen interest as the jurors filed into their seats, one by one. Anxious to read destiny into facial expressions, some observers scrutinized the jurors and whispered their predictions to each other. The court then quieted and came to order, at which point the foreperson identified herself and handed over the verdict sheets. The documents were passed to Judge Damrell, who looked them over thoroughly but without expression. The judge then glanced up, ordering the defendants to rise for the verdict. He handed the documents to his clerk to read aloud.

This was the moment of truth, and the buzzing pulse of anxiety in the room was nearly overpowering. The clerk began to read, beginning with the charges against Fry, and the tension coagulated.

First came a guilty verdict, and the moment of its announcement was punctuated by the eruption of heartbroken sobs in the gallery. More and more declarations of guilt followed, one right on the heels of the other in what became like a repetitive chant of condemnation. The plaintive crying continued throughout the reading of the verdicts, and when it finally came to an end, both defendants had been found guilty on all charges and all elements.

The findings on the plant counts turned out to be nearly as damning, offering just a single point of consolation. The jury found that the plant number exceeded one hundred in all instances except one – the substantive cultivation charge against Fry was determined to have involved less than a hundred plants. It was a disappointingly small slice of vindication to be served, sliver-thin and bittersweet.

Although juror interviews would be a more accurate measure, it seems likely that this finding is directly related to Fry's statement on an undercover surveillance tape that 45 plants had died under the care of her semi-permanent houseguest. On the tape, Fry said she "tried to help" Harvey, a claim the prosecution repeatedly painted as an admission that Fry assisted in the cultivation of the plants. Though a matter of interpretation, this tape was essentially the only evidence that linked Fry to marijuana cultivation.

Dr. Fry broke into tears as the verdict was announced. Sketch by Dr. Care.

Serra requested that the jury be polled, and, right down the rows, each juror affirmed the verdicts. The court clerk then ceremonially declared the obvious to the judge, "The verdict is unanimous, your honor."

Judge Damrell then began expressing his appreciation to the jurors. "This case was relatively brief, as far as criminal cases go, but it was charged with emotion," he summarized. "It was obvious there were strong feelings expressed in the courtroom. A case like this is not easy. The law is not always easy."

Nonetheless, the judge made it clear to the jurors that the outcome was one of value. "The court respects your verdict," he assured them. "The community respects your verdict."

The judge then listed the difficult things the jurors had done: coming together as strangers to sit on a case for nearly three weeks, deliberating in the jury room and coming to a unanimous verdict. "These are not easy tasks," Judge Damrell assessed, turning to address the significance of these actions. "They are a vindication of our system of justice," he pronounced.

The Verdict, With A Quickness

After another of the judge's gushes of gratitude, the jurors were excused and left the room in single file. Once the door shut behind the departed jurors, it was time for the second heightening of tension. Whispered voices and worried eyes wondered if the defendants would be taken immediately into custody.

The judge ordered Fry and Schafer to come forward to the podium in front of his bench, and they complied. Fry put herself between her husband and Lichter, her hands linked with both men as she stood up straight and waited.

After a formal reading of the new convictions, Judge Damrell told Fry and Schafer that he was referring them to probation. There, they would provide information to be included in a report that would assist him with the sentencing. The supporters in the audience listened breathlessly, mixed as they were amongst a little crowd of federal prosecutors and a heavier handful of prosecutors-in-training. In the first row of the gallery seats, the children sat and watched, riveted by the moment. Their faces were simultaneously brave, apprehensive and lamenting, as they waited to see if their parents would be snatched away. For a few moments, it seemed like time flowed thin and evaporated.

Finally, the judge came to the matter of custody. "I will allow you to remain at liberty," he said plainly. "The government hasn't commented, but that is my ruling."

Judge Damrell proposed a sentencing date in late October, but offered to push it back at the defense counsel's request. The new date nearly settled into the middle of November, but on final thought the judge made another delay. "Let's do it *after* Thanksgiving," he suggested pleasantly. The hearing was then scheduled for November 26th at 10am in his courtroom.

"Anything further?" he asked the attorneys.

There was just one thing. "Thank you for allowing them out," Serra said graciously as the proceedings wrapped up.

Outside the courthouse, several news reporters hovered in anticipation of the defendants' statements to the press. Schafer inserted a quick commentary. "They don't allow you to defend yourself," he claimed of U.S. District Court.

Fry was quick to pick up that idea and run with it. "They interpreted the laws retroactively," she complained, "which means I would have had to been psychic to know which laws to follow at the time." She scoffed at the thought, "I'm sorry – I'm a really talented *physician*, but I'm not a *psychic*."

Serra echoed these thoughts, but through his broadly historical perspective. "The federal law, with respect to medical marijuana, is in the Dark Ages," he reflected, "and this was a dark day in the Dark Ages."

It was not, however, the final word. "On an appellate level, I believe we will be vindicated," the defense attorney predicted, only to be met with the question of whether Fry and Schafer would be allowed to remain out of custody during appeal. "Since this is a meritorious issue, I believe the answer is yes," he replied.

"This was a compassionate judge – he understands their frailties," Serra added.

Still, at the end of the day, the defendants were in a very unfortunate position. It was a harrowing, years-long struggle, and they emerged as convicts facing mandatory minimum prison sentences. It left one to wonder – considering the devastating setback, had Mollie Fry's famous faith been shaken?

"I still believe that God is in my corner," she said to reporters with a kind of gritty optimism. "And I still believe that God is going to allow my children to survive without a mother."

The Road to Sentencing

Judge Damrell had intended for Fry and Schafer to be sentenced after the Thanksgiving holiday, but he couldn't have known *how long* afterwards it would be.

Beginning in November, the hearing date underwent a long series of delays. Winter began and progressed, the new year arrived, and gradually, the emergence of spring became undeniable. Each change of season, it seemed, brought a new postponement.

At the end of February 2008, over six months after the verdict was handed down, the defendants and their attorneys finally came before Judge Damrell. However, the appearance was not a sentencing hearing. Rather, Serra and Lichter were asking for the judge to consider a pair of pre-sentencing motions.

One of these motions was a request to vacate the verdict and order a new trial, a proposal the defense attorneys justified with the results of some recent polling of the jury. Investigating the reasons behind a jury's verdict is, as Lichter put it, "unusual," and it is undoubtedly a sensitive matter. Much care must be taken to protect the confidentiality in the decision-making process, and, as such, the defense attorneys filed the motion under seal. Nonetheless, the *general* issues raised by the jury polling were argued on public record, and the issue of financial gain emerged as the central one.

Fry seemed both amused and incredulous upon learning that the jury had thought her to be wealthy. Before the hearing, while adjusting her youngest son's tie, she half-humorously mentioned one of the conclusions of the jury poll. "They said my kids looked like little rich kids," she revealed about the jurors' comments.

Indeed, the Fry/Schafer flock was always properly attired and groomed for court, sitting together demurely in the front row of the gallery during the trial. Perhaps skeptical that teenaged siblings could be so well-dressed and well-behaved, it seemed that the jurors had been suspicious of these appearances. From over in the jury box, they could smell money in the neatly straightened ties and the nice haircuts. Certainly the defendants' offspring had the sweet smiles and the wholesome good looks of a family in a magazine advertisement, but some jurors couldn't discern that the sunny glow came from care rather than currency.

According to the defense attorneys, however, it wasn't merely the appearance of the children that led a few jurors to the conclusion that Fry and Schafer were greedy. After all, Pings used plenty of speculative arithmetic in her rhetoric at trial, especially while cross-examining Schafer. These calculations were slanted to suggest a strong profit motive, and the defense attorneys claimed they were not prepared to adequately counter the questioning because the subject wasn't even supposed to come up.

Shortly before sentencing, Dr. Fry gave a whisper of reassurance to her youngest son Cody. Photo by Vanessa Nelson.

Lichter reminded the judge that the legitimacy of Fry's medical practice was ruled an irrelevant topic for trial, and this ruling presumably included speculation about whether her patient fees were reasonable compensation or greedy exploitation.

Serra characterized the situation more dramatically. "They implicitly and explicitly attributed the motive to greed with respect to my client," he said of the government. "They got their side in to the jury. It was because you tied our hands that we were not allowed with full force and vigor to present *our* side to the jury."

The Fry/Schafer children, as it turned out, may have been too well groomed for the jury's taste. Photo by Vanessa Nelson.

The government, naturally, had a different view. The validity and the profits of Fry's practice had been irrelevant, the prosecution argued, but only so long as the defense didn't open the door and bring up the topic for self-serving purposes. Prosecutor Flynn took up the final statements on this topic, reading to the judge in a declaratory voice, "It was the defense who asked on direct examination about the motive of greed," he pointed out. "The recommendation income directly refuted the defendant's self-serving testimony."

Furthermore, Flynn continued, the motion was invalid because it was made 182 days after the verdict and was not based on any new information, as required by the evidence code. He then went the extra step and clarified that statements from the jurors do not qualify as new information under federal law.

Judge Damrell confirmed that the motion was late, and rejected the notion that there had been any misconduct with the presentation of evidence. "The defense asked about financial versus charity motives, the government had a proper cross-examination, and the defense never raised an objection," he summarized. At any rate, he said, he couldn't grant the motion because of a precedent set by the Tanner case, which "prohibits this or any court to examine the decision process of a jury to overturn the verdict."

The defense's second motion involved the concept of sentencing entrapment, and was aimed at reducing the jury's findings to less than a hundred plants for both Fry and Schafer. The argument here was that Sergeant Ashworth of the El Dorado County Sheriff's Department had acted as a federal agent by working with the DEA throughout 2001, while at the same time encouraging the defendants to grow the crop that would finally bring their cumulative plant count up to the hundred-mark.

As revealed during trial, Ashworth had visited Fry and Schafer in 1999 and 2000 at the defendants' request – they wanted the sheriff to examine their grow and verify that it was in compliance with law enforcement guidelines for medical marijuana. Fry and Schafer, of course, had no clue that these yearly plant counts were part of a running total that would ultimately be prosecuted by the federal government. All they knew was that their grow was visited and approved by the friendly sheriff who always extended his visit with a cup of coffee and casual conversation. And the defendants certainly didn't imagine that their amiable sheriff buddy was working in tandem with the DEA in 2001 when he encouraged them to grow their final crop, which brought the cumulative plant count up to the level that could earn them a mandatory minimum prison sentence.

This was entrapment, the defense agued, and, more specifically, it was *sentencing* entrapment. That is to say, the undercover agent had lured his targets into increasing their activity so that they would qualify for a higher tier of punishment when prosecuted.

"In each of the three years, 1999-2001, Ashworth observed the defendants growing marijuana, and did not arrest them or seize their crops," the motion stated. "Instead, he actively encouraged it…repeatedly assuring them they were complying with the law."

312

The motion asked the judge to make a ruling that would reduce the plant number in the defendants' convictions to less than a hundred, and thereby avoid the mandatory minimum sentence. The government questioned whether such a move was legally permitted. "It is not clear whether the court is authorized to make a post-trial finding of plant quantity which contradicts the jury's finding," the prosecutors responded in an opposition brief.

Pings in particular scoffed at the viability of the defense's argument. "This is analogous to a motorist who speeds on the freeway everyday and when finally pulled over argues that they can't be charged with speeding because they sped everyday and had never been arrested before."

"It's more like they were pulled over everyday, but were told to *keep* speeding, and to go *even faster,*" said defense committee representative Bobby Eisenberg, amending the prosecutor's analogy. "We can show that, all throughout 2001, Bob Ashworth and [DEA Special Agent] Brian Keefe were sitting side by side and calling Dale and encouraging him to grow marijuana."

According to the sentencing entrapment motion, it wasn't just Ashworth who induced the defendants to grow over a hundred plants. Other officials mentioned in the document included California Attorney General Bill Lockyer as well as

Bobby Eisenberg, a spokesman for the Fry/Schafer defense committee, argued that the defendants were victims of entrapment. Photo by Vanessa Nelson.

El Dorado County District Attorney Gary Lacy, who was said to have encouraged the defendants to grow for other local medical marijuana patients. The defense subpoenaed a list of key witnesses to give testimony on this point, but they never made it to the stand. The judge denied the sentencing entrapment motion outright, telling the defense attorneys they had made no showing.

Judge Damrell may have been quick and firm in his denial, but it was followed by argument from counsel nonetheless.

While acknowledging that the motion was categorically denied, Serra proceeded to inform the judge that the defense was filing documents asking for reconsideration about whether or not there was a federal nexus in the investigation. "If our clients were allowed to testify at an evidentiary hearing, they would tell you of the multiple colloquies they had with the agents where they were encouraged to proceed, and if they hadn't gotten encouragement, they would have desisted."

"It's difficult to tell when Sergeant Ashworth began working with federal authorities," Judge Damrell observed. Concentrating, he flipped through his notes from trial testimony and recited key points: that the defendants were growing marijuana before Ashworth's first visit, that Fry was the first to call the sheriff and invite him to come over, that the defendants showed Ashworth around their property voluntarily, and that Ashworth gave the information to federal authorities a year and a half later. "He testified he was acting undercover for the feds at that time," Damrell noted.

"I disagree" Pings broke in. Ashworth had not been working undercover for the DEA, she argued, but for his own agency, the El Dorado County Sheriff's Department. "State law is not a free for all, as many people think it is. It's a situation that still requires law enforcement monitoring," she explained.

It was difficult to grasp the concept of a sheriff working undercover as a sheriff and representing himself openly as a sheriff. "This is a very unusual case – I don't think there's another case like it in America," Lichter speculated. "The local officers looked on the defendants as criminals and treated them as friends... They became the strangest kind of undercover officers, in full uniform."

"It's like the undercover agent trying to get the defendant to sell more drugs so he can get a bigger sentence," Serra equated. "Only in this case it's more egregious because my clients believed what they were doing was legal under state law."

314

"At the same time he was going to roundtable meetings about compliance, he was also going to the feds and working for them," Lichter added, referring to Ashworth. "The defense has submitted affidavits from other roundtable participants in El Dorado County."

Pings was dismissive of this claim, saying that the defense had chosen not to use the taped interviews with these witnesses because they contained no evidence. "The defense didn't submit the tape of the interviews because at no time during those meetings did the agents stand up and say, 'I'm here for the federal government, and I allow you to grow marijuana.'"

Lichter then scrambled to put the recorded interviews into evidence. "I would like to play the tape Ms. Pings said we were afraid to play."

Judge Damrell's brow furrowed. "You can't just bring it in willy-nilly," the judge said, his voice betraying irritation.

"We tried to introduce it before," Lichter said, trying to explain. "It would bolster our testimony and we're not afraid of it."

"Ok...ok..." Judge Damrell broke in, annoyed, just as Pings's mouth opened for retort. To appease the defense, he formally acknowledged that Lichter was not afraid to play the tape. The judge then moved on, eager to finish the eulogy for the motion.

"The defendants argue that Sergeant Ashworth encouraged them to expand their crop...the record does not support that assertion," Judge Damrell concluded. Entrapment had to involve active behavior, he stated, and Ashworth's attitude had been passive. "I don't think it can be established that the defendants were tricked into doing what they did by the conduct of Sergeant Ashworth. It hasn't been shown that he induced them to grow more plants than they would otherwise grow."

The judge was nearing the finish line with the discussion of entrapment, and he was already looking ahead. "It might be interesting before the 9th Circuit Court," he commented, "but this court does not make that finding."

The sentencing was re-set for March, and, as it appeared, the mandatory minimum prison terms would still apply.

But there was one last breakdown on the long, slow road to resolution: on the scheduled March 6th sentencing date, Serra was a no-show.

Everyone else was there: Lichter, the defendants and their family, the Pings & Flynn duo, a delegation of future U.S. Attorneys with their notepads and their awkwardly ambitious gleam, journalists and curious federal defenders vying for the deluxe seats in the jury box, the familiar faces of medical marijuana activists and the extra regiments of marshals deployed to control them, a court reporter, a court clerk, and, most importantly, a very angry Judge Damrell.

As it turned out, Serra was some fifty miles away in Stockton, CA, awaiting a verdict in a "shaken baby" murder case. The jury had deliberated longer than expected, and Serra had not had the foresight to request a continuance.

Exasperated, Judge Damrell called Schafer to the podium. "You're apparently here without your lawyer," he said to the defendant. There was volatility in his voice, leaving the audience breathlessly unsure of what would come next. Schafer just stood there with serenity, watching through his perpetually sad-looking eyes.

"See that first door over there?" the judge asked rhetorically, flinging his finger out to point at the side of the courtroom. "It goes to a holding cell. If you get sentenced, this could be your last day of freedom for many years. Would you like to have your attorney here? ... What do you think of that?"

"I'm not happy about it either," Schafer said calmly. "I feel like I'm caught in the middle here. But I don't blame Mr. Serra. I understand. He's waiting on a murder verdict."

In spite of Schafer's smoothness, the judge was still steaming, and Pings, piping up, seemed to want him to boil over. She chose that moment to inform the judge that it was her understanding that Serra's absence was due to the fact that he considered it "bad luck" to leave a courthouse while a jury is deliberating. Pings delivered her grenade with chirpy cheerfulness, then slunk slyly back to watch the explosion from a distance.

"I find this conduct reprehensible! Reprehensible!" Judge Damrell was bellowing now, in a fit of supremely righteous indignation. "Because Mr. Serra didn't want to leave the courthouse, someone from your firm – I mean, your community of individual practitioners – said that he wouldn't be here. He didn't ask for a continuance."

The semantic slip seemed to ruin the flow of Judge Damrell's outrage. It also served to remind those in the know about the tense months leading up to the trial, when a ruling about whether Serra's law office was a "firm" or a "community of sole practitioners" decided whether the defense attorneys got to stay on the case.

"You have not been well-served by Mr. Serra," the judge announced, turning towards Schafer again and lecturing with urgent emphasis. "This is a very big day in your life," the judge lectured the defendant with urgent emphasis. "This is the biggest casino for you!"

Setting a new date for sentencing was equally maddening for the judge. He had referred to Lichter as "the alter-ego of Mr. Serra," but Lichter claimed to know nothing about his colleague's schedule and availability. Judge Damrell looked to be at his wit's end after reciting several dates and getting only shrugs from the defense. Finally, he set a 'drop-dead' date for the sentencing, then stormed out of the courtroom with his robes streaming behind him. For the defendants, it would be another fortnight of freedom, and yet another opportunity to address the reporters that were gathered outside the courthouse, waiting eagerly for the news.

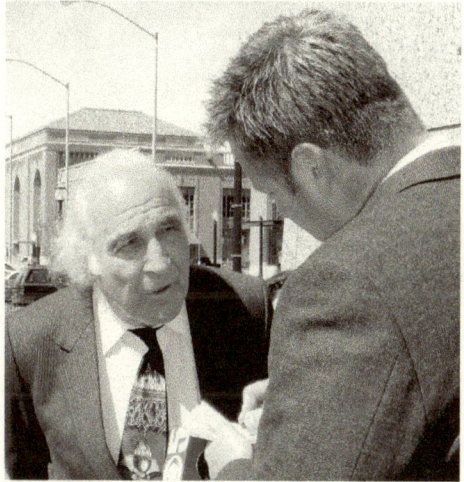

Tony Serra missed Fry and Schafer's first sentencing hearing because he was awaiting the verdict in a shaken-baby trial. Photo by Vanessa Nelson

The Sentencing

After a series of delays, failed motions and false starts, Fry and Schafer's sentencing finally began at 2pm on March 19th, 2008. It was a pleasantly warm day on the cusp of springtime in Sacramento, giving the defendants plenty of sunshine for their lunchtime press conference at the courthouse. More importantly, everything and everyone appeared to be in place this time. Judge Damrell had cleared his calendar, giving the matter the latitude of the entire afternoon. The hearing would ultimately exceed this allowance, but, even then, it was appropriately accommodated.

Time allowances, however, turned out to be more flexible than the space accommodations. Activists and inquisitive onlookers packed the courtroom to capacity, forcing the marshals to do extra duty as ushers and as referees. "You can't save seats," they admonished over and over as the gallery quickly filled up.

The seating frenzy soon settled, and all the necessary players assembled in their appropriate places. But just as the hearing began to get underway, it became clear that something was amiss. Judge Damrell, it turned out, had lost much of his voice. It was weak and hoarse, at times cracking into soundlessness. Perhaps because it disrupted the alignment of perfection, because it redirected the flow of flawlessness, this one detail likely got more attention than it was due. The conspicuous affliction was a marvel to the mildly murmuring crowd.

But, with or without reliable vocal chords, Judge Damrell was determined to get on with the proceedings, and they were soon underway.

The defense attorneys, however, had a full list of requests to make before the actual sentencing would take place. Up to the very last minute, Serra persisted in attempts to demonstrate that Schafer qualified for the safety valve and therefore could be sentenced below the mandatory minimum term. "The probation department persists in concluding that my client was an organizer and leader in criminal activity involving five or more persons," the defense attorney complained. "There was activity in which there were *many* roles, based on need...it was an old-fashioned collective, almost 60s-like activity."

Serra was just getting warmed up. With his characteristic increases in volume, he continued his speech by mentioning various traits about the defendants. He called them good, law-abiding people who are moral and religious. What's more, he pointed out, they had believed their activity to be lawful. "I submit to you – it's gray," Serra said to the judge, characterizing the issue of legality. "They don't deserve five years, your honor. They don't deserve *a day*!"

For Pings, however, there were no shades of gray. Her description of the circumstances was, predictably, starkly black-and-white. When she interjected, she insisted there was no testimony during trial that the defendants' operation was a 60s-style collective. "All the evidence was that these two defendants were the profiteers, the organizers, the leaders," she told the judge. In addition, she said, there was plenty of proof that they knew their activities were illegal.

To back up her claims, Pings reminded the judge of several points. The first was testimony that Heather Schafer said the family home was being cleared of marijuana plants because of her father's campaign for District Attorney. The prosecutor also referenced the recording of Fry telling an undercover agent not to buy hydroponics supplies from Greenfire, which was being staked out by police, and advising him to purchase equipment from her husband's business instead. Finally, Pings brought up trial testimony that the people who received marijuana deliveries from the defendants' employees were told to make their checks out to Dale Schafer so that, if they were ever questioned by law enforcement, they could say the payments were for legal consulting services. "They knew their conduct was illegal all along," Pings concluded about the defendants.

None of this swayed Serra's rhetoric, and the defense attorney simply stuck to his pleas for leniency. "You can do this," he urged the judge. "They were not leaders, therefore they should be eligible for the safety valve."

Judge Damrell, however, appeared to side with the prosecutor. "The evidence in this case demonstrates the opposite in my view," he remarked sparsely.

"Reasonable minds can disagree," Serra conceded. "I understand that." That said, it was clear the defense attorney was intent on renewing his urgings, and the judge cut him off preemptively.

"You never argued it," Judge Damrell told Serra, speaking about the leadership issue. "You let your client do it in his own testimony."

Weak though it was, there was some sense of finality in the judge's wavering voice, and Serra backed off momentarily, allowing his colleague to take the floor. Lichter tried to make a showing about leadership roles in the defendants' activities, offering attorney J. David Nick as a witness. Not only did Nick advise the defendants on how to set up their operation, Lichter explained, but he also observed it at work.

The defense attorney read from a probation report. "It says the defendants claim that what they were doing was legal under 9th Circuit law at the time and that they were doing what was encouraged by the state Attorney General," Lichter declared, holding up the paper. "They say we *do* have evidence."

"It's not proper at this time, counsel," Judge Damrell insisted. "I mean, we had a trial, and that's what I'm looking at now – the evidence. What Mr. Nick advised them to do, it's not relevant. It's not germane."

The judge glanced down at his papers for a moment, but continued his speech before the defense attorneys had the chance to interject. "It's abundantly clear from the evidence in the case that the defendants were the nexus of this activity," he concluded. "Dr. Fry and her husband, the doctor and the lawyer…there's no question this would have never happened without them. There's no question the defendants in this case were the leaders and organizers of this enterprise."

"Dr. Fry did not assist my client in the growing of marijuana," Serra said, referencing Schafer's trial testimony that his wife had been far too sick from breast cancer treatments to cultivate marijuana. "We present that as our view in spite of what the judge, the jury, the prosecution and the probation think!"

Lichter had his own version of this argument. "In spite of the fact that the defendants have had a marriage for many years and had a practice together, they are not in the same position with respect to the safety valve," he claimed.

But Judge Damrell wasn't listening. "Mr. Schafer's statements, that Dr. Fry didn't do it," the judge waved his hand dismissively as he spoke, "I'm not going to consider it."

Encouraged by this, the prosecutor made another request – that a formal finding be made that Mike Harvey made in-person deliveries of marijuana in addition to sending packages through UPS.

"But that finding comes from testimony from persons getting leniency," Serra objected.

"I could make argument with all the findings, couldn't I?" Judge Damrell said pointedly. Through that statement alone, whether intentionally or accidentally, the judge highlighted one of the crucial flaws in the government's case.

Serra also insisted that, due to his hemophilia, Schafer could not receive necessary health care in prison. "The probation department says the facilities he would be placed in could provide adequate medical attention," Serra stated. "We object vehemently with that conclusion." He then went on to his next request, which was to introduce additional information about Fry's medical history.

Lichter spoke up at this point, saying he disagreed with parts of the probation report. "Dr. Fry has a mental illness that prevented her from understanding the law," he claimed. "We would like to introduce Dr. Fry's brain scan –"

Judge Damrell glanced at the images with perplexity, muttering, "I'm not sure I know a brain scan from any other scan." Nevertheless, he allowed the brain scan to be admitted into evidence, along with letters from multiple doctors regarding Fry's mental condition.

"Dr. Fry has been in two car accidents since Dr. Gould's evaluation," Lichter said in commentary on the doctors' letters. "[The accidents] have contributed to her chronic painful condition. As your honor knows, she has other conditions due to her being a breast cancer survivor. Dr. Gould said to tell the court that that her conditions have worsened."

Another submission, written by Fry's neurologist, addressed the defendant's mental health. "Dr. Fry has multiple mental disorders that severely impair her ability to function, and these conditions would be worsened by incarceration," Lichter read from the report. According to the neurologist, Fry's "fragile psyche" would either dip into psychotic depression or accelerate into mania if she were imprisoned. Either way, he said, she would be irrevocably damaged by incarceration, and he requested a lenient sentence for this reason.

Pings wasn't convinced, and she accused the defense attorneys of wanting to have it both ways when it came to the matter of Fry's health. "We have this picture of a legitimate physician giving informed, responsible care to those who need it, and now we come in and hear them saying she's brain damaged," the prosecutor said, working up into a frenzied monologue. "It's contradicted by the fact that she goes to work everyday and hangs out…and collects $200 from anyone who wants to smoke medical marijuana!"

Ignoring Pings, Lichter tried to redirect the judge's attention to the tremendous showing of support in the courtroom. "Many people in the community, of all different levels, have come to support Dr. Fry and evaluate what will be justice in this situation," the defense attorney observed. "This is a unique case. This is a case where justice would best be served by creative sentencing rather than incarceration and punishment."

"There's no creative sentencing here – there's a mandatory minimum," Pings argued back. "She chose the path that put her here today."

"The government gave the defendants ample opportunity to resolve this before and after their conviction," Judge Damrell lectured, his tone stern. "I can't understand why anyone would not want to do that." The judge shook his head disapprovingly. "This is a sad commentary."

323

Although this was probably not the introduction she would have preferred, Fry was given her opportunity to make a public address at this point. "I stand before you as a breast cancer survivor," she told the judge, her voice strong. "Medical cannabis turned my life around… If I was some great activist, I would have jumped on the bandwagon from the beginning. I waited until it came to me."

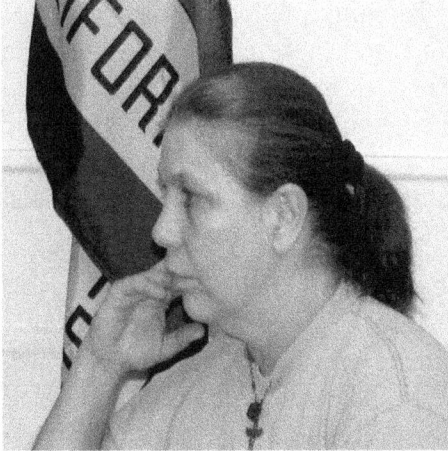

Dr. Fry claimed she was urged by the sheriff's department and the district attorney's office to set up a medical marijuana practice in accordance with state law. Photo by Vanessa Nelson.

She then spoke about a visit she had with Detective Tim McNulty of the El Dorado County Sheriff's Department, who had been serving on a local taskforce organized for "narcotics eradication." According to Fry, McNulty had urged her to do something she had been reluctant to do – set up a practice as a doctor and examine people who needed medical marijuana. She claimed that McNulty said that, if these patients were able to get legitimate physician's notes, then they could grow marijuana and he would leave them alone.

Fry's first reaction had been refusal. "I was sick," she explained. "I didn't want to do anything that would take me away from my children. I didn't want to start a practice up. But I had taken an oath to God when I graduated from medical school that I would help and heal, but first that I would do no harm."

And marijuana, she insisted, was one of the most harmless treatments known to mankind. "This plant has been used for medicine for over six thousand years," Fry pointed out.

Besides, she reflected, she had every reason to believe what she was doing was lawful – District Attorney Gary Lacy had specifically asked her to help medical marijuana patients in the county, and Detective Robert Ashworth repeatedly encouraged her husband to grow within the county's cultivation guidelines. "I thought it was legal. In my

324

mind, it was a blue law – okay to do in one state, but you can't cross boundaries."

At this point, her voice began to waver. "Your honor, my husband and I are sick. We both have many illnesses. My cancer is in remission, but it could come back. I have pain from chemotherapy. I have pain from car accidents. My husband, however, is much sicker than me. He has the most severe form of Hemophilia A. He requires intravenous injections of clotting factors, or it could result in death. I carry these clotting factors with me at all times."

The tears that had been welling up were now flowing freely, but Fry hung tight in her speech. "We set out to heal and educate. We have caused no harm to anyone. There were no victims. There were no ill-gotten gains....The probation report found no damages requiring restitution, no reason for issuing a fine. I have obeyed every order of this court for 32 months. Your honor, I only want to help sick people. I want to be a good wife and a good mother."

Her service had extended beyond the home and the office, however, and the doctor gave a quick list of her community service activities. In particular, she spoke about feeding the homeless two days a month and donating hundreds of pounds of meat that had been raised on her property. Her message was clear – rather than being a danger to the community, she was a boon.

"Your honor, I ask you with all due respect, please do not punish us further," she pleaded. "We have been threatened by the government from day one with a forty-year sentence, that they would put our daughter in jail."

Fry had been crying for most of her monologue now, but this had not had an inhibitory effect on her speech. Rather than stifling her ability to articulate, her emotion appeared to be highlighting many of her points. "If the punishment is to fit the crime, your honor, haven't we suffered enough? Prison is for those who are damaging society. Allow me to keep serving my community and grant me bail on appeal."

Drying her eyes, the doctor concluded. "There is little doubt that I will die of breast cancer. It's just a matter of when. Please, your honor, let me stay with my family for as long as possible."

At her finish, Fry turned to sit back down at the defense table. Before she could reach her seat, however, Judge Damrell called her back up to the podium. This was, after all, a sentencing hearing, during which it is customary for a defendant to stand before the judge. Assessing her state as she returned to the podium, the judge made an offer. "Do you need a break?" he asked. Fry gladly accepted, and while the court held a short recess, she went over to the gallery railing to hug her sobbing daughter.

When the proceedings came back to order, it was Schafer's turn for a statement...but before he began speaking, Serra took the floor to make a speech on behalf of his client.

"Defense lawyers bond with their clients in a form of union that's very personal and intimate," Serra explained as he stood before the judge. "You get to know them like your brother. These two good human beings who conducted themselves as model citizens for a lifetime are about to go to prison for a long time – five years. Five years is irrational! The context is irrational! Medical marijuana will ultimately be accepted by the federal court. Medical marijuana has a vitality that's encompassed in the logo in which it arrives, and that is *compassion*. The federal government here lacked that compassion."

Serra was gesturing passionately now, declaring that the defendants were treated with unnecessary harshness. If the government wanted to put a stop to their activities, he argued, it could have pursued a civil course of action. "It could have been done with an injunction," he insisted. "Shut them down! But don't arrest them!"

The federal government's credibility, as Serra assessed it, was at a remarkably low level. He began listing issues about which the government's position has lost substantial validity. "The Iraq war, weapons of mass destruction or not... no climate change... no recession... no medical efficacy of marijuana..." Serra rattled the topics off in rapid-fire, then went back to directly criticizing agents of the government. "They put their heads in the sand to serve their political agenda."

Serra waved his arm wildly towards the defendants, "These people shouldn't be martyred for that!"

The defense attorney then lowered his voice and calmed his gesticulation. "I am woefully sad and angered by the United States of America when they prosecute medical marijuana," he reflected. "It reminds me of Nazi Germany. We are not Rome throwing Christians to the lions. We are on the side of evolution, not devolution, which is on the other side of the podium here."

In Serra's enunciation, nearly every word was given great emphasis. This technique not only gave the speech a captivating cadence, but it also left the listener with the instinctive sense that each syllable had been meaningful and precious, like a kernel of golden wisdom. But the statement that was most poetic, the one that resonated the deepest in its listeners and echoed in their heads, was Serra's mournful refrain, "Lady Justice weeps today, your honor."

Pings disagreed vehemently with the notion that the government had acted with unnecessary cruelty, and in the pause between Serra's speech and Schafer's statements, she got her rebuttal in. "These defendants have been dealt with with great respect and dignity," she contended. "We did have a discussion about prosecuting their adult son and daughter because they were also selling drugs, but in the government's judgment, did not." The prosecutor then reminded the judge that the defendants had been offered plea agreements that, if accepted, would have let them avoid the mandatory minimum sentences. "The government gave them opportunities to not be here today. If they are martyrs, it's because they *chose* to be martyrs.

Judge Damrell nodded, acknowledging the prosecutor's assertions without commenting on them yet. The floor now belonged to Schafer, and he was eager to take it.

The defendant began reading his prepared statement aloud, his words impassioned and urgent, but he was going so quickly that the court reporter couldn't keep up. Cutting in, she instructed Schafer to start over and speak more slowly. "You're going too fast," she told him.

"Sorry," Schafer said with a calm smile. "My wife complains about the same thing."

The gallery appreciated the comic relief, with more than one titter at the comment's innuendo.

Beginning his speech, Schafer took his listeners back to the fateful day when his wife was diagnosed with breast cancer and given the ever-ominous 30% chance of survival. That marijuana helped his wife cope with aggressive cancer treatments, however, was no surprise to Schafer. He had worked in a hospital in his younger days, when he watched marijuana stop the convulsions of a paraplegic and ease the suffering in a cancer ward where he "saw people die daily." The hospital's policy on medical marijuana was, according to Schafer, "don't ask, don't tell."

By the time his wife fell ill, Schafer knew that the passage of California's Proposition 215 had made medical marijuana legal under state law. The continuing federal prohibition, however, had a dramatic chilling effect on doctors who would otherwise be willing to recommend it. "Mollie's doctor brought it up," Schafer said of medical marijuana, "but he was reluctant to write it down. He just expressed fear of the DEA."

The search for a doctor who would formally recommend marijuana was followed by an even more exhausting search for the medicine itself. "After a nausea-filled eight-hour drive to Dennis Peron's club in San Francisco, she could only get an eighth of an ounce at a time," Schafer explained. It had quickly become clear to him that he would need to find a better way to supply his wife with medicine, and he consulted an attorney about growing marijuana. "David Nick said I could probably grow plants without a problem, but to stay under a hundred," he related. As he testified during trial, Schafer had started with two plants, but this crop didn't yield enough medicine. "It's amazing how fast after harvest a patient can go through a few plants," he commented.

Schafer expanded his crop so that he could grow a few dozen plants at a time, but he checked with local authorities to make sure he was in compliance. "Officer McNulty came out and said I was doing a fine job," Schafer explained. "He wanted us to help others. Not enough people were able to get recommendations."

At that point, Schafer recalled, he did extensive research on marijuana law...and, in front of the whole court, he took the time to share the fruits of his studies, going into a detailed socio-political history of marijuana prohibition. The watchers in the gallery were captivated by the lecture, following Schafer through the entirety of it.

"Dale's statement was historical," defense committee representative Bobby Eisenberg said afterwards. "It was like sitting and listening to a Founding Father."

Schafer started off by explaining the strategically manipulated racism and the economic interests that inspired Congressional hearings on marijuana in 1937. He then recounted the creation of the Marihuana Tax Stamp Act and its demise through the 1969 Supreme Court decision in a lawsuit brought by Timothy Leary. This ruling was followed quickly by the Controlled Substances Act of 1970, Schafer said, and he even employed some evocative quotes from President Nixon that illustrated the prejudices at work behind the passage of this act. Finally, Schafer's narrative concluded with the present-day situation, in which medical marijuana is legal in a dozen U.S. states but not under federal law. In spite of this conflict, he emphasized that free speech protections established by the 2002 case of *Conant v. Walters* prevent doctors from being prosecuted for recommending marijuana to their patients.

"Emboldened by this knowledge, my wife and I set out to help people with medical marijuana," Schafer declared to the packed courtroom. "Mr. Nick said we had to warn people marijuana was still illegal under federal law." In addition to this, Schafer noted, each county in California had different guidelines on the amount of marijuana permitted to each patient. To make sure they complied, Fry and Schafer got actively involved in the formation of the guidelines for El Dorado County. "We sat on the committee for guidelines in our community," Schafer said, noting that he also got involved by running for the office of District Attorney. "People approached us daily to ask how to get medicine. Dispensaries were operating, but the prices were too high."

After the 9th Circuit Court ruling in the *Oakland Cannabis Buyers Cooperative*, Schafer said, he and his wife understood that they had a medical defense in federal court if they were just giving marijuana away rather than selling it. And that's what they set out to do…at least until that 9th Circuit ruling was overturned. "We stopped all distribution once the law changed and we had no medical defense."

While discussing the matter of medical defense, Schafer reminded the judge that his wife was not the only one who suffered from dangerously severe health conditions. It was then that his eyes began to tear up a little. "My body has been ravaged by a lifetime of hemophilia," Schafer stated, his voice strong but tinged with emotion. He then listed the wide array of prescription medicines he now takes daily, concluding all of them "do part of what cannabis did for me."

Schafer then began to widen his speech, getting philosophical. "Now I think I know how Galileo felt when he looked through the microscope and saw that the sun was the center of the universe and the pope said otherwise for religious reasons," he reflected. That a microscope might be ill-equipped for planetary observation didn't seem to occur to Schafer, nor did the fact that the sun is the center of the solar system rather than the universe. The bobbing heads in the audience indicated that nobody else appeared aware of these technicalities either. Schafer's listeners, quite appropriately, were focused on the meaning of the rhetoric rather than its tiny, trifling details.

During his sentencing hearing, Dale Schafer delivered a richly detailed speech that was described as "historical." Photo by Vanessa Nelson.

Bringing up Prohibition of alcohol and terming it a debacle, Schafer made the apt comparison to laws against marijuana. "How many lives must be ruined before science is given its proper place in modern society?" he demanded.

"Neither my wife nor I had the specific intent to commit a crime," Schafer reminded the judge. They only sought to help, he said, "the wretched many," and now they faced an unjust sentence. "Five years is cruel and unusual, but it is also cruel and unusual for sick people to be told they cannot use a medicine they have found to be safe and effective."

Nonetheless, Schafer went on to imply that there was zero chance that he and his wife would re-offend and go through the entire legal ordeal again. "I'm not sure we could repeat this nightmare even if we tried."

Looking squarely at Judge Damrell, Schafer recalled that he learned in law school that federal judges are appointed for life so they don't have to make rulings based on political pressure. "Congress didn't have us in mind when it made this mandatory minimum for a hundred plants," he professed, then softened into a heart-tugging plea. "Our lives are truly in your hands. I hope and pray your honor sees fit to give a sentence that does not destroy our family, and that gives public respect to the courts, not public derision."

Judge Damrell began his own speech at that point, a lecture consisting of equal parts sorrow and reproach. "At some point, it seems to me, that in hearing your stories, you lost control of your life," he told the defendants. "It spiraled out of control. And it's perfectly acceptable that you turned to cannabis to relieve the pain, and that you were able to survive because of it. But at some point in the passion for this drug and its scientific effects, judgment got clouded."

His voice was raspy and thin, but propelled by the intensity of his words, the judge's speech came through with solid strength. "You moved way beyond personal use," he opined. "You set up a business selling recommendations. You moved beyond personal concern for yourself and became a martyr. You're *both* martyrs, and for what?"

The judge took a deep sigh, then made a carefully-balanced concession. "I'm not saying that medical marijuana has no place in modern society, but this nation has laws," he reminded the defendants. "Sometimes we want to rebel against the laws, and sometimes that's a good thing, but here you have *parents* with *children*."

Judge Damrell paused for a moment, then tried to give an example supporting his point. "The court saw pictures of your children trimming marijuana plants, and maybe there's nothing dangerous about that..." he trailed off in that contemplation, but returned from the reverie with the conclusion, "but it may have some ill effect down the line."

The defendants may have had unscrupulous employees, but the judge wasn't letting them off the hook for that. In his view, the associations came through their own fault. "You get caught up with petty drug pushers for a reason – they facilitate you," Judge Damrell theorized. "You should have known that. You should have realized it. But you didn't. You self-aggrandized, and you put your children and their future at risk."

The judge shook his head, looking sternly sorrowful. "I certainly don't want to see you go to prison for five years. That's not the sentence I would choose, but I don't have a choice," he maintained.

"This is a sad day," Judge Damrell went on. "This is a *terrible* day. Not just for you and your children, but for your movement as a whole."

The judge reminded the defendants that they had the option of taking plea bargains before trial, and that they had even been made an offer for a leniency agreement after conviction. Their refusal of these deals, in his view, was egregiously unwise. "You should have taken the opportunity to resolve this case short of the five-year mandatory minimum. So that leaves me with, as I said, no choice. There's only one sentence available. That's it. That's it."

It was time for the pronouncement of the sentence, and it went as Judge Damrell had foreshadowed. For both Marion P. Fry and Dale Schafer – 60 months of imprisonment on each count, to be served concurrently, followed by 48 months of supervised release. The terms of supervised release would include a multitude of restrictions, including no controlled substances and mandatory drug testing.

Lichter spoke up at this point, reminding the judge of the jury's finding that, although Fry *conspired* to cultivate more than a hundred plants, she did not *actually* cultivate more than a hundred plants. In Lichter's understanding, this meant Fry was subject to the mandatory minimum on the conspiracy count but not on the count of substantive cultivation...yet two five-year sentences had been imposed upon her nonetheless. Since she would serve the two sentences at the same time, this point didn't matter much for the moment. Still, it could make a meaningful difference later on, depending upon what developed while the case was on appeal.

The issue was settled succinctly by the government. "The sentence for one count controls the sentence for the other," reported prosecutor Sean Flynn.

And so it was done. The sentences were imposed equally on both husband and wife – five years each in prison, followed by four years of intensive monitoring. For many in the gallery, the tears shed during the defendants' statements had not yet dried, but there was nonetheless a new eruption of sobbing as the reality of the situation set in.

It was no surprise to Schafer, who had commented during a break, "I could probably predict from the day we were arrested, the day they came in with a search warrant, that they were going to hit us with five years. I mean, that's what they were looking for."

That is indeed what the government had sought, painstakingly piecing together evidence to make ends meet above the all-important hundred-plant mark. But, as Schafer suggested, the five-year sentence was also what the judge had sought. "I think it's the problem with the whole system, that you get to the person who makes these decisions and he tells you, 'My hands are tied,'" Schafer said, scoffing. "Now, when I went to law school, we were taught that judges are set for life because they can make the difficult decisions and tell the government they're wrong. He obviously didn't want to do that, and he just perpetuates the system."

Whether or not Judge Damrell was in bondage was a matter of debate. There was one last chance for freedom…and in front of a courtroom full of desperately emotional spectators, as marshals continued to crowd in around the doorways and eye the convicts hungrily, Serra and Lichter launched straight into a crusade to keep their clients out of custody.

After his sentence was imposed, Dale Schafer spoke emphatically to the press. Photo by Vanessa Nelson.

The Bail Motion

The sentences had been given, placing five-year prison terms on the heads of both Fry and Schafer. The gallery was a mess of dismayed spectators, who hugged each other and sobbed. The prosecutors averted their eyes from this spectacle, keeping their focus on court documents like tightrope walkers trying not to look down. Reinforcements for the marshals continued to arrive in waves, ostensibly to handle the custody situation. They stood lining the doorway and the sides of the courtroom, an ominous sign of impending incarceration. But there was one last hope for the defendants – if their attorneys could successfully argue for bail pending appeal, they could remain out of prison for the foreseeable future.

Serra motioned towards the witnesses he intended to call: J. David Nick and Ephraim Margolin. "We brought them to have an opportunity to address you about salient issues," he told the judge. "They're the experts."

Judge Damrell seemed to tip his hand just slightly. "If we need to," he said about the expert testimony. "Let's see if we do."

"There were motions made, all of which, when denied, raise meritorious appellate issues," Serra began. He then laid out a series of four points that he believed, under the *Garcia* criterion, qualified the defendants for bail on appeal. "One – you accept the threshold that there are substantial appellate issues. Two – the defendants are not a flight risk or danger to society. Three – the appeal raises an issue that is not frivolous and can result in a reversed verdict or a different sentence. Four – extraordinary circumstances, and a severe medical condition does fulfill that."

The precedent Serra referenced was the 9th Circuit Court ruling in the United States v. Garcia. This case, which involved a prison guard convicted of conspiring to organize assaults amongst inmates, was decided on the trial court level by Judge Martin Jenkins of the Northern District of California. In spite of Garcia having lymphoma, Judge Jenkins denied the motion for bail pending appeal, saying he was unable to determine whether "exceptional circumstances" existed because there were no guidelines for determining this requirement. Garcia appealed his case to the 9th Circuit Court, which in 2003 issued a ruling that's often cited as the first circuit court decision that meaningfully defines what constitutes "exceptional circumstances."

The *Garcia* ruling gave a detailed analysis of many situations that could qualify as "exceptional circumstances," but did so as guidance for the decision-making of lower courts, and not to establish a comprehensive list. The significant portion of this ruling, as it applied to Fry and Schafer, include "circumstances that render the hardships of prison unusually harsh, such as illness or injury." When it came to such a claim, the defendants had it in the bag...quite literally.

Serra paused, glancing back at the defense table for a moment. "We brought to the court all the medication and syringes, there in a big black bag. I was going to dump it out, but I think you understand this," he said to the judge with a knowing smile. "I am mindful that pre-trial services has recommended bail on appeal. If you don't accept that, I can detail those arguments," Serra promised.

What followed was a tug-of-war over which standards to apply. The defense attorneys argued that bail on appeal could be granted if the defendants demonstrated meritorious legal issues that were not frivolous and that may lead to a reversal on appeal. The prosecutor, however, disagreed on this standard, saying that precedent required the defendants to show that their appeal had a high likelihood of success.

As Pings put it, the defendants had to do more than present an appeals issue that wasn't frivolous. "Given the nature of the case, they must show an unusually strong chance of getting a reversal on appeal," the prosecutor said. Because this was a drug case, she argued, different rules were used. "This standard is applied differently to drug offenses, or to the category that includes drug offenses," she claimed, pointing to a footnote in the ruling.

Judge Damrell had his head in his hands at this point. After reaching its boiling point at the pronouncement of the sentence, the afternoon was now evaporating. Sighing, the judge relented, allowing Serra to call his witnesses to the stand.

Nick was called first. A smartly dressed fellow with small but keen eyes, he started off his testimony by giving details about his legal experience. As he described it, he had handled 150 appeals and argued cases across the United States, resulting in two dozen published decisions. He was called to testify in order to give his expert opinion on the merits of the Fry/Schafer appeal…especially on the advice of counsel issue. "My understanding is that the defendants' entire defense depended on my advice," Nick said on the stand. "The same advice goes to the state of mind. Advice of counsel, mistake of fact or law – it's all wrapped up in the same issue."

Lichter began to ask how Nick knew the defendants, but the judge interrupted. "Let's get down to business here," he said harshly, regaining some of his vocal force. "It's a quarter to five!" he complained.

Wrapping up the direct examination, Lichter asked about the general legal advice he had given the defendants. "I gave advice on the Conant decision," Nick explained. He cited the Conant v. Walters ruling that upheld free speech protections for doctors, allowing them to make medical marijuana recommendations without fear of being prosecuted for it.

Attorney J. David Nick provided crucial testimony during the hearing for the defendants' bail motion. Photo by Vanessa Nelson.

Lichter also asked about advice Nick had given about the Supreme Court decision in Raich v. Gonzales, which affirmed the federal authority to enforce marijuana prohibition in states with medical marijuana laws. "I told them I believed the Raich decision wouldn't come down as it did, that [the Justices] couldn't use the commerce clause," Nick said of his predictions. "It didn't come down like that."

It was an issue Pings seized upon in her cross-examination.

"You didn't tell Dr. Fry to go out and sell marijuana and be protected under Conant, did you?"

"No," Nick responded. "Not under Conant."

"And Raich *was* a commerce clause case," Pings pointed out slyly.

"That was decided *after the fact*," Nick clarified.

Serra broke in with an objection. "We're getting off on a tangent here," he declared, gesturing wildly in the air.

"It was a wide turn in the road," Judge Damrell commented as he again instructed the attorneys to stick to the issues at hand.

It wasn't the only time Serra interrupted Pings, however. He was on his feet almost as soon as the prosecutor began talking about Pier 5, the "community of sole practitioners" to which he and Lichter both belonged.

"Aren't you currently a member of Mr. Serra's office of sole practitioners?" Pings probed.

"I left that office in July of last year," Nick answered.

His response was followed by a bellowing interjection from Serra. "I object!" the defense attorney announced. "It's not *my* office!"

Pings then ran through the history of Nick's role in the revocation of Fry's license to prescribe medicine. As the witness told it, a letter for which he was responsible was never filed, and this factor resulted in Fry's loss in the case. Nick, however, maintained that the blame wasn't his – when asked if he caused harm to Fry, he was insistent. "No," he said. "The letter was put into the mails."

The prosecutor asked Nick about his specialty, inquiring if it was in medical marijuana cases. She donned a shocked expression when the witness didn't accept the description. Several years ago, she claimed, Nick had told her on the phone that he was surprised she hadn't heard of him before, since he was the leading defense attorney for medical marijuana in 2001. "I handle *all kinds* of cases," Nick said dryly.

"Don't you have a personal stake in this?" Pings asked about the current case. When the witness denied it, she pushed her point further. "Wouldn't it be embarrassing if it were resolved and it said your advice was all wrong?"

Insisting that he wouldn't be embarrassed by such a finding, Nick explained his position. "The advice of counsel is like a chameleon," he said, waxing somewhat poetic. "When someone is involved in a conspiracy and they don't have the intent to break the law, it becomes a point."

"So you were articulating the way you hoped the case would be resolved?" Pings asked about the Raich decision.

"That's usually how law goes, yes," Nick said, his voice edged in humor and condescension. On that note, he was dismissed from the stand to make room for the next witness.

The venerable Margolin had an aura of cheerful benevolence about him as he was sworn in. He seemed kindly but clever, looking the part of a favorite old uncle who might pretend to pull a half-dollar piece out from behind your ear. He spoke slowly but with purpose and insight, and never appeared hurried. Margolin's accent betrayed his native Israel, where he clerked in the Supreme Court before coming to the United States. Here, his work is extensive and widely known, with his name appearing on over a thousand reported appeals cases. Most recently, he has specialized in defending lawyers in contempt, the dissolution of law firms, and ethical issues regarding legal practice.

"I represent lawyers and judges," Margolin explained. He then cast a sidelong smile in Judge Damrell's direction. "*State* judges," he clarified with emphasis.

Lichter took the lead in the direct examination, asking what issues in appeal were meritorious. Margolin gives passing mention to the advice of counsel argument, but seemed much more concerned with the entrapment issues. "I was struck by the fact that you have people who invited the local sheriff into their house. For three years, they invited him in… These are people who try to work with local law enforcement and then get indicted by a sovereign, the federal government.

"There is a war on the national level and there are casualties in that war. This case looks to me like an Exhibit A on the casualty list."

"So you agree with the tragic aspects of this case?" Lichter asked.

Margolin was enthusiastic. "Oh, yes."

"Objection!" Pings called out. "This witness is supposed to testify on the merit of the appellate issues."

"Go back to those issues," Judge Damrell instructed Lichter.

Margolin returned to the issue of entrapment created by the way local and federal agents cooperated in the case. He described the sheriff visiting the Fry/Schafer home to check on the marijuana grow, saying the deputies were "lying through [their] teeth" by declaring compliance and then reporting the findings to federal agents. This, in Margolin's view, made the sheriff's deputies into informants and de facto federal agents, and no hearing should be necessary to establish what is plainly obvious in this regard. "That's not how life goes," he commented. "Real life is a situation where a three-year cooperation with the federal government makes the federal government involved."

Margolin was being given impressive latitude for his monologue, and he deftly guided it next into a criticism of Judge Damrell's approach to the sentencing. "Ed Rosenthal got one day in prison," he pointed out. "There is a power in the judge. The judge is not bound to give you the mandatory minimum sentences."

Unblocked, Margolin continued to speculate. "There is something suspect, in my view, something not supported by the law, about [mandatory] minimum sentences," he opined. "In my view, the independence of judges is important–"

At this point, Judge Damrell had enough of the legal commentary and put a halt to it. "I don't want philosophy," the judge reminded the witness. "I just want to know if there are meritorious appellate issues."

Pings objected, claiming that the necessary standard is not merely meritorious issues, but the probability of success for the appeal. Her objection inspired an outburst from Serra, who was on his feet in a flash. "I object," he proclaimed loudly. "That's not it!"

Judge Damrell was visibly irritated. "Mr. Serra, sit down!" he ordered, managing to bring his weak voice close to a bark. The judge pointed at Lichter as he finished reprimanding Serra. "There's a lawyer up here representing your interests!"

Lichter asked Margolin about the standard for bail on appeal, according to the Garcia case, and Margolin replied that there must be a showing that the appellate issues were not frivolous. He also denied that it was necessary to demonstrate the probability of the appeal's success, and expounded on the improbable nature of such a showing. "You can't show the probability of success because you don't know what court will be hearing it," he said in tones of simple logic. "The Supreme Court changes."

With a final key question, Lichter finished up his direct examination. "Do you think bail should be granted for every case on appeal?" he asked.

"No," Margolin said firmly, then repeated his understanding of the necessary criteria.

When Pings began her cross-examination, she kept up the debate over the merits of the appellate issues. "But isn't the burden on the defendants to prove it?" she asked, warming up.

"Yes," Margolin replied, but clarified that this showing did not have to go so far as to convince the trial judge to reverse his own decisions on the issue. "All the judge must consider is if other learned judges would disagree with him... If a judge can entertain the notion that this can be the case, then that can be enough for the conclusion."

Skeptical of the legal basis of the witness's speech on morality, Pings queried, "Do you have cases to support your statements on fairness and equity?"

"No," Margolin answered. "But the Supreme Court has made a decision that judges are not bound by guidelines."

"But this is a mandatory minimum," Pings reminded him, pointing out that it was indeed more binding than a guideline sentence.

Margolin, however, just met her specificity with righteous generality. "This case is an unusual case in many circumstances. It leaves the judge in a position where there is less guidance than there would otherwise be."

When Pings tried again to declare that the Garcia standard used by the defense did not apply to drug cases, Margolin again evaded her by zooming out to the larger picture. He did so, remarkably, with sharp skill and persuasion. "Usually, in a case that is the first of its kind, there are no other cases to rely on," he told the prosecutor plainly. "It is impossible to cite precedent in a new case."

Soon after this, Margolin began a different address, "In California, the voters voted into law–"

Judge Damrell intervened here, holding up his hands. "I've heard enough argument on this," he said, dismissing Margolin from the witness stand.

What the judge wanted to know about particularly was a far different matter, one that had been brought to his attention only shortly before the hearing.

He asked Pings to explain an attachment she filed as part of the government's opposition. It was an exhibit showing recommendations Fry had issued after the time of her arrest and indictment, and the implication was that this could be construed as a violation of pre-trial release. Speaking of the patient, Pings said, "The young man's history laid out mental health issues and drug addiction and 5150 hospitalizations four times, yet Dr. Fry also recommended marijuana for a condition that also includes asthma."

"Dr. Fry issued recommendations to Alice Wiegand and Jeffre Sanderson, who were before me in court now, earlier today," Judge Damrell said, severe disapproval in his tone. "Is that something that's still going on?"

"Because of my mental illness, I accept the examination of a physician's assistant," Fry replied, with a hint of tremulous sorrow in her voice. "I wouldn't necessarily be aware of these two people."

Judge Damrell, indignant, wanted to know if she was aware she had issued a recommendation to one of these defendants for asthma, but

342

acted exasperated when Fry began talking about marijuana as a bronchiodilator. "Are you continuing to issue recommendations for a price?" he asked pointedly, cutting to the chase.

"I approve a physician assistant's examination," Fry said, then shrugged. "A lot of them I *reject*."

"How about for a person who's a meth addict?" the judge asked soberly.

"Here's the thing – there's a new concept in drug treatment that's about harm reduction, " Fry began, but she didn't get very far into her description before Judge Damrell interrupted her.

"Don't you want a more reliable road to follow?" the judge scoffed. "How do you know you've just given it to a meth addict?"

He didn't permit Fry to answer, instead holding up his hand as though being sworn in to testify. "I *know* these people before me," the judge declared. "I *know* their problems."

"I get records from other doctors," Fry claimed, and then explained her approach to her profession. "Medicine is based on trust... You don't wake up in the morning and say, 'I feel great. I need a Tylenol.' You figure [the patients] come to you because they need your help."

"It's not a secret that we don't believe the recommendation process is sincere," Pings said, understating her contempt.

The prosecutor went on, giving another example to illustrate that Fry's recommendations were illegitimate and perhaps even harmful. "Just the other day, we got a call about a man busted for selling. He had a recommendation from Dr. Fry for a broken jaw!" She paused to let her outrage sink in with full effect, then announced about Fry's practice, "We think it's a mockery of state law."

"What's going on here has to stop, but it just goes on and on and on," Judge Damrell reproached. "She keeps trying to get marijuana into the hands of other people."

It was a finding that appeared unfair and inaccurate on its face. There was no indication that Fry was engaged in providing marijuana to anyone, or even, for that matter, to herself. Rather, the opposite conclusion was more warranted, given her flawless results on the random drug testing that the court imposed on her for the two years leading up to trial. If she was continuing to write medical marijuana recommendations, it could arguably have been a violation of her bail conditions, but issuing a piece of paper approving of its use was a far cry from actually putting marijuana in someone's hands. And, besides, making a medical recommendation was Fry's duty as a physician as well as her firmly-established 1st Amendment right.

But here, in this place and at this moment, Judge Damrell's assessments would reign supreme. "I have a hunch Dr. Fry is not going to pay attention to the order I make," he speculated, frowning sternly.

"Her husband will make sure she does!" Serra broke in, his index finger raised upward with confidence as he made the declaration.

"If the court wants her to limit her practice as a condition of bail, she will," Lichter said about his client, speaking in a tone of certainty.

Judge Damrell had revealed that he was considering the option, but there had been no solid assurances. Reading his face as he paused in contemplation, one saw symptoms of agonized conflict but no signs of how it would resolve. As the clock's hands continued their slow spin and 6pm approached, the mood in the courtroom was unmistakably one of anxiety.

Finally, the judge reached his conclusion. "Under the statute, the court must detain a defendant unless it finds he is not doing harm to the community and that the appeal is not being taken for the purposes of delay," he summarized. "I think, in terms of what's required for bail on the appellate issue, it has to have exceptional circumstances and reasons."

The watchers in the gallery were giving the proceedings the fullest attention. Those who had been sobbing at the pronouncement of the sentence were now collectively dry-faced. The focus required for concentration on the judge's words and the tension of the climaxing suspense had them captivated.

"I believe there could be a number of exceptional circumstances," Judge Damrell continued. "The defendants do not appear to me to be a risk to flee. Dr. Fry's conduct would pose a danger to the community if she continued to recommend marijuana as she has."

After calling such conduct "aberrational," Judge Damrell finally looked down at Fry and made his decision fully apparent. "The court would have to impose very strict conditions on you," he told her gravely.

"I accept," Fry promised immediately, at once breathlessly eager and genuinely earnest.

Judge Damrell noted her statement with a nod, then went on with his speech about the merits of the appeal. "Whether the visits to the home make this a case of entrapment is a strong issue," he stated. "The advice of counsel…it's an issue, but I'm not as enamored of it." That the judge recognized the strength of the entrapment argument was an unusual revelation given the fact that he had denied pre-trial and post-conviction motions that claimed entrapment.

As a condition of bail, Dr. Fry had to swear that she would stop issuing medical marijuana recommendations. Photo by Vanessa Nelson.

"Among the exceptional circumstances are the defendants' health," Judge Damrell continued. "I *am* concerned about the defendants' health. I don't think there's any malingering here – these are serious issues." Making a brief pause, he mused. "I believe the defendants, without the onset of their enthusiasm for marijuana, would have lived a model life. This is clearly a departure from their previous life."

After this brief speculation, the judge finally made the official pronouncement. "I'm not dead-on for reversal, but I'm going to grant bail on appeal," he declared. Simultaneous sighs of relief followed the pronouncement, and the buzz of happy excitement eclipsed everything else in the room. Tears resurfaced in the gallery, but, this time, the crying was brought on by joy rather than devastation.

The intensity of focus on the judge's words had instantly eased, but he nonetheless went on to detail the bail conditions. They would be the same as what had already been imposed, he ruled, but he wanted to specifically address the issue of Fry's medical practice. "The defendant shall be restricted from recommending marijuana to others, either directly or indirectly, while on bail pending appeal," Judge Damrell said slowly and carefully, staring at Fry intently. "Do you understand those conditions?"

"I do," the doctor replied, matching the judge's emphasis.

For Pings, however, this condition had not been phrased carefully enough. The prosecutor wanted the requirements laid out in specific language, unambiguous and irrefutable. "When referring to recommending marijuana... that means she can't employ a physician's assistant or nurses to pay to do so in her stead."

"I understand," Fry said with firm certainty, "and I accept."

"Okay," Pings eyed the defendant for a second, then continued making her requests to the judge. "Given their status as felons, could they be ordered to surrender the five firearms in their home?"

As soon as they heard the words, both of the newly-minted felons balked simultaneously.

"We already did," Schafer asserted.

Fry chimed in, saying with emphasis, *"Years ago."*

Pursing her lips, Pings went to her last point. As she claimed, Judge Damrell had used the wrong set of requirements to determine the appropriate conditions for bail on appeal. "For the record, the government continues to believe that the standard for bail on appeal is subsection 1, not the subsection that your honor used," she announced. The prosecutor knew this wouldn't make a difference, however, and immediately clarified her intent. "But, we're okay on that. It's just for the record."

Judge Damrell spent a few moments in perplexed scrutiny of the various documents sprawled out on his bench, but quickly concluded that it was a moot point whether or not he had used the appropriate set of conditions.   "It's not going to change my decision," he said resolutely.

It was music to Serra's ears. His hands clasped respectfully behind his back, the defense attorney beamed up at the judge. "Thank you for hearing us out, your honor," he gushed, nearly giddy. "That was the right decision."

Predictably, television and newspaper reporters had staked out the exit of the courthouse, and the excitement was electric when the convicted couple and their attorneys finally emerged.

The Unsinkable Mollie Fry

"Boy, it was a nail-biter, wasn't it?" Fry gushed with a big grin and wide eyes, quickly getting chummy with the newscameras.

Several reporters had waited the proceedings out, staying steadfast in front of the federal courthouse even after it closed for the day. Finally, at just past 6pm, the reporters were getting Fry's candid reaction to being granted bail during the appeals process.

"It was the worst experience I've ever had in my whole life," she said about the raid and the trial. "But in this whole thing, God is in charge, not me."

Though not a divine authority, Fry did have some plans of her own. "I'm going to sell my business, and that'll be no problem," she said confidently. "I'm sure there are a lot of people who would like an up-and-running business, and that will allow my children to be fed and my

After being granted bail on appeal, Dr. Fry glowed with joy and relief. Photo by Vanessa Nelson.

life to go on." She paused and then added, "And I will obey the court and every order, as I always have."

Freed from the rigors of maintaining an office and a practice, Fry would now have time for something she had a great passion for – medical research. She talked about the possibility with a remarkable show of excitement.

Fry also spoke at length regarding her fears about prison. Specifically, she had been worried that her cancer would return while she was incarcerated, and that her husband would die because his hemophilia could not be adequately treated behind bars. "For him, I was afraid if he got a bleed in his spinal cord, he'd be in a wheelchair, and, if he got a bleed in his brain, he'd be dead."

The couple was safe from that fate for the time being, but the reporters were eager to know how long incarceration could be avoided.

"By the time they finally get to the appeal, it will take a while," Fry told the cameras. "And we're going to be found innocent. This was such a railroad trial. [Judge Damrell] said no to everything we asked and yes to everything [Pings] asked, and, you know, it was almost as though he was going, 'I know they're going to appeal and win, let's make it easy for them.' I really do feel that way. I mean, he made *mistakes*." Then, looking over at her attorney husband, she joked with an endearing smile, "Of course, I'm not a lawyer."

That was Schafer's cue to offer his own reactions and observations. Now that the ordeal of what he called "running the gauntlet" was behind him, he was effusively optimistic. "They wanted to wave us around as people they threw in jail, and they haven't thrown us in jail," Schafer commented about his prosecutors. "It's a very hollow victory for them."

When it came to the issue of his freedom, in fact, he was remarkably confident. "I'm not going to serve it now," he said of his prison sentence, "and there's a good chance I will *never* have to serve it."

Then Schafer noted, "You're locked up with the dregs of society. Most people in prison deserve to be there."

"It's true!" Fry burst in, nodding enthusiastically.

The defendants have maintained that they were unjustly convicted. Photo by Vanessa Nelson.

Schafer continued his description of prison life. "There are predators in there," he said glumly. "In there, you have to be careful who you talk to, who you associate with, and there are gangs –"

"And I'm gullible," Fry added, with a laugh.

In spite of the conviction and its consequences, the couple did not regret the decision to go to trial and felt that the plea deals would have been a far worse fate. Even though one of the bargains had offered no prison time, Schafer said that he and his wife would have essentially had to give up their identities in order to accept the deal.

"They required me and my wife to give up our licenses to practice law and medicine," Schafer revealed about the plea bargains. True, his conviction had resulted in an automatic suspension from the bar, but because his crime was not one of "moral turpitude," he fully expected to regain his status as a practicing attorney.

There was another factor that dissuaded Schafer from taking a plea deal, and it was one he couldn't have given up. "We would have had to give up our right to appeal," he said, his voice conveying the significance of this fact. For him and Fry, sacrificing their chances of appeal would have meant the loss of all hope.

And Schafer believed his chances for a favorable appellate decision were remarkably good. As he spoke, he demonstrated great optimism about its potential to set a precedent on the issue of entrapment. "It's an area of the law that's still evolving," he explained. "Frankly, I think our case is going to put some corners on this law."

The critical error, Schafer realized in hindsight, was having confidence in the integrity of his local sheriff's department. "I wanted to trust them and work with them," he said, his eyes solemn. "I found out you just can't trust them."

He had specific advice to give on this matter, and he summed up his comments succinctly. "Don't tell them any more than you have to," Schafer advised about law enforcement. "Keep your cards close to your chest, and don't grow more than a hundred plants in five years, *please.*" He spoke with emphasis, conveying the moral of his story in clear, direct language.

Nearly seven years had elapsed between the raid and the sentencing, and enduring it had been enormously draining. But for Schafer, the suffering had meaning and purpose if it was instructional for other people. This was his most fervent point, and, concluding, he pled with his supporters to protect themselves.

"There are lessons from this case," Schafer said, giving a final urging. "Learn from what happened to me and Mollie."

As for Serra, he appeared ecstatic about winning the bail on appeal motion. "We're pleased, we're excited, and we hope to prevail on substantive issues at the appellate court," he declared. "We're in a celebration mood now, and we...love...the...judge!"

"*Today,*" Fry interjected, amending the statement.

"Today," Serra agreed, grinning wide enough to flash a gold tooth.

When asked about the appeal's potential for success, Serra's optimism was more guarded than that expressed by Fry. It was a matter of great uncertainty, as he saw it. "With the appellate court, the decisions are so variable," Serra explained. "It depends on what justices you get and how they react, so I would say the odds are 50/50."

Tony Serra ended the case by delivering a playful declaration to the press. Photo by Vanessa Nelson.

In spite of the fact that nearly a decade had already passed between investigation and sentencing, and although the day's proceedings had an atmosphere of finality, the Fry/Schafer case was still far from resolution. Much, it seemed, would be subject to chance and circumstance, and the world would have to watch and see what developed.

But this uncertainty did nothing to spoil the mood of what Serra considered a victory. "The health of the clients is going to be preserved," he assured the press. Then, in an explosion of jubilance, he announced, "I'm so delighted I may go home and light up a medical marijuana joint!"

About the Author

Vanessa Nelson is a U.C. Berkeley-trained journalist who worked in travel publishing before putting her efforts into covering medical marijuana court cases. Her articles on this subject have appeared in a variety of online and print publications since 2004. She quickly earned a reputation for combining detailed accuracy with passionate courtroom storytelling, thereby gaining a large readership within the activist community. Her debut book, U.S. v. Ed Rosenthal 2.0: The Re-trial of the Ganja Guru, was published in the fall of 2007 and was received with rave reviews. She continues to cover medical marijuana prosecutions in the northern half of California, following cases on both the state and federal levels. She also advocates on behalf of inmates serving time for medical marijuana offenses and maintains a pen-pal service for these prisoners.

www.ingramcontent.com/pod-product-compliance
Lightning Source LLC
Chambersburg PA
CBHW022052210326
41519CB00054B/315